COMPUTER
BOOK SERIES
FROM IDG

Internet E-Mail For Dummies®

Cheat Sheet

Your Own Customized Cheat Sheet

Build your own cheat sheet! Fill in the details — using information from the appropriate chapters in the book — to describe your personal mail setup:

My e-mail address: _____@_____ (Chapter 1)

My mail system: _____ (Chapters 8 through 19)

The rest of these items can be cribbed from the chapter that describes your mail program. Make note of the pages where they're described so that you can check for details.

To start my mail program: _____ (page _____)

To retrieve incoming messages: _____ (page _____)

To create a new message: _____ (page _____)

To send outgoing messages: _____ (page _____)

To reply to a message: _____ (page _____)

To forward a message: _____ (page _____)

To file away a message: _____ (page _____)

To delete a message: _____ (page _____)

To open the address book: _____ (page _____)

E-Mail Addresses You'd Hate to Lose

_____

_____

_____

_____

_____

_____

Favorite Nicknames (Aliases)

Fill in the names you pick when you make a nickname

_____

_____

_____

_____

_____

D1214148

. . .For Dummies: #1 Computer Book Series for Beginners

Internet E-Mail For Dummies®

Cheat Sheet

COMPUTER BOOK SERIES FROM IDG

Ten Tips for Effective Mail Use

1. Include a clear and specific subject line.

2. Edit any quoted text down to the minimum needed.

3. Read you own message thrice before you send it.

4. Ponder how the recipient will react to your message.

5. Check your spelling and grammar.

6. Do not curse, flame, spam, or use ALL CAPS.

7. Do not forward chain letters.

8. Do not use e-mail for illegal or unethical purposes.

9. Do not rely on the privacy of e-mail, especially from work.

10. When in doubt, save your message overnight.

The Golden Rule of E-Mail:
That which you find hateful to receive, do not e-mail to others.

Host Name Zones

Internet host name zones are represented by a three-letter abbreviation at the end of an address.

Name Zone	Host
com	company or individual
edu	educational institution
gov	government
mil	military
net	network organization
int	international organization
org	non-profit or other non-commercial organization

Internet E-mail Address Formats

To Send To	With This Address	Use This
America Online	SteveCase	stevecase@aol.com
BITNET	user@node	user@node.bitnet *or* user%node.bitnet@cunyvm.cuny.edu
CompuServe	77777,7777	77777.7777@compuserve.com
Delphi	jsmith	jsmith@delphi.com
EasyLink	1234567	1234567@eln.attmail.com
FIDONET	MarySmith 1:2/3.4	mary.smith@p4.f3.n2.z1.fidonet.org
GEnie	J.SMITH7	J.SMITH7@genie.geis.com
MCI Mail	555-2468	5552468@mcimail.com
MSN	BillGates	billgates@msn.com
Prodigy	ABCD123A	abcd123a@prodigy.com

Commonly Used Smileys

Smiley	Definition
:-)	Simple Smiley
;-)	Winking Smiley
:-(	Frowning Smiley
8-)	Smiley with Big Eyes
B-)	Smiley with Glasses
:-P	Smiley with Tongue Out

. . .For Dummies: #1 Computer Book Series for Beginners

®

Reference for the Rest of Us!®

COMPUTER BOOK SERIES FROM IDG

Are you intimidated and confused by computers? Do you find that traditional manuals are overloaded with technical details you'll never use? Do your friends and family always call you to fix simple problems on their PCs? Then the . . .*For Dummies*® computer book series from IDG Books Worldwide is for you.

. . .*For Dummies* books are written for those frustrated computer users who know they aren't really dumb but find that PC hardware, software, and indeed the unique vocabulary of computing make them feel helpless. . . .*For Dummies* books use a lighthearted approach, a down-to-earth style, and even cartoons and humorous icons to diffuse computer novices' fears and build their confidence. Lighthearted but not lightweight, these books are a perfect survival guide for anyone forced to use a computer.

> "I like my copy so much I told friends; now they bought copies."
>
> Irene C., Orwell, Ohio

> "Quick, concise, nontechnical, and humorous."
>
> Jay A., Elburn, Illinois

> "Thanks, I needed this book. Now I can sleep at night."
>
> Robin F., British Columbia, Canada

Already, hundreds of thousands of satisfied readers agree. They have made . . .*For Dummies* books the #1 introductory level computer book series and have written asking for more. So, if you're looking for the most fun and easy way to learn about computers, look to . . .*For Dummies* books to give you a helping hand.

™

IDG BOOKS WORLDWIDE

INTERNET E-MAIL FOR DUMMIES®

by John R. Levine, Carol Baroudi,
Margaret Levine Young, and Arnold Reinhold

IDG Books Worldwide, Inc.
An International Data Group Company

Foster City, CA ♦ Chicago, IL ♦ Indianapolis, IN ♦ Braintree, MA ♦ Southlake, TX

Internet E-Mail For Dummies®

Published by
IDG Books Worldwide, Inc.
An International Data Group Company
919 E. Hillsdale Blvd., Suite 400

Foster City, CA 94404

Library of Congress Catalog Card No.: 96-75409

ISBN: 1-56884-235-X

Printed in the United States of America

10 9 8 7 6 5 4 3 2 1

1B/SW/QT/ZW/IN

Distributed in the United States by IDG Books Worldwide, Inc.

Distributed by Macmillan Canada for Canada; by Computer and Technical Books for the Caribbean Basin; by Contemporanea de Ediciones for Venezuela; by Distribuidora Cuspide for Argentina; by CITEC for Brazil; by Ediciones ZETA S.C.R. Ltda. for Peru; by Editorial Limusa SA for Mexico; by Transworld Publishers Limited in the United Kingdom and Europe; by Al-Maiman Publishers & Distributors for Saudi Arabia; by Simron Pty. Ltd. for South Africa; by IDG Communications (HK) Ltd. for Hong Kong; by Toppan Company Ltd. for Japan; by Addison Wesley Publishing Company for Korea; by Longman Singapore Publishers Ltd. for Singapore, Malaysia, Thailand, and Indonesia; by Unalis Corporation for Taiwan; by WS Computer Publishing Company, Inc. for the Philippines; by WoodsLane Pty. Ltd. for Australia; by WoodsLane Enterprises Ltd. for New Zealand.

For general information on IDG Books Worldwide's books in the U.S., please call our Consumer Customer Service department at 800-762-2974. For reseller information, including discounts and premium sales, please call our Reseller Customer Service department at 800-434-3422.

For information on where to purchase IDG Books Worldwide's books outside the U.S., contact IDG Books Worldwide at 415-655-3021 or fax 415-655-3295.

For information on translations, contact Marc Jeffrey Mikulich, Director, Foreign & Subsidiary Rights, at IDG Books Worldwide, 415-655-3018 or fax 415-655-3295.

For sales inquiries and special prices for bulk quantities, write to the address above or call IDG Books Worldwide at 415-655-3200.

For information on using IDG Books Worldwide's books in the classroom, or ordering examination copies, contact the Education Office at 800-434-2086 or fax 817-251-8174.

For authorization to photocopy items for corporate, personal, or educational use, please contact Copyright Clearance Center, 222 Rosewood Drive, Danvers, MA 01923, or fax 508-750-4470.

is a trademark under exclusive license to IDG Books Worldwide, Inc., from International Data Group, Inc.

About the Authors

John R. Levine was a member of a computer club in high school — before high school students, or even high schools, had computers. He met Theodor H. Nelson, the author of *Computer Lib/Dream Machines* and the inventor of hypertext, who reminded us that computers should not be taken seriously and that everyone can and should understand and use computers.

John wrote his first program in 1967 on an IBM 1130 (a computer roughly as powerful as your typical, modern digital wristwatch, only more difficult to use). He became an official system administrator of a networked computer at Yale in 1975. He began working part-time, for a computer company, of course, in 1977 and has been in and out of the computer and network biz ever since. He got his company on to Usenet early enough that it appears in a 1982 *Byte* magazine article in a map of Usenet, which then was so small the map fit on half a page.

He used to spend most of his time writing software, but now he mostly writes books (including *The Internet For Dummies, UNIX For Dummies,* and *Internet Secrets*, published by IDG Books Worldwide, Inc.) because it's more fun and he can do so at home in the tiny village of Trumansburg, New York. He also teaches some computer courses and publishes and edits an incredibly technoid magazine called *The Journal of C Language Translation.* He holds a B.A. and a Ph.D in computer science from Yale University, but please don't hold that against him.

Carol Baroudi first started playing with computers in 1971 at Colgate University where two things were new: the PDP-10 and women. She was lucky to have unlimited access to the state-of-the-art PDP-10 where she learned to program, operate the machine, and talk to Eliza. She taught Algol and helped to design the curricula for Computer Science and Women's Studies. She majored in Spanish and studied French, which, thanks to the Internet, she can now use every day.

In 1975 she took a job doing compiler support and development, a perfect use for her background in languages. For six years, she developed software and managed software development. For a while, she had a small business doing high-tech recruiting (she was a headhunter). Though she wrote her first software manuals in 1975, her *job* has been writing since 1984. She's described all kinds of software, from the memory management system of the Wang VS operating system to e-mail products for the PC and Mac. For the last several years, she's been writing books for ordinary people who want to use computers. Her books include *The Internet For Dummies* and *Internet Secrets.* She's exchanged tens of thousands of e-mail messages and hopes that's just the beginning.

She's the mother of a fantastic five-year-old. She loves acting and singing and will fly to France on any excuse. She believes that we are living in a very interesting time when technology is changing faster than people can imagine. She hopes that as we learn to use the new technologies, we don't loose sight of our humanity. She feels that that computers can be useful and fun but are no substitute for real life.

Margy Levine Young has used small computers since the 1970s. She graduated from UNIX on a PDP/11 to Apple DOS on an Apple][to MS-DOS and UNIX on a variety of machines. She has done all kinds of jobs that involve explaining to people that computers aren't as mysterious as they might think, including managing the use of PCs at Columbia Pictures, teaching scientists and engineers what computers are good for, and writing and co-writing computer manuals and books, including *Understanding Javelin PLUS* (Sybex, 1987), *The Complete Guide to PC-File* (Center Books, better known as Margy and her Dad, 1991), *UNIX For Dummies, MORE Internet For Dummies, WordPerfect For Windows For Dummies,* and *Internet FAQs: Answers to the Most Frequently Asked Questions.* Margy has a degree in computer science from Yale University and lives with her husband, two children, and chickens in Lexington, Massachusetts.

Arnold Reinhold has been programming computers since they had filaments. His first introduction to the hype/so what?/wow! cycle that governs computer industry evolution was the invention of the transistor. He has gotten to do cool stuff in spacecraft guidance, air traffic control, computer-aided design, robotics, and machine vision. Arnold has been on and off the Internet for over ten years. Recent writing includes *The Internet For Dummies Quick Reference,* 2nd Edition and "Commonsense and Cryptography" in *Internet Secrets,* both from IDG Books.

Arnold studied mathematics at CCNY and MIT, and management at Harvard. You can check out his home page at `http://world.std.com/~reinhold/`.

ABOUT
IDG
BOOKS
WORLDWIDE

Welcome to the world of IDG Books Worldwide.

IDG Books Worldwide, Inc., is a subsidiary of International Data Group, the world's largest publisher of computer-related information and the leading global provider of information services on information technology. IDG was founded more than 25 years ago and now employs more than 7,700 people worldwide. IDG publishes more than 250 computer publications in 67 countries (see listing below). More than 70 million people read one or more IDG publications each month.

Launched in 1990, IDG Books Worldwide is today the #1 publisher of best-selling computer books in the United States. We are proud to have received 8 awards from the Computer Press Association in recognition of editorial excellence and three from Computer Currents' First Annual Readers' Choice Awards, and our best-selling ...*For Dummies*® series has more than 19 million copies in print with translations in 28 languages. IDG Books Worldwide, through a joint venture with IDG's Hi-Tech Beijing, became the first U.S. publisher to publish a computer book in the People's Republic of China. In record time, IDG Books Worldwide has become the first choice for millions of readers around the world who want to learn how to better manage their businesses.

Our mission is simple: Every one of our books is designed to bring extra value and skill-building instructions to the reader. Our books are written by experts who understand and care about our readers. The knowledge base of our editorial staff comes from years of experience in publishing, education, and journalism — experience which we use to produce books for the '90s. In short, we care about books, so we attract the best people. We devote special attention to details such as audience, interior design, use of icons, and illustrations. And because we use an efficient process of authoring, editing, and desktop publishing our books electronically, we can spend more time ensuring superior content and spend less time on the technicalities of making books.

You can count on our commitment to deliver high-quality books at competitive prices on topics you want to read about. At IDG Books Worldwide, we continue in the IDG tradition of delivering quality for more than 25 years. You'll find no better book on a subject than one from IDG Books Worldwide.

John J. Kilcullen

John Kilcullen
President and CEO
IDG Books Worldwide, Inc.

Credits

Senior Vice President and Publisher
Milissa L. Koloski

Associate Publisher
Diane Graves Steele

Brand Manager
Judith A. Taylor

Editorial Managers
Kristin A. Cocks
Mary Corder

Product Development Manager
Mary Bednarek

Editorial Executive Assistant
Richard Graves

Marketing Assistant
Holly N. Blake

Acquisitions Editor
Tammy Goldfeld

Assistant Acquisitions Editor
Gareth Hancock

Production Director
Beth Jenkins

Production Assistant
Jacalyn L. Pennywell

Supervisor of Project Coordination
Cindy L. Phipps

Supervisor of Page Layout
Kathie S. Schnorr

Supervisor of Graphics and Design
Shelley Lea

Reprint/Blueline Coordination
Tony Augsburger
Patricia R. Reynolds
Todd Klemme
Theresa Sánchez-Baker

Project Editor
Tim Gallan

Copy Editors
Christa Carroll
Suzanne Packer
Tamara S. Castleman
William A. Barton

Technical Reviewer
Dennis Cox

Editorial Assistants
Constance Carlisle
Chris H. Collins
Kevin Spencer

Associate Project Coordinator
Debbie Sharpe

Project Coordination Assistant
Regina Snyder

Media/Archive Coordination
Leslie Popplewell
Melissa Stauffer
Jason Marcuson

Graphics Coordination
Gina Scott
Angela F. Hunkler

Production Page Layout
Shawn Aylsworth
Elizabeth Cárdenas-Nelson
Maridee V. Ennis
Jill Lyttle
Ron Riggan
Kate Snell
Marti Stegeman

Proofreaders
Joel Draper
Jenny Kaufeld
Christine Meloy Beck
Dwight Ramsey
Robert Springer

Indexer
Steve Rath

Cover Design
Kavish + Kavish

Acknowledgments

We particularly thank our editors at IDG, Mary Bednarek and Diane Steele, whose support and trust encouraged us to do what we all knew perfectly well was impossible.

John thanks Tonia Saxon, for taking such good care of both him and The Bug during the often exciting process of writing this book.

Carol thanks Joshua, whose Lego creations adorn her every surface, Philippe, whose e-mail correspondence requires a disk of its own, and her e-mail friends whom she hopes to meet in person someday.

Margy would like to acknowledge Barbara Begonis and the folks at Lexington Playcare, without whom she would have been typing with one hand while holding two kids. She would also like to thank Meg and Zac, the two kids in question, for being such extraordinary people.

Arnold thanks Barbara Lapinskas for her help with the cc:Mail chapter and many useful suggestions, Joshua Reinhold for his tour of the Eiffel Tower, and Max and Grete Reinhold of blessed memory.

Thanks to Tim Gallan for rallying to the cause and producing this book despite all odds.

The entire contents of this book were submitted by the authors to the publisher using e-mail over the Internet. Edited chapters were returned for review in the same way. We thank TIAC (Bedford, Massachusetts), CENTNet (Cambridge, Massachusetts), and Lightlink (Ithaca, New York), our Internet providers.

(The publisher would like to give special thanks to Patrick J. McGovern, without whom this book would not have been possible.)

Dedication

John dedicates his part of the book (the words that start with the letters N through Q) to Tonia and an increasingly evident but as yet unnamed person.

Carol dedicates her part of the book, the invisible part, to her friends who remind her that only the impossible is worth doing.

Contents at a Glance

Cartoons at a Glance

By Rich Tennant

Fax: 508-546-7747 • E-mail: the5wave@tiac.net

page 321

page 7

page 135

page 303

page 197

page 97

page 231

Table of Contents

Introduction

• •

*E*lectronic mail, henceforth *e-mail*, sure has become popular. Everyone seems to have an e-mail address on their business cards, and messages fly around offices (and even around the world). The occasional sage predicts the death of the post office. We're not too worried about the post office, but we can't imagine going back to life before e-mail. It's like life without the telephone.

A Whole Book on E-Mail?

You bet. When someone first suggested we write a book on e-mail, we thought, "It's so simple; the book would only be 25 pages long." But the more we thought about it, the more we realized that the problem wasn't finding material, it was picking the best of all the material we had and squeezing it into these 400 or so pages.

First, e-mail is a little like driving a car: it's easy once you know how, but you have to learn about it first. There are some nerdy aspects to e-mail that you may need to know about in order to use it: different e-mail programs, service providers, computer platforms, operating systems, and so on. And there are many different situations, some kind of confusing to deal with. You may already know how to send e-mail to someone in the next office or to your kid in college, but what about that urgent message your boss wants sent to Switzerland? And how do you obtain people's addresses, keep your e-mail private, or figure out if someone has gotten your message? We cover these issues and a lot more.

Second, there is a lot more you can do with e-mail than most people realize. You can join any of more than ten thousand e-mail mailing lists out there, which cover almost every topic conceivable. You can use e-mail to access almost every service on the global Internet. We'll tell you all about this stuff, too.

Finally, e-mail differs from other computer applications. Once you learn to use a word processor, you can write letters, memos, and even books to your heart's content. To communicate using e-mail, however, the people you write to have to know how to use it as well. Even if you are cool with the technology, this book can help you bring your friends and colleagues up to speed. We know not everyone is comfortable with using a computer. In a country where most people still can't program their microwave oven, we will hold their hand and guide them through the process.

And remember, a gift of *Internet E-Mail For Dummies* means "I want to stay in touch with you, wherever you are!"

Who Are You?

In writing the book, we assumed that

- ✔ You have or would like to have access to e-mail.
- ✔ You want to use it to communicate effectively with others.
- ✔ You are not interested in becoming an expert on building worldwide e-mail systems; you just want to learn how to use them.

About This Book

We understand that e-mail is pretty utilitarian stuff and won't be offended if you don't read every page of this. Part I gives you a general understanding of e-mail.

We cover many different e-mail programs and systems in Parts II, III and IV. Obviously, you won't be interested in all of them. The ones we cover include

- ✔ Eudora
- ✔ Netscape
- ✔ America Online and GNN
- ✔ CompuServe
- ✔ Prodigy
- ✔ Microsoft Network and Exchange
- ✔ Netcom's NetCruiser
- ✔ UNIX Pine
- ✔ cc:Mail
- ✔ Microsoft Mail
- ✔ Lotus Notes Mail and Lotus Notes R4

Part V covers some advanced topics including mailing lists (there are oodles of great ones) and e-mail security (no, that isn't an oxymoron). Part VI contains some interesting top-ten lists.

How to Use This Book

To begin, please read the first four chapters. You can skip Chapter 2 if you already have e-mail service. These chapters give you an overview of e-mail and some important tips and terminology. Besides, we think that they're interesting.

After that, use this book as a reference. Look up your topic or command in the table of contents or the index, both of which can refer you to the part of the book where we describe what to do and perhaps define a few terms (if absolutely necessary).

In order to emphasize e-mail addresses and other important things that you may need to type in, we present that information in the book like this:

```
cryptic command or address
```

If you want type in this information (say it's an address to a mailing list you'd like to join), just type it as it appears. Use the same capitalization we do — some systems care very deeply about CAPITAL and small letters.

How This Book Is Organized

This book has seven parts. The parts stand on their own — you can begin reading wherever you like, but you should at least skim Part I first to get acquainted with some unavoidable Internet jargon and learn how to get your computer on the Net.

Here are the parts of the book and what they contain:

Part I: What Is E-Mail All About?

In this part, you discover what e-mail is and why it's interesting (at least why we think it's interesting). It discusses how you get on e-mail. Also, there's stuff about vital e-mail terminology and concepts that will help you as you move through the later parts of the book.

Parts II: The Two Big E-Mail Programs

If you use an Internet service provider, you probably use either Eudora or Netscape to read and send mail. Here's the inside scoop on both of them.

Part III: Using Online Services for E-Mail

Every online service offers e-mail, both to other users of the same service and to everyone connected to the Internet. Here's blow-by-blow directions on how to use each of the services' e-mail systems. We also cover Pine, the mail system used on most workstations and available on most Internet providers who offer "shell access" dial-up accounts.

Part IV: Using E-Mail at Work

If your office has computers with a local network, you probably have a mail system on that network. We look at the three biggest local network mail programs here.

Part V: Advanced E-Mail Topics

We cover a bunch of fun stuff here, including how to find someone's e-mail address, how to use mailing lists, and how to keep snoopy people from reading your e-mail.

Part VI: The Part of Tens

This part is a compendium of sound advice on e-mail (which, we suppose, suggests that the rest of the book is full of bad advice).

Part VII: Glossary and Appendixes

The two appendixes contain some useful information pertaining to Internet e-mail addresses. The glossary will aid you in deciphering Internet- and e-mail-related jargon.

You will also find a comprehensive **Index**.

Icons Used in This Book

Lets you know that some particularly nerdy, technoid information is coming up so that you can skip it if you want.

Indicates that a nifty little shortcut or time-saver is explained.

Arrrghhhh! Don't let this happen to you!

We really want this to stick in your mind, as in "It's cold out, wear a sweater."

What's on the CD

If you haven't already noticed, this book has a CD-ROM stuck to its inside back cover. This CD-ROM runs on Windows 3.1, Windows 95, and Macintosh computers, and it contains the following software:

- ✓ CompuServe (a popular online service) for Windows 3.1, Windows 95, and Macintosh
- ✓ Eudora Light (a popular e-mail application) for Windows 3.1, Windows 95, and Macintosh
- ✓ Netcom's NetCruiser (a popular Internet service provider's software) for Windows 3.1 and Windows 95.

This software is a sort of bonus for buying the book. You don't need to load any of it to understand what we're covering throughout the book. In fact, you may already have access to an e-mail package, online service, or Internet service provider. For those of you who don't, however, we just thought it'd be nice to give you some cool Internet software to try out.

Appendix C provides detailed installation instructions for all of the software on the CD-ROM. Please note that inside the plastic CD-ROM envelope are two cards containing important installation, sign-up, and registration information for both CompuServe and NetCruiser, so please don't throw them away. Again, Appendix C explains the whole process.

Feedback, Please

We love to hear from our readers. If you want to contact us, please feel free to do so in care of

IDG Books Worldwide, Inc.
7260 Shadeland Station, Suite 100
Indianapolis, IN 46256

Better yet, send us e-mail at email@dummies.com. (We answer our e-mail a lot more quickly than we answer our paper mail. E-mail is like that.) You can also visit our new World Wide Web home page at http://dummies.com where you'll find the latest updated information on this and other . . .*For Dummies* books that we've written. These electronic addresses just contact the authors of this book; to contact the publisher or authors of other . . .*For Dummies* books, send e-mail to info@idgbooks.com or write to the postal address we just provided.

Part I

What Is E-Mail All About?

The 5th Wave   By Rich Tennant

PLEASE

In this part . . .

*E*verybody's talking about e-mail these days, but if you've never seen it, it seems pretty scary. We start with the very basics and gently guide you through the important concepts. We help you understand how e-mail can enhance our businesses and enrich our lives. We even have one chapter in this section for those eager for the technical details, but you can skip it and we'll never know.

Chapter 1

If You Can Type, You Can E-Mail: A Gentle Introduction to Electronic Mail

* *

In This Chapter

▶ What is e-mail?

▶ How is it different from other kinds of mail?

▶ Why is it so great?

* *

*E*lectronic mail, or *e-mail,* is a way for people to send and receive messages using computers. It is rapidly becoming a primary communication tool for both business and pleasure. Millions of people are using e-mail now, and thousands more are signing up every day. As more and more people use e-mail, it is getting to be very likely that someone you care about is reachable by e-mail. Many of us feel that e-mail is the greatest invention in the history of humanity since the Cuisineart.

The basic idea of e-mail is simple enough:

- ✔ You type your message on a computer keyboard.
- ✔ You type in someone's e-mail address — it's sort of like a phone number but usually has letters in it.
- ✔ You press a button.
- ✔ Almost instantly, your message appears on that person's computer screen, anywhere in the world.

In many cases, e-mail really is about that easy. Best of all, it is usually free, even for messages sent half way around the world.

Here is what a typical e-mail message looks like:

```
From carol@iecc.com  Fri Jan  5 01:08:51 1996
Mime-Version: 1.0
Content-Type: text/plain; charset="us-ascii"
Date: Thu, 4 Jan 1996 20:08:51 -0500
To: Margaret Levine Young <margy@gosport.com>,
    reinhold@world.std.com (Arnold G Reinhold),
    Mary Bednarek <mbednarek@idgbooks.com>,
    Waterside Productions <75720.410@compuserve.com>
From: carol@iecc.com (Carol Baroudi)
Subject: Paris contact info

I arrive Saturday, January 6th and return Tuesday, January 16th.

I'm at the Hotel d'Albe

011 33 1 46 34 09 70 phone
011 33 1 40 46 85 70 fax

Carol Baroudi (carol@iecc.com)
CoAuthor The Internet for Dummies, Internet Secrets
```

What's So Great about E-Mail?

Why all the fuss? Couldn't you make a phone call instead or send a fax, or just put a stamp on a letter and drop it in the mail box? Well, in many ways, e-mail combines the best characteristics of all the methods of communicating that preceded it and adds important new benefits of its own. To understand what e-mail is like, let's compare it with the other communication methods in turn.

The letter

Postal mail is slow. Overnight delivery is the best you can expect, and you can't rely on that unless you pay a lot of money. Overseas surface mail can take weeks or even months to reach its destination. E-mail, by contrast, often arrives within seconds. Because it is so slow compared to e-mail, postal mail is often called *snail-mail* in the electronic world.

Letters are written on paper. You can read them again if you want, photocopy them and pass them on to someone else, and file them for later reference. But you'd better have stationery, envelopes, and stamps on hand to send a letter, and it is awkward to correct a mistake in a handwritten note. You can edit e-mail with a flick of your mouse and you never have to weigh your e-mail message to figure out the right postage. Just as easily, you can forward a message to a zillion of your closest personal friends and file it on your disk.

You need to know where people live to address letters to them. The post office has a tradition of delivering mail that is poorly addressed, but when you move, after a few months' forwarding grace period, you are expected to inform correspondents of your new address. Unless you change e-mail service providers, you can usually keep your e-mail address when you move.

On the other hand, a personal letter is still perhaps the warmest way to communicate. The sender's aura is somehow affixed to the piece of paper. E-mail, by contrast, can feel quite cold. Experienced users work to keep their messages from sounding too harsh. We'll tell you how in Chapter 4, "The Finer Points of E-Mail."

The telephone

Phoning is the most immediate form of electronic communication. Most of us use it many times per day. We often get as much information from pauses and tone of voice as we do from the words. Getting emotions across in e-mail is a lot harder. Some people have taken to using cute abbreviations in e-mail to make their feelings a little clearer. We tell you all about those in Chapter 2.

A big problem with the telephone is that the other person has to be there to answer your call. Answering machines and voice mail have helped somewhat, but it is tough to get a long message just right, and your only option if you don't is to re-record the entire message. Also, it is very hard to save a voice message in any useful way. By contrast, a typical computer hard disk can store thousands of e-mail messages, all neatly indexed by subject, correspondent, and date.

The need for the other person to be there to get a phone call is a particular problem for calls to different time zones. France is 9 hours ahead of California, and Japan is 11 hours ahead of New York, for example. E-mail makes communicating across the planet a breeze.

The phone is also very intrusive. Most of us have a Pavlovian need to answer a ringing phone no matter what. Frequent calls make it very hard to put quality time into one's work or life. But *you* decide when to read your e-mail.

Because the phone is so intrusive, many busy people have their calls screened. The "Whom shall I say is calling?" followed by a pause, followed by "I'm sorry but Mr. Gates is out of the office right now" routine can get pretty tiring. Most people still read their own e-mail or at least scan the subject lines that start off most e-mail messages.

The phone system is persnickety about phone numbers. If you goof on a single digit, you will get a wrong number or a nasal recording saying, "The number you have reached is not in service." E-mail will also bounce if you get a single letter or number wrong in the address, and the error messages are just as unfriendly.

Within North America, phoning is fairly inexpensive, though you can get socked with all kinds of charges when you're away from home. Calling overseas is another matter. People with overseas relationships can run up hundreds of dollars every month in phone bills. E-mail is usually close to free.

The fax

The facsimile machine, or fax, is a recent addition to the general public's communication vocabulary. Because most fax transmissions take place over ordinary phone lines, it shares some of the characteristics of the phone call, including phone numbers and calling rates.

There are two big ways in which a fax is less like a phone call and more like e-mail: A fax is a written form of communication, and the recipient usually doesn't have to be there to receive it. These features have made the fax the medium of choice for international commerce, though e-mail is rapidly gaining a foothold.

Now that you can buy fax machines that use plain paper instead of that yucky thermal stuff, the biggest problem with fax is that the messages cannot be easily and accurately read by computers, which makes it hard to automate the handling of fax messages. If someone faxes you text to include in a document, you typically have to retype and proofread the text. With e-mail, you can paste the text in electronically with complete accuracy.

Another advantage of fax is its capability to easily transmit graphics and messages in any language including the logographic characters used in China, Japan, and Korea. The latest e-mail systems can also do this.

E-Mail Is the Best of All Worlds, Sort Of

E-mail combines most of the best — and a few of the worst — characteristics of the more well known methods of communicating described in the preceeding section.

- It is written. You get to review and edit your message before you send it, and the other person can re-read it, forward it to someone else, or file it away.

- The other person doesn't have to be there. E-mail is great for international conversations.

- E-mail addresses are as persnickety as phone numbers — you usually have to get every letter in the address right — but they can also follow you around when you move. And many e-mail providers let you pick up your messages even when you are out of town. (We've picked up our e-mail in

Australia, Hong Kong, and Japan, as well as all corners of the United States.) We'll talk a lot more about e-mail addresses in Chapter 3.

✔ E-mail is fast — at least usually. It is not uncommon for messages to be delivered halfway around the world in seconds.

✔ E-mail is cheap. After you've paid for the computer, modem, phone line and access account, e-mail is usually free. It doesn't matter how long the message is or how far away the recipient lives. A few services still charge per message, but they usually compensate by letting you call in to pick up or leave off messages for free.

✔ E-mail is non-intrusive. You can set aside a fixed time each day to read and respond to your e-mail, or you can read it whenever you have time.

✔ People who would never take your call are often reachable via e-mail. Senior managers can get feedback from every level of their organization without being swamped. The head of a large semiconductor plant recently sent all 1,400 of his employees an e-mail message asking, "What are we doing that is keeping you from doing your job to the best of your ability?" and expects to read all the responses.

E-mail's unique advantages

You can do several things with e-mail that are difficult or impossible with any other form communication. These e-mail advantages include

✔ It's easy to send your message to more than one person. You just type in several e-mail addresses. You can also keep mailing lists on your computer, which allows quick distribution to many people, thousands even.

✔ Most e-mail systems have a reply button that lets you include all or part of the original message when you are writing a reply. This feature is a small one, but it really speeds replying to messages. In composing a letter or even when making a phone call, people spend a lot of time establishing a context for your reply. Here is an example:

```
Subject: Re: ST:A Final Unity for Mac?

     It's out now!

     Best,

     Peter
     Spectrum HoloByte Tech Support Rep
```

```
——————————Reply Separator——————————
Subject: ST:A Final Unity for Mac?
Date:    12/21/95 11:32 AM

Good Morning!

Would you please tell me if you have plans to put out
a version of "Star Trek: A Final Unity" for the Mac,
and if so, when?

Many thanks!
Happy Holidays!
```

✔ You can attach drawings, sounds, video clips, and other computer files to your e-mail.

✔ You can easily save thousands of e-mail messages and search message files electronically.

✔ You can paste all or part of an e-mail into other computer documents.

✔ You can use e-mail to access vast pools of information stored on the Internet.

E-mail's disadvantages

Okay, so e-mail isn't perfect. Here are some of the pitfalls:

✔ While the post office goes everywhere and phones are nearly universal in developed countries, most people don't have e-mail yet.

✔ Your messages won't be received until the recipients check their e-mail. While most active users check their mail daily, many people who don't get mail often can't be counted on to check their mail regularly.

✔ E-mail isn't always as reliable. Messages between different e-mail systems can be held up for days by computer glitches.

✔ Because it can pass through many multiuser computers on its way, e-mail lacks privacy, particularly when you e-mail from work. But there are programs available that will protect your messages with secret codes. See Chapter 22, which covers e-mail security.

These disadvantages not withstanding, e-mail will become a part of most of our lives in the 21st century. We hope the rest of this book will help you make e-mail a valuable and pleasant way to communicate.

Chapter 2
Getting Started

. . . .

In This Chapter

▶ What you need from a computer to get connected

▶ What to look for in a modem

▶ How to find cheap software

▶ What your e-mail software can do

▶ What e-mail providers can offer

. . . .

*G*etting hooked up to e-mail can be much harder than using it. The process can be hard on new users. We'll try to help.

You may already have e-mail — most college students do and many employees of large corporations get their accounts the first day on the job. If so, you can skip this chapter, although parts may come in handy later as a reference. If you are part of an organization that has e-mail but you don't yet have an account, talk to your supervisor or look for someone with the name "System Administrator" on her door. Tell her *Internet E-Mail For Dummies* sent you and bring cookies.

If you are an individual or part of a small organization and want to communicate using e-mail, grab your favorite beverage and settle in someplace comfortable while we lead you through the process.

To use e-mail, you'll need access to the following:

✔ A computer

✔ Unless your computer is already connected to a network, a modem and phone line

✔ Some software that lets your computer talk to other computers

✔ Some software that lets you send and receive e-mail

✔ A copy of this book

I have e-mail at work.
Does this mean I'm on the Internet?

Maybe yes, maybe no. Many companies hook their computers together with other computers at the same company to form a *network* of computers. Some then connect that network to the Internet, the worldwide association of computer networks all linked together. If so, you can use your computer at work to send e-mail to anyone anywhere on the Internet — for business purposes only, of course.

Other companies are not connected to the Internet either because they don't want to be or because they haven't gotten around to it yet. If your company is one of those non-Internet types, you can exchange e-mail with coworkers but not with outsiders. This fact does not mean you should put this book back on the bookstore shelf and browse elsewhere. We have a lot to tell you about making more effective use of the e-mail you already have, and we'll prepare you for the day you get Internet access at work (it's coming, trust us). You may even want to get your own e-mail account at home. It will give you a real leg up on your coworkers.

Different kinds of internal e-mail software exist. Some companies run e-mail programs on their mainframes — large, very expensive computers that live in rooms with glass walls and false floors and that need special air-conditioning. IBM's PROFS and Digital Equipment Corporation's

All-In-One are examples of such packages. Other companies wire together all their personal computers into a local area network or *LAN*. Novell, Appletalk, Lotus Notes, and Banyan are names you might see if you company is hooked up this way. Some organizations have even set up their own internal version of the Internet. These systems are called *Intranets* and use much of the same software, such as Netscape and Eudora, that we describe in this book.

The best way to find out if your organization's e-mail system is on the Internet is to ask a coworker. You might also try sending an e-mail message addressed to email@dummies.com This is the address of the Dummies Authors Central e-mail robot. We'll send a reply if we get your message, and you'll know you are on the Internet. If you don't get a reply, or if you get a reply saying your message cannot be delivered, it's a bad sign, but it doesn't mean for sure that you are not connected. You may have to do something special to get mail out to the Internet. Again, ask.

If you get fired just for trying, send a message to sympathy@dummies.com. If that message is returned to you as undeliverable, it means that you are actually a decent person with a great future and should accept this minor career setback as a learning experience.

Some users, typically at universities and large corporations, are lucky enough to have a *direct connection* for e-mail. These people do not need a modem or phone line, but they may need a network interface card. Almost every organization that provides direct connections has someone, usually the System Administrator, who can help you get started.

You won't need exclusive control of a computer system, though e-mail will be more convenient and private if you do. You can share. One thing you will need for your very own is an e-mail account. This will give you an e-mail address — the letters and numbers that people type into *their* e-mail system when they want to send mail to you — and a place where mail for you is kept until you get around to reading it. Your account is set up on a computer called a *mail server*. This computer is usually *not* the one on your desk. It may be in your building or at a *service provider* — a company that connects you to the Internet so that you can send and receive e-mail.

Buying a Computer for E-Mail

If you don't already have access to a computer, you need to borrow or buy one. Computer salespeople will try to sell you the most expensive model they can. Actually, almost any computer will do for e-mail. What follows is some advice if you need to go shopping. (You can find a more extensive version of this discussion in our *Internet For Dummies Quick Reference,* 2nd Edition.)

- ✔ Pretty much any computer built in the past decade can handle some sort of e-mail hookup so long as it has a modem.

- ✔ Make sure that whatever computer you're planning to use can run the software you want to use. This is particularly important if you're buying a used computer.

- ✔ Most people need help getting their computers set up. If you have friends with computers (particularly if they already have e-mail), consider getting the same kind of computer they have. Also, look for user groups, and try and buy from a store that provides useful support.

- ✔ There are lots of different kinds of modems available. When you buy one, make sure that it supports at least one of V.32, V.32bis, or V.34, standards that define the way your modem connects to the modem at your service provider. (There are other V.*xx* standards, but these are the only ones that matter.) Also make sure that your modem works with the kind of computer you have, and if it's not the kind that mounts inside your computer, also make sure that you have a suitable cable.

Mommy, what's a protocol?

When your phone rings, you pick it up and say something short like, "Hello," "Bonjour," or "White House, how can I direct your call?"

If the other person recognizes your voice or the name of your organization, he then says who he is or what he wants, and the conversation proceeds.

If the other person doesn't recognize who picked up, he will ask, "Is this 617 555 2368" or "I was trying to reach Dummies Central?"

And so on.

When your conversation is nearly over you might say the following:

"It's been nice chatting, but I have to get back to work."

"We should do lunch."

"Give me a call."

"Bye."

Computers have similar rules for starting and ending phone calls and dealing with any problems that may arise. Protocols are just sets of rules that computers use to establish a conversation between each other. Computers use different sets of rules, or protocols, for different purposes, just like people have different rules for calls to business acquaintances, friends, and lovers. And, like people, computers rarely do lunch.

A few modem tips

 ✔ If someone picks up an extension phone while you are logged in, your connection usually breaks and you have to call back.

 ✔ If you have call waiting, put *70 in front of the number of your e-mail service provider in your communication software to turn off call waiting while your modem is on the phone. Otherwise those incoming calls may break your e-mail connection.

 ✔ If your modem isn't working, check that all the cables are plugged in nice and tight at the computer, the modem, and the phone jack; that the power supply is plugged into the wall; and that the modem on-off switch, usually hidden in back, is on, usually up.

 ✔ If your modem dies, buy a new one. Modems are usually not worth repairing.

 ✔ While a zillion brands of modems exist, they all buy the key internal parts, called the chip set, from one of a handful of manufacturers. This chip set actually determines how a modem works.

Telephone line tips

Your ordinary phone line is all you need to connect to your e-mail. If you end up tying up the phone a lot, you may want to get a second line. Here are some other tips:

- ✔ If your phone company gives you a choice of local service options, pick one that lets you call your e-mail provider without per-minute charges.

- ✔ You need a modular phone jack, the same kind of jack that telephones use, to plug in your modem. If you don't have one, Radio Shack stores carry a wide line of adapters and wiring stuff.

- ✔ If you do get a second line, don't add on extensions and don't get call waiting. Just use it for your computer.

- ✔ Business service costs a lot more than residential service.

Selecting an E-Mail Provider

Once you have a computer and a modem, you need a service provider. A provider is a business that offers electronic communication services, usually for a fee. You have to call them up to ask for an account, either by voice or using your computer and modem. Many provide free disks with everything you need to get started. You will be asked for your name and address and for a credit card number. You will be billed monthly for the services you use. Some providers ask you to pay in advance or offer a discount if you do. Providers get a lot of deadbeats.

Your provider forwards the mail you send on to its destination — directly if the addressee uses the same provider; otherwise, by way of the Internet. Mail addressed to you is held by the provider until you call up and log in to check your mail. You don't have to worry about missing mail when your computer isn't connected.

Types of service providers are described in the following sections as value-added online services and local service providers. Competition between the different types of service providers is intense, and the boundaries between them are blurring.

Value-added online services

This type of provider tries to offer much more than basic e-mail access in order to get you to use its services. Needless to say, these providers charge more as a result.

The most popular value-added providers include America Online, CompuServe, Prodigy, Microsoft Network, eWorld, Delphi, and GEnie.

Reasons for picking a value-added online service include the following:

- ✔ User-friendly software that provides all the tools you need in a single package
- ✔ Additional services that are only available to customers of that provider
- ✔ The capability of logging in from any major city just by making a local phone call
- ✔ Better security. The bigger companies have a lot more to lose and take security more seriously (we hope).
- ✔ Longevity. At least the top four are likely to be around for a while. Harry's Internet and Pizza Emporium may switch to Harry's Tattoo Removal and leave you stranded with an e-mail address that no longer works.
- ✔ Lots of user support

The value-added online services provide a great deal of user support, but when something new comes along in Internet technology, months (or even years) may pass before they can offer it.

If you call, the major value-added providers will send you a starter kit with the software you need and usually some promotional offer, like ten free hours. A listing of the top online services phone numbers follows in Table 2-1.

Table 2-1	Major Online Service Providers
Service	*Phone Numbers*
America Online (AOL)	800-827-6364; 703-448-8700
CompuServe	800-848-8990; 614-529-1340
Prodigy	800-776-3449; 914-448-8000
The Microsoft Network (MSN)	800-386-5550 (Windows 95 only)
eWorld	800-775-4556; 408-996-1010 (Macintosh only)
Delphi	800-695-4005; 617-491-3393
GEnie	800-638-9636; 301-340-5216; TDD 800-238-9172

America Online has launched a new subsidiary called Global Network Navigator (GNN) that provides services similar to the local providers but with AOL's network of phone connections. You can contact GNN at 800-819-6112.

Local Internet e-mail providers

Local service providers come in two flavors:

- Terminal or shell dial-up
- SLIP/PPP dial-up

Terminal or shell dial-up service connects you to a computer, usually one using the UNIX operating system. You can send and receive your e-mail using a UNIX e-mail program, like Pine. See Chapter 16 to learn how these UNIX e-mail programs work. This kind of service is great if you have an older computer that cannot run the latest graphical interface software.

SLIP or PPP service connects you directly to the Internet, and you can use (and will need) a powerful Internet e-mail program like Eudora or Netscape. SLIP stands for *Serial Line Internet Protocol* and PPP stands for *Point to Point Protocol.* (See the sidebar "Mommy, what's a protocol?" earlier in this chapter.) These protocols do pretty much the same thing. Ask your service provider which one they support. If you have a choice, PPP is slightly more reliable and a lot easier to set up. For more information on SLIP and PPP, see *The Internet For Dummies,* 3rd Edition (IDG Books Worldwide, Inc.).

Why go with the little guys?

Reasons to go local include the following:

- Lower cost. Many local providers offer a flat monthly rate, though the hourly rate may make more sense if you only plan to use e-mail. Either way, they are usually cheaper than the value-added providers.

- Choice of access tools. Many programs are available for reading e-mail, such as Eudora and Netscape, and with a SLIP or PPP account, you can use any program you want. Competition is fierce, and new features are being added all the time. If you go with a value-added service provider, you are generally locked into the e-mail program they provide.

- Ability to use the latest Internet services as soon as they hit the Net. The value-added providers usually take half a year to a year to add a new capability — if they ever do.

- Less censorship. CompuServe recently cut *all* its customers' access to some allegedly racy Internet newsgroups due to pressure from the German government. Local providers tend to be more nimble.

- Higher status in the Internet pecking order. If your e-mail address ends in `aol.com` or `compuserve.com`, some people on the Internet will peg you as a newbie, or newcomer, and take you a bit less seriously. We think you shouldn't take people like that seriously, but they're out there. One message we saw referred to America Online accounts as "Internet training wheels."

Here are the best ways we know to find a local service provider close to home:

- ✔ Check the business pages of your local newspaper for advertisements from local access providers.
- ✔ Ask your public library's research librarian or online services staff.
- ✔ Look in your local Yellow Pages under "Online service providers." For some reason, not all service providers are listed in the Yellow Pages.
- ✔ Ask anyone you know who already has e-mail what service she's using and if she likes it.
- ✔ Many cities have *freenets*, public access online systems that you can use for free (except in Los Angeles). They all offer e-mail. Your public library should know whether there's one in your city.

Consider the following things when picking a local service provider:

- ✔ Flat fee versus hourly charge. Monthly Internet access is available for $30/month or less in all major U.S. cities and a surprising number of rural areas. (One of your authors is typing this while connected to his local provider in Trumansburg, NY, pop. 1,733). Some providers charge less for e-mail-only use. A flat monthly fee is a great buy if you will be using other Internet services besides e-mail. An hourly rate might be a lot cheaper if you are only using e-mail.
- ✔ Local phone access. In most areas in the U.S. phone calls are free or at least not charged by the minute if they don't go too far. If at all possible, select a service provider that has an access phone number that is within your local (free) calling area.
- ✔ System availability during peak periods. The cheaper providers cut costs by not having enough equipment to provide good service during peak periods. The result is busy signals when you try to dial in and painfully slow response when you do get through, especially on weekday evenings. If you can get by checking your mail at other times, the low-price outfits may be the way to go.
- ✔ Modem speeds. If you go out and buy a fast 28,800 bps modem, make sure that your provider has modems that are as fast as well as big enough computers to keep up.
- ✔ Ability to call in from remote locations. Some providers, like The World in Brookline, MA, have arrangements with large data networks to allow their customers to dial in from the road by making a local call, and some like ClarkNet in Washington, DC have an 800 number for use on the road. They usually charge extra for this service.
- ✔ Support for neophytes. If the provider's technical support staff has no patience for questions from a beginner, look elsewhere.
- ✔ If you are a Macintosh user, make sure that your provider offers whole-hearted support for Macintosh e-mail applications.

Don't feel unreasonable if you want to try several services before picking the one you like best. But remember, once you start giving out your e-mail address, you may find it harder to switch services.

Understanding Your E-Mail Program

An e-mail program is software that runs on your computer and lets you read and compose your e-mail. If you are using a value-added service provider, your e-mail program will be included in the program disk you use to start your service. We talk about using online services for e-mail in Part III.

If you are using a local Internet service provider, you will generally need to choose an Internet e-mail program. The two most popular programs, Eudora and Netscape Navigator, are described in Part II. This part will also tell you how to get copies of these programs.

If you are using a shell account, you might want to use the UNIX e-mail program Pine described in Chapter 16.

Finally, if you are using e-mail at work, you'll likely be told which e-mail program to use. We'll tell you about the most common types in Part IV.

Common features of e-mail programs include the following:

- ✔ Selecting and reading e-mail. Most e-mail programs present a list of incoming messages from which you can select.

- ✔ Composing, addressing, and sending outgoing messages. E-mail programs usually provide you with a built-in word processing program that allows you to type in your message and make edits until you are satisfied with what you wrote. Some even have spell checkers.

- ✔ Replying to a message that someone has sent you. You can usually include all or part of the message that was sent.

- ✔ Forwarding a message you receive to someone else with your comments.

- ✔ Redirecting or bouncing a message to someone else without any edits or changes.

- ✔ Saving and organizing your messages. Many programs let you set up a number of folders on your computer and make it easy to put each message in the right folder.

- ✔ Filtering and threading incoming messages. Some e-mail programs have features that let you tell the program to put different types of mail into a separate list so you can easily read them in order of the priority you choose. Mail from your boss can be read first (or last!), for example.

✔ Saving and organizing e-mail addresses.

✔ Creating a short block of text that is automatically added to the end of messages you send. These files are called *signature files*.

✔ Creating personal nicknames, or aliases, that you can use to address mail without typing the entire address.

✔ Creating personal electronic mailing lists that let you send messages to a number of people at once.

✔ Importing a computer file into an e-mail message so its text is part of the message.

✔ Attaching files to an e-mail message. These files might be anything from a word processing document, to a picture, to a video clip.

Whew!

We've given you an awful lot of information in this chapter. Don't panic if you haven't absorbed it all: In later chapters we get down to the nitty-gritty, step-by-step operations, and you can always come back here when you have a general question.

Chapter 3
Basic E-Mail Concepts

• •

• •

*T*he amazing information superhighway is still under construction. Just like a real highway construction project, only the access roads are open in many areas. The access road for the information superhighway is e-mail. In this chapter, we tell you the essential things you need to know in order to use e-mail. We cover some of the finer points of e-mail in Chapter 4. Chapter 5 has some techy stuff that you certainly don't need to know about to get started, but you will be very glad it is in here if you ever *do* need it.

The basic concepts we talk about here apply whether you are on an isolated e-mail system and can only talk to people in your own company, say, or your e-mail system is connected to the Internet and you can talk to any other Internet-connected e-mail user in the world. We start at the top with e-mail addresses.

What's the Story with E-Mail Addresses?

Understanding addresses may be the hardest part of learning e-mail — and definitely the most important. To send an e-mail message to someone or something (some e-mail goes to robots), you have to have his, her, or its address. An e-mail address is a lot like a phone number. Phone number styles vary somewhat around the world — some countries have 6, 7 or even 8 digit local numbers, for example — but e-mail address styles vary a lot, too.

Here is the good news! If your computer has a cut and paste feature — as all Macintosh and Windows computers do — you can usually copy e-mail addresses and paste them where they are needed. Just be sure to copy the correct address, the whole address, and nothing but the address, so help you. If you just started using a computer for the first time and you don't know what we mean by "copy and paste," don't worry, typing works just fine. In your spare time, pick up *Macs For Dummies* or *Windows For Dummies* and read at your leisure — you might find the background helpful even if it's not absolutely necessary for your task at hand.

Local e-mail addresses

Local e-mail addresses, or *mailbox names,* are usually just a bunch of letters and numbers like `margy`, `john1`, `Carol_Baroudi`, or `AGR12745`. Often your local e-mail address is the same as the name you use when you log in to your computer — your *login name.* Many services let you pick any e-mail name you want, just so long as it isn't taken already. Often this means you end up with a name like `joshua819` on a big, popular service like America Online.

CompuServe, for reasons having to do with long forgotten computer operating systems, uses a pair of numbers separated by a comma for its e-mail addresses — for example `102554,3060`.

That pesky comma in CompuServe addresses is a source of considerable confusion because Internet mail uses a comma to separate the different addresses when you want to send e-mail to multiple recipients. We'll see how this conflict is handled later. (Okay, if you can't stand the suspense: you replace the comma with a period in an Internet address. But please don't tell the other readers yet.)

Capitalization normally does not matter in e-mail addresses. Or, as computer-types say it, e-mail addresses are not *case sensitive.* This means that e-mail addressed to `margy`, `Margy`, and `MARGY` will all end up at the same place. On the other hand, `margy`, `margaret`, and `margy1` are all different, of course. (In fact, a few ancient systems still care about capitalization, but unless you're really unlucky, you'll never run into one.)

The general rule is that you can use the local e-mail name by itself whenever you are sending mail to someone who uses the same e-mail provider that you use. For example, if you use America Online, you can send mail to other America Online users without tacking "aol.com" after the username. If you are sending a message to someone on a different e-mail service, you usually have to use a full Internet e-mail address.

Internet e-mail addresses

So what's an Internet address? Roughly speaking, an Internet e-mail address consists of the following parts:

- ✔ A mailbox name
- ✔ @ (the *at* sign)
- ✔ A domain name

For example, here is a typical address: elvis@iecc.com.

Here, elvis is the mailbox name and iecc.com is the domain name. We tell you more about domain names in Chapter 4.

Internet e-mail addresses are more complicated than local addresses for several reasons:

- ✔ Internet e-mail connects millions of people today, and that number will grow to billions in the next century. We can't all have a simple e-mail address like Bob.
- ✔ The Internet has to accommodate addresses from many different e-mail systems. Each of these systems were developed separately, and the developers had different ideas of what an e-mail address should look like.
- ✔ The computer programmers who invented the Internet never expected it to go on as long as it has without being re-designed. Had they known, they might have made it a bit more user-friendly (then again, they might have done worse).

Some e-mail services make you put an access code in front of the address to tell your mail system that this message is destined for the Internet. It's kind of like dialing 9 to get an outside line. Here are some examples:

Internet:elvis@iecc.com

SMTP:elvis@iecc.com

SMTP in this example, stands for Simple Mail Transfer Protocol, the optimistically named set of rules that say how Internet e-mail is transferred from one computer to another. For the most part, you never have to pay attention to these rules; your e-mail program takes care of them.

One rule that you do have to pay attention to says that Internet addresses can contain the following:

- ✔ letters
- ✔ numbers
- ✔ some punctuation characters such as periods and underscores

It also says that Internet addresses should *not* contain the following:

- ✔ commas
- ✔ spaces
- ✔ parentheses

The most common situation in which these restrictions cause problems is for CompuServe addresses, which consist of two numbers separated by a comma. When converting a CompuServe address to an Internet address, change the comma to a period. For example, 71053,2615 becomes 71053.2615@compuserve.com.

Another common problem is spaces in AOL mailbox names. For example, John Doe's mailbox name would be John Doe.

If, for some reason, you must send mail to an address that does include commas, spaces, or parentheses, enclose the address in double quotes, like this: "John Doe"@aol.com.

America Online in fact lets you leave out the space so you don't have to quote the name, but there are some other mail systems that are not so forgiving.

Where am I on the Internet?

The most important address you need to know is your own. You should keep a copy in you wallet until you have it memorized. That way you will be prepared when someone asks, "What's your e-mail address?"

If you are accessing the Internet through a service provider, your address is most likely

```
yourloginname@yourprovider'sdomainname
```

The domain name is usually your provider's domain name. In the case where your company or school is your provider, it's your company's or school's domain name. If your login name is *elvis* and your computer is shamu.strat.ntw.org, your mail address may be

```
elvis@shamu.strat.ntw.org
elvis@strat.ntw.org
elvis@ntw.org
```

or even

```
elvis-presley@ntw.org
```

If you're using a computer such as a PC or a Mac that doesn't require you to log in, your mail is probably handled by a central mail server. In this case your e-mail name will probably be the login name you use when you contact the mail server.

If you're not sure what your e-mail address is, send an e-mail message to *Internet For Dummies* Central at email@dummies.com.

Our mail robot will send back a note containing the address from which your message was sent, which is your e-mail address. While you're at it, add a sentence or two telling us whether you like this book because we authors do read all the mail, too.

Knowing your own e-mail address is all well and good, but what you really need is the address of the person to whom you want to send that hot e-mail message. We tell you how to find out someone else's e-mail address in Chapter 20. Spoiler: the best way is to call them on the phone and ask them.

You should now know enough about addresses to get you started. We return to this fun topic in Chapter 4, where we tell you how to decode those intriguing domain names and deal with something called X.400 addresses, which you will encounter only if you have done something really bad in a previous life.

Using Your E-Mail Program

To use e-mail, you need a mail program, or *mailer.* Mailers typically let you do the following:

- ✔ Read your incoming mail.
- ✔ Send new mail.
- ✔ Reply to messages you receive.

✔ Forward messages to other people via e-mail.

✔ Save messages for later.

✔ Read saved messages.

The bad news is that dozens of mailer programs are out there — programs that read and write electronic mail messages. They are available as freeware, shareware, commercialware, and somekindofware that probably came with your computer. The good news is that they all do more or less the same thing, since they are all e-mail programs, after all.

Sometimes you have a choice of which mailer to use. Other times you don't. If you use AOL, you will use their mailer. In this book, we cover the following mailer programs:

Eudora (Macintosh and Windows)

Netscape Navigator 2.0 (Macintosh and Windows)

America Online (Macintosh and Windows)

CompuServe (Macintosh and Windows)

Prodigy (Macintosh and Windows)

Microsoft Network and Exchange (Windows)

Netcom NetCruiser

Pine (UNIX)

cc:Mail

Microsoft Mail

Lotus Notes

Although many other mailers are in use, the basic principles are pretty much the same. In this chapter, we paint a broad picture of what a generic mailer is supposed to do. When you are actually ready to send mail, for the picky details, turn to the chapter that deals with your very own mailer.

Where is my mail, anyway?

When your mail arrives, unless you are one of the lucky few whose computers have a permanent Internet connection, the mail doesn't get delivered to your computer. Your messages are delivered instead to a *mail server,* a computer that is sort of like your local post office. In order for you to actually get your mail, your *mail program* has to contact your mail server and ask for your messages. To send mail, your mail program has to take it to the post office — that is, transmit it to the server.

If you're using a shell account or a commercial online service, the mail server is in the same group of computers you connect to when you're dialed in. So when you run your provider's mail program, the mail is right there for you to read, and it can drop outgoing mail directly in the virtual mail chute.

If you're using a SLIP/PPP account, when your mail program picks up the mail, it sucks your messages from your provider to your PC or Mac at top speed. After you have your mail on your local computer, you can disconnect — a good idea if your provider charges by the hour. Then you can read and respond to your mail while the meter isn't ticking — that is, while you're *offline*. After you're ready to send your responses or new messages, you can reconnect and transmit your outgoing mail to the mail server, again at top network speed.

A five-step program for sending e-mail

You complete these five steps to send an e-mail message:

1. **Tell the mailer that you want to send a new message.**
2. **Address the message.**
3. **Fill in the subject line.**
4. **Compose the message.**
5. **Tell your computer to send the message on its way.**

Most mailers have a command like "New Message" that lets you create new e-mail. Usually a window or screen appears with fields for the address, subject, and the actual text of the message, often called the *message body*.

Where to, buddy?

Normally you address the new message by typing or pasting the recipient's e-mail address into a To field. Simple enough. Most mailers let you keep an address book on your computer. If your mailer does, you can just select the recipient's name from a list, assuming you've entered the address into the address book beforehand.

You can send your message to more than one recipient. Most mailers will let you enter several addresses into the To field. Most mailers ask you to separate different addresses with commas — but not CompuServe.

Mommy, what's carbon paper — ccs and bccs

You will also notice fields labeled cc and maybe even bcc. The abbreviation *cc* stands for "carbon copy." Way back when, typists made multiple copies of a letter by inserting a sandwich of stationary separated by sheets of carbon paper. Use the cc field for the addresses of people who aren't the primary recipients of your message but who need to be kept informed. Everyone who gets the message will see the cc field and know who else has received the message.

Some mailers have a *bcc* field. This abbreviation stands for "blind carbon copy." A person whose address is entered into the bcc field gets a copy of the message, but, because the other recipients don't see the bcc field, they have no clue that this person got a copy. Use this feature judiciously. If someone thinks her communication with you is private and confidential, only to find you've been copying her mail to someone else, you'd best have your ducks all lined up.

What's the message all about?

Another universal feature of mailers is a Subject field. It's a place for you to enter a short description of what the message is about. The recipient will see the subject and your name in her incoming message list when she picks up her mail (many e-mail users find a hundred or more messages on their computer every morning). Your recipient can choose in what order to read her messages, so state your subject as clearly as possible. Here are some examples of subject lines:

Poor: "Need Information"

Fair: "Real Estate Question"

Better: "About the Binkley sale"

Best: "What's the closing date for Binkley?"

Most mailers will let you have a blank subject, but we wish they would at least warn you when you forget the subject line. Always include a subject.

I have something to say

You are now ready to type in the text of your message. This text is often called the *message body*. On most mailers, you can get to the field or box where you will enter the message body by clicking in it with the mouse or by using the tab key. Once you get there, you just type in what you want to say.

Once you are done, we recommend that you read over your message carefully. Most mailers have built-in editing features like cut and paste that let you correct what you have written. A few mailers even have a built-in spell checker.

If your mailer lacks a spell check feature, you can always copy the message, paste it into your word processor, and spell check there.

See Chapter 4 for some ideas on writing more effective e-mail.

You can also include text in your message that is in a file on your hard disk. To do so, look for a message import command in your mailer or open the file with your favorite word processor, select and copy the text you want included, and then paste that text into the mailer's message body field.

Many mailers let you *attach* one or more local computer files to your message. These files can be word processing documents, graphics, sounds, or even video clips. Make sure that your recipient has the necessary programs to read the files you are sending to her. See Chapter 5 to learn about some of the more popular formats for e-mail attachments.

Ship it

After you are really, really sure your message says what you want it to say, you are ready to send it on its way. Most mailers have a send button or command. If you are online to your provider, just click this button and your message is on its way.

Most mail systems have no provision for recalling a message once you have sent it. In fact, e-mail messages are often delivered in less than a minute.

If you are working offline, you can put the message aside for transmission the next time you connect with your service provider. If your mailer is equipped to do this, you will see a command like "Drop mail in out-box" or "Send later." Not only does this way of working save on connect time charges, but it also gives you some time to reconsider.

Receiving mail

You follow four steps to read your mail:

1. **Get the mail from your service provider.**
2. **Review your list of messages.**
3. **Select and open messages.**
4. **Dispose of messages.**

Beam them up, Scotty

You usually have to connect to your e-mail service provider or connect to your mail server to get your e-mail. Once you do this, you may have to enter a command like "Check mail." You then get to wait a moment while your messages are brought over the network to your computer (if you are using a UNIX shell provider, you don't have to go through the "check mail" step).

Your mailer will present you with a list of incoming e-mail messages (see Figure 3-1). This list typically contains a line for each message containing the date, sender, and subject of that message. The list usually includes old messages that you have not dealt with and new messages at the end. Different mailers use different codes and icons to indicate the status of each message on the list: new, old-but-unopened, read.

You can now select a message to read, usually by double-clicking on the message line using the mouse or by using the arrow and Tab keys to move to the message line you want and then pressing Enter.

You can read your message on the screen, print it out, or close it and read it later. You can also send a reply message or send the message on to someone else. We'll talk about those options later in this chapter.

File this message, please

Finally, you can dispose of your message, either by throwing it out or by saving it for later reference. Different mailers have different names for the place in the computer where messages are saved. Most call them *mailboxes*. You can create as many of these mailboxes as you want and give them whatever names you want. Many mailers let you organize your mailboxes into *folders*.

Most mailers let you open any of these mailboxes and see a list of the messages that are in it. You can then select a message and open it, read it again, copy stuff out of it, send a belated reply, or whatever.

Mailers also usually let you save individual messages as separate text files that you can then open with a word processor, spreadsheet program, or some other type of software.

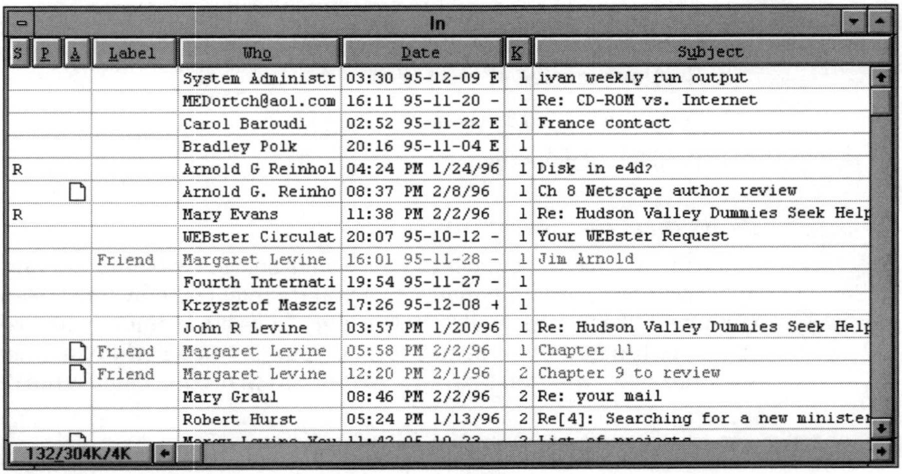

S	P	A	Label	Who	Date	K	Subject
				System Administr	03:30 95-12-09 E	1	ivan weekly run output
				MEDortch@aol.com	16:11 95-11-20 -	1	Re: CD-ROM vs. Internet
				Carol Baroudi	02:52 95-11-22 E	1	France contact
				Bradley Polk	20:16 95-11-04 E	1	
R				Arnold G Reinhol	04:24 PM 1/24/96	1	Disk in e4d?
		🗋		Arnold G. Reinho	08:37 PM 2/8/96	1	Ch 8 Netscape author review
R				Mary Evans	11:38 PM 2/2/96	1	Re: Hudson Valley Dummies Seek Help
				WEBster Circulat	20:07 95-10-12 -	1	Your WEBster Request
			Friend	Margaret Levine	16:01 95-11-28 -	1	Jim Arnold
				Fourth Internati	19:54 95-11-27 -	1	
				Krzysztof Maszcz	17:26 95-12-08 +	1	
				John R Levine	03:57 PM 1/20/96	1	Re: Hudson Valley Dummies Seek Help
		🗋	Friend	Margaret Levine	05:58 PM 2/2/96	1	Chapter 11
		🗋	Friend	Margaret Levine	12:20 PM 2/1/96	2	Chapter 9 to review
				Mary Graul	08:46 PM 2/2/96	2	Re: your mail
				Robert Hurst	05:24 PM 1/13/96	2	Re[4]: Searching for a new minister
		🗋		Margaret Levine You	11:43 95-10-23	2	List of projects

132/304K/4K

Figure 3-1:
Your basic
incoming
mail.

If you choose to save a message, you can use two general organizational approaches: filing by sender and filing by topic. Whether you use one or the other or both is mostly a matter of taste. Some mail programs (such as Pine) help you file stuff by the sender's name, so if your friend Fred has the username `fred@something.or.other,` when you press S to save a message from him, Pine asks whether you want to put it in a folder called `fred.`

For filing by topic, you come up with the folder names. The most difficult part is coming up with memorable names. If you're not careful, you end up with three folders — for example, *Accounts, Bills,* and *Finances,* with different names, each with a third of the messages about a particular topic. Sometimes you should just use the first name you come up with. That way you are more likely to pick the same name again to save future messages with similar topics.

When in doubt, throw it out

The hard disk manufacturers' association doesn't want us to tell you this but, umm, you really don't have to save all your incoming messages. In fact saving them all is usually a really bad idea. This issue may not be high on your list of concerns if all the e-mail you've gotten so far is the welcome letter from the president of your service provider and the response from the *Internet For Dummies* Central robot (see "Where am I on the Internet?" in this chapter). But, trust us, your incoming mail volume will pick up as people find where you are, and if it doesn't, try subscribing to a few mailing lists (see Chapter 21). We delete 98 percent of the mail we receive after we read it, and we still have thousands of saved messages.

Replying to a message

Another thing you can do when a message is open on your screen is send a reply message. You start this process by giving the reply command. Your mailer then opens a new outgoing message automatically addressed to the sender or senders of the original message with the subject line filled in. The subject will be the subject of the original message with the letters *Re* placed in front. ("Re" is short for "Regarding," or for the Latin speakers among us, *in re.*)

Many mailers also include the text of the original message in the body of the reply. To set off your reply, a left angle bracket (">"), colon (":"), or tab indentation appears in front of every line of the original message. This reformatting is called *quoting* the original message.

When messages bounce back and forth a number of times, the quoted text can get quite complicated, with three, four, or even five angle brackets in front of some lines, forming a kind of high-tech court transcript. Computer types, who are used to puzzling out complex program files, may find this angle bracket build-up acceptable. Many others find it very tedious and confusing.

Edit the quoted text in a reply message so that it is clear and no longer than necessary to remind the original sender of what you are replying to.

Forwarding and redirecting (bouncing) mail

Another option you have when a message is open is to *forward* it to someone else. The forwarded message will indicate that it came from you. The text of the message you are forwarding often appears in a quoted format. Usually, you can add your own comments to the forwarded message.

Redirecting a message — also called bouncing a message — is a lot like forwarding one, only the mail is sent as though it came from the original person directly. The message isn't quoted, and the sender and reply-to information are left intact. This way, if the new recipient of the mail wants to reply, the response goes to the original sender, not to you just because you passed it on.

Forwarding a message says, "I think you might be interested in this." Bouncing a message says, "This should have been sent to you."

Forwarding or redirecting e-mail along to someone else is easy and cheap. It's one of the handiest things about e-mail, and at the same time it can make you very unpopular if misused. It's handy because you can easily pass along a message to someone who needs to know. It can get you a reputation as a pain-in-the-modem if you send out floods of messages to recipients who would just as soon not hear about yet another important cause or bon mot. So please, please think a little about whether you will really be making your e-mail friends' day by forwarding that message to all of them. Better still, ask, "From time to time, I get interesting e-mail on the plight of the Antarctic phyto-plankton. Would you like me to send them on to you?"

Inspect the list of recipients carefully when forwarding mail. Some mail addresses are really mailing lists that redistribute messages to many other people. Make sure you know where your e-mail is going.

Filters

You can easily get inundated with incoming mail, especially if you subscribe to automated mailing lists (see Chapter 21). Not only can you take a long time to slog through hundreds of incoming e-mail messages every day, but you can easily miss the one important message in all that drek. To help you deal with this problem, some mailers offer a feature called *filters*.

Filters are sets of rules that you create in your mailer program. When your mailer gets new incoming mail, it uses those rules to sort your mail into different piles based on who sent the mail and what the subject is, sort of like an efficient secretary used to do back in the twentieth century. The piles of messages then show up in different incoming mailboxes. Some filters also highlight key messages on the incoming message list with colors or priority codes.

You can ask your mailer program to put e-mail from mailing lists into separate mailboxes for each list. Mail whose subject mentions a project you are working on can go into yet another box. And, of course, mail from your boss or significant other can be given the priority it deserves.

Headers: the basics

Headers are the seemingly indecipherable lines of text that appear at the beginning of every incoming e-mail message. The most common format for headers is that used on the Internet. Other mail systems have their own format for headers, but the information is usually pretty much the same.

```
From carol@iecc.com Sun Jan 28 15:09:17 1996
Mime-Version: 1.0
Content-Type: text/plain; charset="us-ascii"
Date: Sun, 28 Jan 1996 16:09:17 +0100
To: reinhold@world.std.com (Arnold G Reinhold)
From: carol@iecc.com (Carol Baroudi)
Subject: josh's tooth paste
```

Table 3-1 is a guide to what the most important parts of an Internet mail header mean.

Table 3-1	The Parts of an Internet Mail Header
Header	*Description*
Subject:	Describes the message (recommended)
To:	Lists recipients of the message (at least one required)
Cc:	Lists "carbon copy" recipients (optional)
Bcc:	Lists "blind carbon copy" recipients; these recipients' names are not sent with message (optional)
From:	Address of message author (required and provided automatically)
Reply-To:	Address where replies should be sent if different from the From line (optional)
Date:	Time and date the message was sent (required, provided automatically)
Expires:	Date after which message expires (optional, rarely used)
Message-ID:	Unique machine-generated identifier for the message (required, provided automatically)
Mime-Version:	Version of MIME being used (see "Sound! Pictures! Action!" in this chapter)
Content-Type:	What MIME data format is being used (see "Sound! Pictures! Action!" in this chapter)
Content-transfer-encoding:	How MIME is transmitting this message (see "Sound! Pictures! Action!" in this chapter)
Lines:	Number of lines of text in the message (optional, provided automatically)

Note: Many other optional header lines exist. None of them are of great importance.

A picture is worth a million bytes

Sooner or later, plain old, everyday e-mail is not going to be good enough for you. Someone's going to send you a picture you just have to see, or you're going to want to send something cool to your new e-mail pen pal. Some mail systems can handle graphics and other non-text data right in the message body. Sometimes the entire message is in a special format (such as *MIME*, which we talk about soon), and sometimes people *attach* things to their mail.

Getting attached

To exchange things such as computer programs, drawings, photographs, and video clips using electronic mail, you may need to send or receive them as attachments. The e-mail message acts sort of like a cover letter with a package. You have to unwrap the attachment separately.

Attachments come in many flavors. You may or may not have the software you need in order to read the package you receive, but Chapter 5 tells you how to know what you're looking at and what your likely next step is toward making it comprehensible.

Meanwhile, we tell you now about MIME, a convention for including stuff other than plain text in e-mail messages. MIME stands for *m*ultipurpose *I*nternet *m*ail *e*xtensions, by the way.

Sound! Pictures! Action!

MIME supports a long list of all kinds of stuff, ranging from slightly formatted text using characters (such as `*emphasis*` for *emphasis*) up through color pictures, full-motion video, and high-fidelity sound. The group that designed MIME had enough sense to realize that not everyone has a computer that can handle all the fancy high-end stuff, so a single MIME message can contain alternative forms of the same thing, such as beautifully formatted, typeset text for people with fancy video screens and plain text for people on simple terminals. Because MIME also handles nested messages, a single MIME message might contain a document and a couple of illustrations that go with it.

All kinds of computer data links exist out there in network-land, and some of them are hostile or at best unhelpful. About the only thing they agree on is text. So MIME disguises all its fancy formats as plain old text (at least it looks like text to computers. To us, it looks more like `QW&IIdfhfFX97/$@`). You can recognize a MIME message by looking for special mail headers that look something like this:

```
MIME-version: 1.0
Content-type: TEXT/PLAIN; CHARSET=US-ASCII
Content-transfer-encoding: 7BIT
```

The first line says that the message is using Version 1.0 of the MIME standard (the only version defined so far). The second line says that this particular message contains just text. The third line says that the text is represented in the message as the simplest kind of text that's out there (computers are so dim that even this isn't obvious to them). Different kinds of messages use different Content-type headers. At this point, they all use the same Content-transfer-encoding.

- ✔ If you are using a mail program that is *MIME-compliant,* you'll know when you have a MIME message because, as you're reading your mail, a window pops up all of a sudden with a picture or formatted text, or perhaps your computer begins singing the message to you (remember singing telegrams?). Eudora, Netscape, and Pine are MIME-compliant, and America Online can send and receive MIME mail.

- ✔ If your mail program doesn't know about MIME and you get a MIME-ized message, it shows up as a large message in your mailbox. If it contains text, it might be readable as is, give or take some ugly punctuation. The sound and pictures, on the other hand, are totally hopeless because they are just binary digitized versions of the images and not any sort of text approximation.

- ✔ If you get a picture or sound MIME message and your mailer doesn't automatically handle it, clunky but usable methods may exist for saving the message to a file and extracting the contents with separate programs. Consult your Internet service provider's help desk.

How Can E-Mail Be Free?

At the beginning of this book, we told you that e-mail is usually free. If you have gotten as far as sending your first message, you might feel we misled you a bit. After all, you've had to get a computer (maybe a thousand bucks or two — but hey, they're supposed to be good for balancing your checkbook, storing recipes, and, most important, playing Myst, too). Your modem cost you $50 to $300, but it's small and makes cute noises. And you needed an extra phone line. (Well, you had to have one of those anyway. Whaddya mean your kids made you get a second line?) And don't forget the Internet service ($5 to $50 per month, zero to three bucks an hour — okay, that's extra).

What we *really* meant to say is that on most providers, you are not charged for each e-mail message, no matter where it goes. You can correspond with dozens of people all around the world or subscribe to bunches of mailing lists and see a thousand messages per day (we get hives just thinking about it), all at no extra charge.

So how do they do that? A common misconception is that the U.S. government is paying for all this. That used to be true, at least in part, but the Internet has been private for a couple of years. Here is the real story.

A hiccup is worth a thousand bytes

Almost all Internet data is sent over circuits developed for telephone communication. Nowadays, all long-distance telephone lines are digital, meaning that the sound of your voice moves across the country as electronic ones and zeros just like computer data. The standard speed for a voice call, established way back in the 1960s, is 8,000 bytes per second. Because a byte can hold a single letter or number and your average e-mail message is less than eight hundred letters long, it can be sent on one of these lines in about a tenth of a second, less time than a hiccup takes. A residential customer is charged about $0.12 per minute for a long distance call within North America. Wholesale rates are far less. So an e-mail message can go from New York to Los Angeles for a small fraction of a penny.

Put that in your pipe . . .

Rather than try to keep track of all these tiny usage charges, the Internet asks providers for a fee based on how fast they *could* send data. This measure is called *size of your pipe* pricing. The provider, in turn, divides up those fees and includes your share in your monthly bill.

Some people think newer Internet services, like the World Wide Web and Internet telephone service, may force providers to charge you for the actual amount of data you send. Others think the present system can go on indefinitely. Even if you do end up paying usage charges, competitive pressures will likely keep the cost of a basic e-mail message so low that you'll hardly notice.

Chapter 4
The Finer Points of E-Mail

*I*n the previous chapters, we covered the basics of e-mail — sending and receiving messages and filing them away. Now it's time to talk about the subtler issues, like what to write and how to write it. We also address addresses one more time, to tell you more than you probably want to know about domain names and what they mean, and to introduce the evil empire of e-mail, X.400.

The Psychology of E-Mail

We humans have evolved many methods to communicate in person: speech, eye contact, body language, and touch. And we have invented many more ways to communicate over distance: letters, telegrams, telephone, fax, and now e-mail. Each has its own power and limitations. Many of e-mail's strengths are also its limitations:

✔ E-mail's speed discourages thoughtful replies.

✔ Its low cost can lessen its impact.

✔ Its textual basis makes it hard to catch nuance and inflection.

✔ In volume, it's easy to overlook.

Marshall McLuhan told us that the medium is the message. The message of e-mail is casual, flip, cold, shot from the hip, matter of fact. All you need to get your messages to stand out above the clutter are a little thought, a little effort, and, most of all, a little empathy: How would you feel if you received the message you are about to send?

E-Mail Etiquette

You may take a while to cotton to e-mail style, but before you dive in and alienate your friends and your would-be friends, take some hints from our years of e-mail experience. All we say here applies to *all* your e-mail, be it to friend, family, or coworker. It applies quadruply to e-mail you send to mailing lists on which people haven't the slightest idea of who you are, where the only impression you make is with your e-mail.

If you use e-mail for any length of time, you *will* get a message from someone that just makes you seethe with rage.

```
To: you
From: Boss

When will the Simson contract be ready?

Boss
```

Doesn't he know you were in the office until 3 a.m. this morning working on the stupid thing? Doesn't he realize it would have been done already if he had told you last week about those changes Simson requested? Doesn't he know you were planning to take your kids to a ball game this afternoon?

Well, your boss was just getting ready for his boss's staff meeting and needed to know what to tell her if the subject came up. What seemed to him like a harmless request for a status update sent you over the edge. It might have been more palatable if he had written

```
To: you
From: Boss

Thanks for the extra effort on the Simson contract. Could you
give me an idea when you think you'll have it done? I need an
estimate for Sue's 10 am meeting.

Boss
```

Our dictionary defines *etiquette* as proper behavior or courtesy. The speed and impersonal nature of e-mail make respecting social conventions even more important. Here are a few suggestions regarding more effective e-mail style:

- ✔ Watch your tone. E-mail can seem brusque even when you don't intend it to be. Try to read it from the recipient's point of view before sending.

- ✔ Avoid foul language. Just because Senator Exon is trying to ban dirty words on the Internet doesn't mean you have to use them.

✔ Don't send messages full of pointless and excessive outrage — what we netoids call a *flame*. Here's an example:

```
u bozos are going to tell me how to write my
messages?
```

✔ Irony and sarcasm are easy to miss without the raised eyebrow. Double-check your humor. Sometimes, adding a *smiley* helps to let your reader in on the joke:

```
u bozos are going to tell me how to write my
messages? ;-)
```

✔ When in doubt about your message's tone, save the message overnight and read it again in the morning before you send it, or ask someone else to read it over before you send it. Many's the message we wrote and later threw away unsent.

✔ If you *do* get involved in a vitriolic exchange of messages, known as a *flame war,* the best way to stop is to let the other guy have the last word.

✔ Your Subject line should tell the recipient as much as possible about your message without getting too long. "Don't park in the back lot this Thursday" is much better than "Parking Announcement."

✔ Check your spelling. You may have to use a word processor if your mailer lacks a spell check feature. Typos can twist the meaning of your message so badly that you end up saying exactly what you didn't want to say. And proofread it again. A spell checker makes sure that your message consists of 100 percent actual words, but it doesn't check that they're the words you want to use.

✔ Remember that e-mail is not particularly private and that a glitch can cause the system to deliver your mail to the wrong recipient on the wrong system (like your boss or your kids).

✔ Don't pass on chain letters. Here are some common examples that have made the rounds several times by now:

- A dying boy who wants lots of greeting cards (he's not and he doesn't).

- They want to tax modems (the proposal was squelched in 1987).

- Letters about the "Good-news" virus — it's a hoax.

- Make money fast just by putting your name at the bottom of the list and forwarding this message to 10 friends. (These schemes are invariably illegal, guaranteed to annoy your friends, and a waste of time and money.)

✔ If you don't get a response from someone to whom you sent e-mail, or if the response is very different from the one you expected, politely ask for clarification:

```
I sent you a note about your chapter. Did you get a chance
to look at it?
```

or

```
Yikes, maybe I wasn't making myself clear. What I meant to
say was...
```

Or pick up the phone and call if it's appropriate. Try to nip e-mail misunderstandings in the bud. Never blame the other person. Assume your message wasn't clear or that the message never got there. If you have to blame something, start with the technology.

Subjects and Kings

General W. G. Pagonis was in charge of all the logistics for the 1991 Gulf War — moving all the equipment and supplies for 600,000 soldiers to Saudi Arabia in six months, getting everything ready for battle, and then moving the stuff back out when the war was over. The general used an eccentric management style: all messages to him from people in his command had to be written on a 3×5-inch index card. If he wanted more, he'd ask. The idea was simple and powerful. Confining subordinates to a 3×5 card made people think about what they wanted to say, and the general could listen to comments from many more of his troops because each message was so short.

A friend of ours, who was working for Harvard Business School Press at the time, read about General Pagonis in a news magazine. She thought a book by him would sell, but she had no mutual contact. So she wrote a note on an index card and mailed it to him. His book, *Moving Mountains,* was published in 1992.

Important people who are hooked up to e-mail get tons of messages each day. They simply cannot read them all. All they will ever read of most messages is the subject line, and then the messages are bounced to a subordinate or trashed. If you want your message read, make that subject line work for you. Think of General Pagonis's 3×5 cards. You've got about 60 characters to get their attention.

Sign on the Dotted Line

E-mail doesn't leave a lot of room for artistic creativity. One place where people do try to add a special touch to their e-mail is the signature. Many people turn their signatures into a personal letterhead, or letterfoot, to be more accurate. Here's John's signature, for example:

```
Regards,
John R. Levine, Trumansburg NY
Primary perpetrator of "The Internet for Dummies"
and Information Superhighwayman wanna-be
```

Typing a fancy signature like that into each message you send would be a pain. Fortunately, almost all mail programs let you set up a special file called a *signature* file. Text in the signature file will automatically plop down at the end of all your outgoing messages. The only problem is that people sometimes get carried away, filling their signature with whole paragraphs lifted from their favorite book or page-long *ASCII art,* pictures drawn in letters, numbers, and special characters. Here's an example of an ASCII art signature:

```
                            _...-'_-'-...__
                      ======================================
        ,_____.-/'    '-..._____...-'
       (_____||_) . . .-'
       /  /.-'       '/  Michael Mathiesen
      '_____- - - - -_/    phantom@nevada.edu
          '_____'
```

The traditional rule is "keep your signature to four lines or fewer." This is still not a bad policy. Long signatures are a problem on articles bound for mailing lists and newsgroup postings that get sent and resent thousands of times as they make their way around the globe. But we've seen obnoxious one-line signatures and ten-line sigs that made us smile. We're not your mother. Just keep your signature in good taste, and remember that your regular correspondents are going to see your signature dozens if not hundreds of times.

While most mailers will let you turn off the automatic signature feature, you probably won't remember to do so when you send that one message to someone you really want to impress.

Managing Addresses

Many e-mail programs have handy little features built in to help you manage the many e-mail addresses that you have to handle. Some let you make up a short nickname or alias that you can use instead of typing in a long, awkward Internet address, for example. Others let you set up an e-mail address book inside the mailer. You can then select your recipient from a pulldown list or other graphical gimmick.

Another useful feature that some mailers offer is mailing lists. These are not as complex as the automated mailing list systems we describe in Chapter 21. They are a simple way to assign a name to a set of e-mail addresses, everyone in the department, say, or everyone working on the Simson account. These kinds of mailing lists can be very handy.

If your mailer does not have these features and you can't upgrade to one that does, don't despair. You can use a database program or even a word processor to manage your e-mail list. Just create a text document and type in the addresses you use, one to a line, like this:

```
letters@globe.com        Boston Globe, letters to the editor
news07b@aol.com          Channel 7 News Boston
president@whitehouse.gov Bill Clinton
root@whitehouse.gov      Hillary Rodham Clinton
email@dummies.com        Dummies Central
info@idgbooks.com        IDG Books
70277.2052@compuserve.com Rush Limbaugh
wesun@npr.org    National Public Radio Sunday Weekend Edition
scitimes@nytimes.com Science editor, New York Times
```

When you want an address, just open your e-mail list in your word processor, copy the address you want, and paste it into your mailer's address field. You can even set up a simple mailing list by typing all the addresses in a single group:

```
Media list:
letters@globe.com, news07b@aol.com,
70277.2052@compuserve.com,
wesun@npr.org, scitimes@nytimes.com
```

Finally, don't forget to let people know about your e-mail address. Many people remember to put it on their business cards, but what about stationery, fax cover sheets, and even the answering machine message? In Chapter 20, we tell you how to find someone else's e-mail address. Some of the resources described there are good places to list your e-mail address.

It's 3 O'clock. Do You Know Where Your E-Mail Is?

In Chapter 3, we warned you to take a close look at the address fields of your message before you click the send button. If your message says something you wouldn't want everybody in the company to read, you need to be extra careful, particularly if you are writing a reply message. Don't simply verify that every address in the to:, cc:, and bcc: fields points to someone you want to see what you are saying. You also have to think about where each recipient might forward your message and then think about where each of *those* recipients might ship it. Clicking that Forward button is just so easy. E-mail that you send to three colleagues in the morning can be all over the building and in half your branch offices by that afternoon.

Putting a note in your message saying "For your eyes only" or "Don't forward this to Meg" only compounds the problem. Meg will be even more annoyed, and the forwarder might not have sent her a bcc if you hadn't reminded him. Office politics can get nasty.

The best way to protect yourself is never to write an e-mail message that would make you squirm if it was posted next to the water cooler. If you have to write something negative about someone's performance or pet idea, write it in such a way that you could still look her in the eye were she ever to get hold of it. Better yet, send her a copy in advance and ask for her comments before you send it on. Acting like a mensch can take the sting out of your criticism.

If you really need to communicate confidentially, encrypt your message and send it to just one address. If you can communicate in person, do so. If you can call and talk about the matter on the phone, do. But don't leave on voice mail what you wouldn't send in e-mail. Though voice-mail systems aren't as easy to hack as e-mail systems, many voice-mail systems have forwarding capabilities, and major systems are often backed up so that messages are saved.

Reading Your Mail Offline

No big deal, but here's an idea that can save enough money to pay for this book: If you are using a mail service that charges by the hour for connect time, you should try to read and compose your e-mail offline. Many of the value-added services, as well as mailers like Eudora and Netscape Navigator, let you do this easily. You just log in, retrieve your mail, and log out again. You can then read your messages, reply to whichever ones need answers, and create new messages without having to worry about online charges. You save your outgoing mail in an outbox. After you are finished, just log in again and send your outgoing messages. That's all there is to it.

If you're using a shell account or a service that doesn't let you easily download your mail, you can still pinch a few pennies. For shell users, your terminal emulator, that program that connects you to your provider, often logs your whole session. When you've finished reading your mail, you in fact have a giant transcript of everything you just read. Save any lengthy replying you have to do until after you've disconnected. Compose your responses in text files that you can later cut and paste into an outgoing message.

Likewise, while you're connected to your provider, you can copy mail that you're reading into a text file on your machine and save the replying for when you're off the meter.

Abbreviations, Smileys, and Emoticons

Most e-mail systems only allow straight text in the body of the message, though this may change in the future. If you find this restriction boring, you are not alone. E-mail users have used a variety of techniques to liven up their messages. One of the simplest is *emphasis*. Because **bold** and *italics* are usually *not* available options, the e-mail convention is to bracket words you want to stand out with an asterisk or underscore character. Here is how you might include the above sentence in an e-mail message:

```
Since bold and italics are usually *not* available options,
e-mail convention is to bracket words you want to _stand out_
with an asterisk or underscore character.
```

Other techniques used to liven up e-mail are abbreviations, smileys, and emoticons.

Abbreviations, smileys, and emoticons are the e-mail equivalent of slang, so you probably shouldn't use them in formal messages.

In any case, if you use abbreviations and smileys, use them sparingly. Don't do this:

```
FYI WRT smileys FAQ:
IMNSHO e-mail users have **no** self-
discipline! AFIK YMMV :-> ROTFL NRN
BTW, seen any new TLAs? TIA
TTFN CUL 8-)
::clicks on _send_ button::
```

Abbreviations

Abbreviations serve several purposes in e-mail. They help prevent repetitive stress injury by cutting down on typing. They conserve scarce electrons by making transmitted messages shorter. Perhaps the most important function they perform is to let people know that you are part of the club. We think they are overused and often stupid, and the club is stupid too. But you should know what the most common ones mean. Table 4-1 shows some of the most widely used abbreviations.

EUOMUNA (*E*-mail *u*sers *o*ften *m*ake *u*p *n*ew *a*bbreviations)! No list of e-mail abbreviations can ever be complete.

Table 4-1	Commonly Used Abbreviations
Abbreviation	*What It Means*
AFAIK	As Far As I Know
AKA	Also Known As
BFN	Bye For Now
BTW	By The Way
CUL	See you later (Warning: also a rude word in French)
FAQ	Frequently Asked Questions (actually a list of answers)
FYI	For Your Information
HNN	Hey Nonny Nonny or Hey Nonny No
IMHO	In My Humble Opinion
IMNSHO	In My Not So Humble Opinion
IMO	In My Opinion
NRN	No Response Necessary
LOL	Laughing Out Loud
RSN	Real Soon Now (don't count on it)
ROTFL	Rolling On The Floor, Laughing
ROTFLOL	Rolling On The Floor, Laughing Out Loud
RTFM	Read The Manual (you should have looked it up yourself)
SNAFU	Situation Normal, All Fouled Up
TIA	Thanks In Advance
TLA	Three-Letter Acronym

(continued)

Table 4-1 *(continued)*

Abbreviation	What It Means
TTFN	Ta Ta For Now (good-bye)
WRT	With Respect To
WYSIWYG	What You See Is What You Get
YMMV	Your Mileage May Vary
73	Best Regards (from ham radio)
88	Love and kisses (from ham radio)

For lots more abbreviations and acronyms, check out Babel: A Glossary Of Computer Oriented Abbreviations and Acronyms on the World Wide Web at

```
URL: http://www.access.digex.net/~ikind/babel95c.html
```

If you want to know about URLs and surfing the World Wide Web, check out *The Internet For Dummies,* 3rd Edition, written by people who care.

Smileys and other emoticons

Not long after you start getting e-mail, you begin to wonder if people have gone a little crazy with the punctuation keys. You start seeing unmatched parentheses, oddball colons, and misplaced semicolons, and you start to wonder what you're missing. Well, if you bend your head to the left as far as you can manage, you'll often see a kind of smiling (or frowning) face known as a *smiley*. Smileys come in an infinite number of flavors, but Table 4-2 shows you some common ones to give you the idea.

Table 4-2   Smileys

Smiley	What It Means
:-)	The basic smiley
;-)	Winking smiley ("Don't hit me for what I just said!")
:-(	Frowning smiley
:->	Sarcastic smiley
;-(	Crying smiley
:-p	Smiley with its tongue stuck out (nyah nyah)
:-@	Screaming smiley

Smiley	What It Means
:-o	Uh oh! smiley
8-)	Wearing sunglasses
::-)	Wears glasses normally

Lots, lots more are out there. If have access to the World Wide Web, you can download a long list of smileys from either of the two following URLs. Most of them are not in circulation among e-mail users, but they are very entertaining if you are in a properly silly mood.

- The Smiley Dictionary (`http://www.netsurf.org/~violet/Smileys/`)

- The EFF's Guide to Internet Smileys (`http://www.germany.eu.net/books/eegtti/eeg_286.html`)

Smileys are part of a bigger class of e-mail paraphernalia known as *emoticons*. How's that for a nineties word? Emoticons are stylized conventions developed in e-mail and in forums, chat rooms, and newsgroups. They try to bring subtlety of inflection and tone to written communication. We tend to want to type the way we talk, but our tone of voice doesn't come across the wire. Emoticons help bridge the gap and soften the harshness of less-than-polished text. Here are a few emoticons outside of the smiley category:

`_\,,/`	I love you (from American Sign Language)
`<g>` or `<grin>`	Same as :-)
`<sigh>`	Sigh!
`::`	Action markers, as in `::removes cat from keyboard::`

Action markers can be useful to those of you who are planning your online wedding or other theatrical venture.

More about Addresses

As we said in Chapter 3, addresses are the hardest part of e-mail *and* the most important. So here is some more information on this scintillating topic that never ceases to amuse and entertain us. For example, did you know that you can learn a lot about where a piece of e-mail comes from by looking at its domain name? Did you know you can own a domain name of your very own for only $50 per year? And if you ever ran into an X.400 address, would you know what to do with it? Stay tuned for the rest of this chapter.

We suggest that you glance through this section so that you know what's here, and then use it as a reference when you need it.

Domain names

The part of an Internet address that comes after the at-sign (@) is the *host name*. *Hosts* are just computer systems that are attached to the Internet — for example, xuxa.iecc.com.

Notice that host names have several parts strung together with periods. You decode a host name from right to left:

- ✔ The rightmost part of a name is its *zone* (in the example, com).

- ✔ To the zone's left (iecc) is the name of the company, school, or organization.

- ✔ The part to the left of the organization name (xuxa) identifies a particular computer within the organization.

In large organizations, host names can be further subdivided by site or department.

A partial name is known as a *domain*. For example, xuxa is in the iecc.com and com domains.

Who said that?

Forging e-mail return addresses is not that hard, and people sometimes leave their logged-in computers unattended, allowing spurious mail to be sent. So if you get a totally off-the-wall message that seems out of character for the sender, somebody else may have forged it as a prank.

Many people on the Internet adopt fictional personas. The lonely flight attendant you are corresponding with may be a 15-year-old boy. A famous *New Yorker* cartoon shows a mutt at a computer terminal thinking, "On the Internet, no one knows you're a dog."

Not every mail address has an actual person behind it. Some are for mailing lists (see Chapter 21), and some are *robots*. Mail robots have become popular as a way to query databases and retrieve files.

Don't zone out now

Three categories of zone names are in common use:

- ✔ Organizational
- ✔ Geographic
- ✔ Other

Organizational zone names

If the zone is three letters long, it is an *organizational name*. The three-letter code indicates the type of organization, and the part just before the zone indicates the specific organization.

Most systems that use organizational names are in the United States. Table 4-3 describes the organizational names currently in use.

Table 4-3	Organizational Names in E-Mail Addresses
Zone	**Type of Organization**
com	Commercial organization
edu	Educational institution
gov	U.S. Federal Government body or department
int	International organization (mostly NATO at the moment)
mil	U.S. military site (the site can be anywhere in the world)
net	Networking organization
org	Anything that doesn't fit elsewhere, such as a not-for-profit group

Geographic zone names

If the zone name is two letters long, it is a *geographic name*. The two-letter code specifies a country, and the stuff in front of the zone is specific to that country. For example, ac means academic in many countries.

The us domain, used by some schools and small organizations in the United States, is set up strictly geographically. It is usually preceded by a two letter state code. For example, John's machine in Trumansburg, NY is called iecc.trumansburg.ny.us.

A host can have more than one name. John's machine is also known as ivan.iecc.com.

Table 4-4 lists popular geographic names. For the most part, the two-letter country names come from an International Standards Organization (ISO) standard. See Appendix A for a full list.

Table 4-4	**Geographic Names in E-Mail Addresses**
Zone	*Country*
br	Brazil
ca	Canada
fr	France
jp	Japan
mx	Mexico
nl	Netherlands
no	Norway
ru	Russia
es	Spain
se	Sweden
ch	Switzerland
uk	United Kingdom (The official ISO code is actually gb, but everyone uses uk, and it's too late to change.)
us	United States

Other zone names

You may encounter a few other zones, including the following:

- **arpa:** Left over from the ARPANET, the Internet's predecessor
- **bitnet:** Unofficial zone used for mail to BITNET, a network of mostly IBM mainframes
- **uucp:** Unofficial zone used for mail to sites on a system called UUCP, a crusty old network that uses dial-up modems

X.400 addresses

In case you ever have to send mail to an X.400 system, here is a brief guide to X.400 addresses. X.400 is an e-mail standard that competes with the Internet's SMTP standard. Its main virtue is that it's been blessed by the UN's International Telecommunications Union, the same people who set the V.xx modem standards. X.400 is more popular in Europe than it is in the U.S., although the

U.S. military, the people who invented the Internet, are basing their new worldwide command and control system on X.400 — your tax dollars at work. Some commercial e-mail systems such as Sprintmail also use X.400.

An X.400 address is a great deal more like a postal address than a phone number. X.400 addresses are made up of a bunch of different *attributes*. If you have enough of these attributes to single out one recipient, the mail should go through. If you don't, back it comes. The most common attributes and the codes used to represent them are

- ✔ **Given name (G):** The recipient's first name
- ✔ **Initials (I):** First or middle initial (or initials)
- ✔ **Surname (S):** The recipient's last name
- ✔ **Generational qualifier (GQ or Q):** Jr., III, and so on
- ✔ **Administration Domain Name (ADMD or A):** More or less the name of the mail system
- ✔ **Private Domain Name (PRMD or P):** More or less the name of a private system connected via a public ADMD
- ✔ **Organization (O):** The organization with which the recipient is affiliated
- ✔ **Organizational unit (OU):** The sub-organization with which the recipient is affiliated
- ✔ **Country (C):** A two-letter country code; see Appendix A
- ✔ **Domain Defined Attribute (D, DD or DDA):** Any code that identifies the recipient, such as username or account number

Write each attribute to include the code, followed by an equal sign (=), followed by the value of the attribute. Use the slash character (/) to separate attributes in an address.

For example, suppose you want to send e-mail to Samuel Tilden at Tammany Hall in the United States using Sprint's X.400 Telemail service, which is connected to the Internet via `sprint.com`. The address would be

```
/G=Samuel/S=Tilden/O=TammanyHall/C=US/ADMD=TELEMAIL/@sprint.com
```

Grown men and women who are bright and well educated thought this up and actually proposed it as the world standard for e-mail addresses. It boggles the mind.

You are allowed to simplify an X.400 address when the only attribute needed is the recipient's name. Instead of

```
/G=Rutherford/I=B/S=Hayes/
```

you can write

```
Rutherford.B.Hayes
```

If someone tries to sell you a mail system based on X.400, throw that person out of your office.

Sending Mail from One Service to Another

Many value-added networks have their own mail addressing schemes. Table 4-6 tells how to address Internet messages to these systems. In this table

- ✔ *Username* is the name that the recipient uses to log onto the system.

- ✔ *Usernum* is the recipient's numerical user ID.

- ✔ *Hostname* is the name of the particular computer within the remote network.

Table 4-6	E-Mail Addresses for Some Online Services	
System	*How to Address Messages*	*Notes*
America Online	*username*@aol.com	
AppleLink	*username*@applelink.apple.com	
AT&T Mail	*username*@attmail.com	
BITNET	*username*@*hostname*.bitnet or *username*%*hostname*.bitnet@ mitvma.mit.edu or *username*%*hostname*.bitnet@ cunyvm.cuny.edu	
BIX	*username*@bix.com	
CompuServe	*usernum.usernum*@compuserve.com	*usernum.usernum* is the numerical CompuServe ID with a period replacing the comma. For example, if the person's CompuServe ID is 71234,567, send mail to 71234.567@compuserve.com.
Delphi	*username*@delphi.com	

System	How to Address Messages	Notes
Easylink	*usernum*@eln.attmail.com	*usernum* is the seven-digit user ID number.
eWorld	*usernum*@eworld.apple.com	
FIDONET	*firstname.lastname*@ p4.f3.n2.z1.fidonet.org or *firstname.lastname*@ f3.n2.z1.fidonet.org	Replace the numbers with parts of the person's Fido node number. For example, this user's Fido node number would be 1:2/3.4 or 1:2/3.
GEnie	*mailname*@genie.geis.com	*mailname* is based on the user's name, not the user's random login access name.
MCI Mail	*usernum*@mcimail.com	*usernum* is the person's numerical MCI mail address, usually written in the form 123-4567. You can leave out the hyphen.
Microsoft Network	*username*@msn.com	
Prodigy	*usernum*@prodigy.com	The person's Prodigy account must be set up for Internet mail.
Sprintmail	/G=*firstname*/S=*lastname*/O=*orgname*/ C=US/ADMD=TELEMAIL/@sprint.com	
UUCP	*username*@*hostname*.uucp or *hostname*!*username* @internet_gateway	The first UUCP form works only for registered addresses. The most common gateway is uunet.uu.net.

Dear Ms. Postmaster

Every Internet host that can send or receive mail has a special mail address called `postmaster` that is guaranteed to get a message to the person responsible for that host. If you send mail to someone and get back strange failure messages, you might try sending a polite message to the postmaster.

For example, if mail sent to king@bluesuede.org returns with an error, you might send e-mail to postmaster@bluesuede.org asking, *"Does Elvis the King have a mailbox on this system? TIA, Ed Sullivan."*

The postmaster is also the place to write if you believe someone is seriously misusing a mail account. This action is the Internet equivalent of reporting someone to the police, so use this judiciously.

The postmaster is usually an overworked system administrator, so pestering her unnecessarily is considered poor form.

Chapter 5
Some Technical Stuff

 *I*n this chapter, we cover a grab bag of relatively technical topics related to e-mail. We suggest that you skim or skip this the first time through the book and come back here when a technical question bothers you. This chapter may also be useful in stubborn cases of insomnia.

What's a Demon Doing in My Computer?

No, wait, there's no need to call an exorcist. A *demon* or *dæmon* (spelled that way because on some early computers, file names were limited to six letters and they didn't want to waste any) is just a special kind of computer program. Most non-dæmon programs run when somebody wants to do something — for example, when you want to edit some text, you run a text editor. A dæmon, on the other hand, lurks in the background waiting for something to do, and does it, usually silently and without human intervention. It may sound a little creepy, but in fact, it's quite useful and benign. Dæmons aren't entirely independent of people since someone has to arrange for them to start running in the first place, but they quite often run for weeks or months without human intervention.

The e-mail angle is that almost all e-mail is actually processed and delivered by dæmons. When you compose a mail message, the program you use is known as a *mail user agent* (MUA). The mail agent doesn't actually try to deliver the message itself. Rather, it hands your message to a *mail transfer agent* (MTA) to do the actual delivery. MTAs are invariably dæmons, working in the background to process the mail. If a message is destined for a user on the same computer, the MTA delivers the mail directly. If not, it communicates over the Net to another MTA on the destination computer to deliver the mail there.

This division of labor is, for the most part, a good idea. Delivering the message may take awhile (what if the other computer isn't on the Net right now, or the connection is really slow?) and most users have better things to do than to hang around and wait for delivery to finish. Also, most systems have several different MUAs — on our system, for example, different users prefer Pine, Elm, and several versions of Eudora, but because they all use the same MTA, they all exchange mail without trouble.

Normally, all of the MTA stuff happens without you having to worry about it, but two situations involving your MTA will grab your attention:

✔ When you send mail to an invalid address

✔ When the MTA is broken

Tales from the dæmon

When you send a mail message, your mail program (that is, your MUA) can make only the most general checks that the addresses you specify are valid. Once you've written your message, valid or not, your MUA hands it to the MTA for delivery.

If the address isn't valid, you'll get back a message like this:

```
From: <MAILER-DAEMON@iecc.com>
Newsgroups: local.junkmail
Subject: mail failed, returning to sender
Date: 2 Feb 1997 15:57:06 -0500
Message-ID: <mOtiSXZ-001TKpC@ivan.iecc.com>
Reference: <mOtiSXY-001TKoC@ivan.iecc.com>


|——————— Message log follows: ———————|
 no valid recipients were found for this message
|——————— Failed addresses follow: ———————|
 <elvis@iecc.com> ... unknown user
|——————— Message text follows: ———————|
Message-Id: <2.2.16.19960202205659.0e1f49cc@ivan.iecc.com>
Date: Fri, 02 Feb 1997 15:56:59 -0500
To: elvis@iecc.com
From: John R Levine <johnl@iecc.com>
Subject: Yo, King!

Anyone home?

Regards,
John R. Levine, Trumansburg NY
Primary perpetrator of "The Internet for Dummies"
and Information Superhighwayman wanna-be
```

The dæmon deep in your mail system wakes up and writes you back to complain about the invalid address. For addresses on the local system, you'll generally hear back in a few seconds. But for addresses destined for remote systems, hours or sometimes days can pass before the error message comes back.

In a perfect world, error messages would be in a standardized format so that, for example, your mail program could check to see if the address is in your address book and offer to delete it. But no, that would be too easy. No standard exists for mailed error messages, so although most of them look pretty much like the one above, enough variation occurs that even experienced human users can't always figure out what the problem was.

It's dead, Jim

Now and then, the mail dæmon (that is, the MTA) in your system might just stop working. (This problem has occurred once or twice when our system manager made a tiny little change that turned out not to be quite as tiny as he thought. Oops.) The most common symptom is that all mail delivery stops, but sometimes you get all mail, whether addresses are valid or otherwise, returned to you.

The most common MTAs are called `sendmail` and `smail`. If you start getting error messages saying something like `sendmail: not found`, contact your system manager immediately.

Considering the nature of the problem, this situation is one of the few times when a phone call is definitely preferable to e-mail.

More about Headers

Back in Chapter 3, we talked about mail headers, the stuff at the front of the message that describes who a message is to and from, what it's about, and so forth. Well, lots more headers are out there besides the ones we listed. Here's a typical message with *all* the headers:

```
From jqpublic Tue Jan 30 22:58:43 1996
Return-Path: <jqpublic@sample.org>
Received: from babbitt.sample.org by ivan.iecc.com with smtp
(Smail3.1.29.1 #11) id m0thTgx-001TOJC; Tue, 30 Jan 96
22:58 EST
Message-ID: <310EE8B4.4A74@sample.org>
Date: Tue, 30 Jan 1996 22:57:40 -0500
X-UIDL: 823060777.001
```

(continued)

```
(continued)
From: John Q Public <jqpublic@sample.org>
Organization: The Sample Organization
X-Mailer: Mozilla 2.0b6b (Win16; I)
MIME-Version: 1.0
Content-Type: text/plain; charset="us-ascii"
To: email@dummies.com
Subject: book report
Status: RO

... actual contents of the message here ...
```

So what are all those headers? Table 5-1 shows a rundown of the ones we didn't discuss in Chapter 3.

Table 5-1	Headers
Header	*Meaning*
From	A "From" line as the first line of the message with no colon is a UNIX mailbox separator. It shows when the mail was put in your mailbox and who seemed to have delivered it.
Return-Path:	The address from which the message was sent. This needn't be the same as the "From:" address if the message was sent through a gateway system or via a mailing list.
Received:	Each time a message is processed by a mail transfer agent (MTA, discussed in "What's a Demon Doing in My Computer?" in this chapter), the MTA adds a "Received:" line. The contents are utterly technoid, but they are very useful to mail experts who are trying to figure out how a message went astray, or from where a mystery message came.
Organization:	The name of the author's organization (optional).
Status:	The status of the message in the mailbox. *R* means you've read it, and *O* means it's old (was in the mailbox the last time you ran your mail program). Unlike all the other header lines, this line is created and updated by the *receiver's* mail program.

X doesn't mark the spot

Mail programs are allowed to add any old nonstandard headers they want as long as they put X- in front of them. Table 5-2 shows what typical nonstandard headers include.

Table 5-2	Nonstandard Headers
Header	*Meaning*
X-UIDL:	Unique identifier, used by POP mail programs such as Eudora to figure out which messages they've already downloaded.
X-Mailer:	The name of the program used to create the message. In the earlier example in which all headers are shown, "Mozilla" is the developers' code name for Netscape they evidently never bothered to remove.

What's the Difference between an E-Mail Address and a URL?

This is an e-mail address

```
email@dummies.com
```

and this is a Universal Resource Locator (URL):

```
http://www.dummies.com/books/toc-email.html
```

What's the difference? You use them for entirely different things. You send mail to an e-mail address — the normal thing to do with one is to type it on the To: line in your mail program.

A URL, on the other hand, is the name of a "page" of information in the World Wide Web. You use it to tell your Web browser, Netscape, Mosaic, or Lynx, for example, what page to retrieve. URLs and e-mail addresses are not interchangeable, and you have to use the right kind of program to handle each. This task is made somewhat easier if you use a multipurpose program like Netscape that handles both Web pages and mail. In Netscape, you select File⇨New Mail Message to start sending mail, but you use File⇨Open Location to tell it to go to a URL.

Telling URLs and e-mail addresses apart is easy. E-mail addresses are shorter and always contain an at-sign (@). URLs start with a code, usually `http:`, followed by the host name of a computer and the name of the page on that computer.

In the interest of maximized confusion, a special kind of URL is actually an e-mail address. It looks like `mailto:email@dummies.com`.

This kind of URL tells the Web browser to open a mail window (or sometimes, to start up a separate mail program) and start a message to that address. These URLs aren't very useful for humans because going to the mail window directly is easier, but they sometimes appear in other Web pages to make sending mail to the owner of the page easier.

IP Addresses

We've told you dozens of times by now that computers on the Internet have multi-part names like chico.iecc.com. Well, we were simplifying a little bit. They do have names, but they also have numbers, similar to phone numbers. These numbers are used by the underlying Internet protocol, which moves data from one place to another on the Internet, so they're called IP Addresses.

An IP address is written as four numbers separated by a dot, like this: 205.238.207.67. Quite a lot can be said about the structure of IP addresses, none of which will be said here because it's not all that interesting (see *The Internet For Dummies,* 3rd Edition if you like).

You can send Internet e-mail to IP Addresses, an option that is useful now and then when some piece of the name system goes West. You put the IP address in square brackets, like this: email@[205.238.207.67].

You might think that every name on the Net corresponds to one IP address, but that's not true (it's not like every name in the phone book corresponds to a single phone number, either). Many computers on the Internet have more than one IP address if they're connected to more than one network. Some computers, particularly those used for internal network functions, have an IP address but no name at all. And some names correspond to more than one computer. For example, delphi.com corresponds to five different IP addresses on five different computers.

Fortunately, if a computer has more than one IP address, you can use any of them, and if a name corresponds to more than one address on more than one computer, you can still use whichever one you want because all of the computers are invariably set up to do the same thing.

Some names don't correspond to any IP addresses at all, including some major ones like aol.com. Those are called *mail exchange* or *MX* names. If a system has an MX name, some other computer has arranged to receive mail for it. In AOL's case, four computers named a.mx.aol.com through d.mx.aol.com stand ready to receive AOL's mail. Unless your mail system's configuration is messed up, a situation that happens occasionally, mail to and from MX names works exactly the same as mail to regular names, so you don't have to worry about it.

I'm So Attached to You

Internet mail for many years only officially handled text, not pictures, word processor documents, or any other kind of file. The relatively new MIME standard now provides an official way to send around non-text material, but as you might suspect, people were sending files around for years before MIME came along using nonstandard hackery.

MIME

As we mentioned in Chapter 3, you can recognize a MIME message by the MIME headers at the beginning of the message, which look something like this:

```
Mime-Version: 1.0
Content-Type: multipart/mixed; boundary="=====================
==_823336045==_"
```

If you have a modern mail program like Eudora, Pine, or Netscape, your mail program will automatically recognize a MIME message and will reconstitute the file contained in it. Some of the cleverer ones even will figure out what kind of file it is and will run an appropriate program to display it for you.

Unfortunately, some older mail programs don't handle MIME, in which case you're out of luck. This problem occurs frequently with LAN mail systems attached to the Internet through a gateway system — on one LAN system we deal with, we've been asking them to get MIME working for two years, and they haven't been able to do it yet.

If your mail system is MIME-impaired, you can still usually use one of the other older, informal attachment schemes that we describe next.

Uuencode

Back in ancient days (like about 1979), a mail system named UUCP worked over dial-up modems. It didn't handle attached files, so a couple of students whipped up a pair of programs called uuencode and uudecode that let them disguise files as text for the purpose of sending them as UUCP mail. These days, UUCP is nearing the end of its useful life (and not a moment too soon), but uuencoding lives on.

A uuencoded file appears in a message bracketed by begin and end lines. The name of the file appears after the word begin (you can ignore the three digit number between them).

```
begin 600 efdb202.bmp
MODT-!'$"""#8$$"'H""30(",'!"'!"@""""',!"""""'
M""""""""'%4"'"J""_P""'E""!5)0"JB4"/\E""2"'
M54@"*I("'#_2""&T"%5M""J;0"_VT"'"2"!5D@"JI("/^2""
... lots more illegible glop here ...
'
end
```

Better mail programs such as Eudora automatically recognize uuencoded files and extract their contents. Even if your mail program doesn't understand uuencoded files, on most systems, you can use a decoding program, such as `uudecode` on UNIX systems and `Wincode` on Windows systems, to extract the encoded file. Ask your system manager which, if any, of them are available.

BinHex

Macintosh programmers invented their own equivalent of uuencoding called *BinHex*. It's most popular on Macs, although it works on any kind of computer. BinHex-ed files start with this surprisingly understandable message:

```
(This file must be converted with BinHex 4.0)
```

(We've never seen a version of BinHex other than 4.0.) Once again, Eudora and a few other mail programs automatically extract BinHex-ed files. Lacking automatic extraction, separate un-BinHexers are widely available on Macs and less so on other systems.

So how should I send my files?

The answer depends on the capabilities both of your mail system and of those of your correspondents. MIME has been available for several years and is quite widely accepted, so in most cases, you should just be able to send MIME messages and expect success. (AOL, for example, supports MIME completely.)

If you find that your correspondents can't deal with MIME, your next best bet is BinHex if they're using Macs and uuencode if they're using anything else.

Graphics Formats

Perhaps you felt that having three different but similar ways to send attached files was too many. Little did you suspect how simple your life was.

"How many different ways can you store a picture in a computer?" you might ask. Dozens, maybe hundreds, that's how many. On your Windows machine, you may have run into BMP, PCX, DIB, GIF, JPG, TGA, and other files, all of which contain various kinds of pictures. If for some reason you want more details on this convoluted state of affairs, you probably won't be surprised to hear that we suggest *Graphic File Formats,* 2nd Edition by David Kay and John Levine (Windcrest) and *Programming for Graphics Files in C and C++* (Wiley), which John wrote by himself.

Fortunately, two picture formats are much more popular than the rest: GIF and JPEG. Lengthy, er, free and frank discussions have occurred on the Net concerning the relative merits of the two formats. Because John is an Official Graphics Format Expert (by virtue of having persuaded two otherwise reputable publishers to publish his books on the topic), here are his opinions:

JPEG

JPEG, named after the Joint Photographic Experts Group that designed it, is a format specifically intended to store digitized photographs.

- Best format for scanned photographs
- Handles "true color" better
- Files are usually smaller than GIF
- Doesn't handle large areas of solid color or sharp edges well
- Slower to decode than GIF

GIF

GIF, a format designed by CompuServe, comes in two slightly different versions, GIF87 and GIF89. Fortunately, the two versions are similar enough that all the GIF-handling programs we know can deal equally well with both.

- Best format for computer-drawn cartoons and icons
- Handles solid color areas well
- Faster to decode

GIF's designers used a compression technique that turned out, after many years, to be patented by Unisys, and in 1995, Unisys started demanding patent royalties. In response, an industry group came up with a replacement for GIF called PNG (Portable Network Graphics), which is patent-free and solves a few other minor GIF deficiencies. GIF will eventually be replaced by PNG, but probably not for several years.

Everything else

The next most popular format is TIFF (Tagged Image File Format), popular with fax programs and graphic design programs. TIFF can in principle be converted easily to other formats such as GIF, but TIFF is fantastically complex with dozens of internal options; so it's dismayingly common to find that a TIFF file written by one program can't be read by another.

Other formats are popular on particular computers, such as BMP and PCX on Windows and PICT on Macs. If you know you're sending a file to someone with the same kind of computer you have, you can just send the file. If not, you should probably convert it to GIF or JPEG to up the chances that your recipient can read it.

Lights! Action! Multimedia

Multimedia in theory means any sort of file or presentation that combines more than one kind of computer output (sound and smell-o-vision, for example), but in practice it means movies. The two most common multimedia formats are QuickTime and MPEG.

QuickTime

QuickTime is a format designed by Apple and is handled quite nicely by Macintoshes because the support is built right into the Mac's system software. Apple also has QuickTime software available for Windows, but it's much less popular.

MPEG

MPEG, the Motion Pictures Experts Group, was down the hall from the JPEG group and built on their work (that's practically unprecedented in the history of standardization). MPEG is more popular on Windows and other non-Mac systems.

Firewalls

Let's say you're a company with an internal network, and you want to hook up to the Internet. That's technically straightforward, involving a *gateway* or *router* computer that passes traffic back and forth between the internal network and the outside. But the Internet has a certain number of, shall we say, undisciplined users who delight in trying to break into computers where they don't belong. If your internal network has 1,000 computers, you'd have to make sure that the security setup on each and every one of those thousand computers was correct, and in practice you never will. What's a network manager to do?

The answer is a *firewall* computer. Rather than passing any old network traffic between the inside and the outside, a firewall strictly limits what can pass. So long as the security on the firewall is set up correctly, the entire internal network is protected. Firewalls frequently act as *proxy servers,* a fancy term meaning a computer that provides a service to the internal network that the proxy in turn has received from the outside (checking to make sure that there's no security breach in the process).

Firewalls tend not to make much difference to e-mail users because even if mail has to be forwarded via a firewall or a proxy server, the addressing and delivery work the same as they always do. But if you use any other network service such as the World Wide Web, you'll have to do extra setup steps so that your program uses the proxy server. In Netscape, for example, you see a Proxy tab on the Network Preferences window.

Protocols

E-mail and the computer networks that make it work depend on numerous protocols that control how data flow around the network. Here's a quick roundup of some of the most important protocols for e-mail.

Most of these protocols are defined by so-called Request For Comment (RFC) documents available on the Internet. (Despite their names, we're about ten years too late to comment on most of them.) See Chapter 24 for advice on retrieving files, including RFCs, by mail.

POP

POP (Post Office Protocol) version 3 is what programs like Netscape and Eudora use to download mail from a central server to the computer on your desk. It's defined by RFC 1725.

SMTP

SMTP (Simple Mail Transfer Protocol) is used to transfer messages from one system on the Internet to another. It's defined by RFC 821.

The difference between SMTP and POP is that SMTP is used to pass mail from system to system until it's delivered to the recipient's mailbox, and POP is used by an individual user to retrieve mail that's been delivered to her mailbox.

X.400

A competitor to SMTP, defined by the International Telecommunications Union (ITU). Much more complex than SMTP, it's much less widely used. We tell you all about X.400 addressing in Chapter 4.

X.500

A "white pages" service defined by the ITU to make it possible to look up people's e-mail addresses. It's alleged to be coming soon but not widely used yet. See Chapter 20 for advice on how to use the X.500 directories that are out there.

DNS

The Domain Name System keeps track of the names of the millions of computers on the Internet, like `dummies.com`. Defined by RFCs 1034, 1035, 1101, and 1348 (it's pretty complicated).

TCP/IP

Transfer Control Protocol (TCP) and Internet Protocol (IP), which together define the way that data is actually sent from one computer to another on the Internet. IP is defined by RFC 791 and TCP by RFC 793. SMTP and DNS use TCP/IP to make the actual connections from one computer to another.

Chapter 6
Putting E-Mail to Work

• •

• •

*W*e found that when we put our collective heads together, we have a lot to say about using e-mail at work. Roughly speaking, it falls into two broad categories: how to use e-mail to improve your way of doing business and practical tips for successful e-mail use in your office.

Using E-Mail and the Internet to Better Your Business

Philippe Le Roux, a founder of the Canadian Internet and the online services consulting company, VDL2, has been working with the Internet and online services for 15 years. VDL2's Internet and online services clients include Via Rail, Canada's Passenger Rail Company, for whom they created an interactive Web site; The Montreal Stock Exchange; and companies in Europe and North and South America. In a personal interview with us, he shared his insight and expertise. The material in this section is taken from that interview and from discussions we've had subsequently.

Reaching the world through e-mail

We know you've heard all about surfing the Net, Web sites, and home pages, but the Web (where the surfing happens) is not the best place for you to start as a business new to the Net. Philippe recommends that you begin with *e-mail*. If you haven't thought about the implications of using e-mail for your business, now's the time to begin. E-mail predates the World Wide Web by more than twenty years, is the only tool used by everyone on the Net, and is a fundamental learning ground for understanding Net culture and potential.

E-mail opens an important new way of communicating within and without an organization. Inside a company, e-mail becomes a powerful tool for company communication and project management. Outside the company, e-mail can help you better your customer support, support your field offices, get help from experts, and even find new customers.

Preparing employees for the world of e-mail

To get the most out of e-mail for your organization, you need to train your users, not just in the "how-to"s of your particular e-mail program, but also in the kinds of uses and capabilities inherent in e-mail. You need to teach them Netiquette — how to behave on the Net. Show them things that they might not stumble across by themselves. Buy them a copy of this book.

Working with E-Mail: Changing the Way We Work

People who use e-mail find that the very technology itself changes how they work. E-mail communication is highly structured, compared to a phone call for example, yet very versatile and easy to use, compared to traditional written communication.

For example, e-mail provides a written point of departure. You present your issues and questions in text that becomes an easy reference point for further discussion. Every e-mail system has a Reply feature that enables the responder to include the original message in the text of the new message, setting off the original text from the new with special characters. Using the Reply feature to structure their response, people generally respond to e-mail point by point. This process allows people to clarify misunderstandings rapidly without typing a lot of separate memos and without countless rounds of telephone tag. Often many rounds of e-mail happen in short order — a matter of minutes — as opposed to hours, days, or weeks that traditional media require.

Improved project management

E-mail facilitates group communications and heightens accountability for projects involving many people. The larger the project, the more you need e-mail. The larger the company, the more you need e-mail. Most projects affect more than just the core people involved.

For example, a new product under development might involve marketing, development, documentation, testing, manufacturing, and shipping. All these different departments need to be aware of what's happening, though they probably don't need to get involved with the daily comings and goings of the project. They don't need to be at the meetings, but they do need to know what happened.

A schedule slip, for example, might throw previously allocated resources into contention. This problem happens all the time. But what mechanisms do you have in place for communicating what's happening? How is everyone who really needs to know going to find out? Well, experienced e-mail managers will tell you that one solution is to set up different mailing lists: mailing lists for the developers, mailing lists for the business team members, and mailing lists that include all the groups.

Mailing lists facilitate group communication. You don't have to think about to whom you should send a message. When you use the appropriate mailing list address, all the appropriate people automatically find out. When a person joins or leaves the team, you change the alias, but the workings of the group continue unaltered.

Even in small companies where people are working on the same project together, using e-mail to communicate makes a lot of sense. For one thing, you cut down on the number of interruptions. For another, people often have time to gather information before they get back to you. And you've created a written log, something very useful for everyone. People are less likely to forget what you asked about — they have your request right there to check.

Virtual meetings

E-mail can eliminate a lot of meetings. For example, if you have a problem to solve, instead of trying to get everyone in the room at the same time, try addressing the problem in e-mail. Include the same people and make sure that they're copied on all the ongoing correspondence. As you discuss the problem in e-mail, you may find you've saved yourself a lot of time. People can respond at a convenient time, and the "meeting" tends to stay more on target. Unless they're on vacation, people usually respond to their mail within a day. Finding a time when everyone could be in the same room at the same time could take a week. By then, you could have solved your problem using e-mail.

E-mail timing

E-mail is often delivered in a matter of minutes, if not seconds. Depending on whether the person on the other end is connected and reading her mail, a dialog can happen as quickly as people can send messages. Even if the response is not instantaneous, generally people respond to short e-mail messages quickly. If you send a lengthy message requiring a lengthy response, expect it to take a while. Generally speaking, however, you can expect a much more rapid turn-around in e-mail correspondence than you can from other traditional media. Communication among several parties is much easier because you don't need to schedule everyone for a conference call. Even if you *do* need a conference call, you're probably better off sending the scheduling request and the call's agenda through e-mail.

Because people read e-mail in their own time, using e-mail to communicate project information saves time in meetings and lessens the need to interrupt someone with phone or office chatting. We don't think that e-mail replaces actually talking to people; we just know that it's difficult to get a lot of work done, and e-mail can go a long way toward reducing interruptions.

Corporate communication

E-mail is probably *the* cheapest way to communicate and absolutely the cheapest way to reach a lot of people around the world. E-mail often reaches its destination in a matter of seconds, and it costs no more to send it to Hong Kong, Lima, or New York City than to an office down the hall. Furthermore, when language is a barrier, reading e-mail in a foreign language is generally easier than understanding subtleties over the phone. (You can even forward the e-mail on to someone else to translate.)

Because e-mail is almost free, it costs no more to send a message to 245 people than it does to one. It costs less to send an electronic newsletter around the world than it does to create a paper newsletter for a department. David Letterman's electronic newsletter is sent to 27,000 people each month for only a few cents. The cost of reaching a large audience is dramatically reduced. Not only do you not have to pay postage, but you also save money on materials, presentation, and printing.

Mailing lists are text-based, so you can't wow your fans with graphics. This restriction means that content becomes extremely important. Unless you have something to say, don't bother. People can easily press delete before they read your mail. Make sure that you aren't cluttering mailboxes with garbage.

When you compare the cost of e-mail with the cost of any other kind of express mail delivery, or even the cost of overseas phone calls, you begin to grasp the impact it can have. Compare the cost of shipping software overseas by FedEx to the cost of sending it by e-mail. Suddenly having good communications with foreign offices and customers doesn't cost a lot.

It pays to collaborate

Suddenly collaborative work is easy. People can quickly and cheaply share files, pictures, even video and sound. We know — we've been creating whole books using e-mail for years. Our book, *Internet Secrets*, involved fifty different contributors e-mailing files from the UK, Canada, Texas, and Poland, among others.

Whether your collaborator is across the hall or in China no longer matters. Because actual word processing files can be sent, everyone can easily stay current with changes others make (though you do need to pay attention and decide on procedures for version control so that you don't create diverging strands from the same source). Independent research groups around the world can share a common database, as genetics researchers do.

C.Y.E.

Using e-mail, people begin to communicate easily with all levels of an organization, allowing information to flow much more freely. Many environments find this liberating; others find it terrifying. However, environments that encourage a free-flow of information (excluding those that involve confidential material) have found that better communication fosters better employee morale, and in turn, greater creativity and productivity. We warn you, however, that old political games die hard and don't suddenly disappear with the appearance of e-mail. Remember the old adage, "Information is power." E-mail can shift fields of power in an organization and threaten egos built by withholding information. If you're in the kind of place where you need to watch your back, you need to watch your e-mail, too.

New customers in the mail

Sure, you can easily envision sending e-mail to your existing customers. Well, maybe not easily, but once you try it for a while, it'll seem perfectly natural. But how about finding new customers with e-mail? We aren't talking about sending out junk e-mail advertisements as a lame imitation of direct mail marketing. We're talking about going to new sources to find out who's looking for your product or service. Those new sources are automatic mailing lists. Similar to Usenet newsgroups, mailing lists exist on almost every topic you can imagine (and many more you haven't imagined — trust us). Indiana University's Support Center catalogs some 12,850 mailing lists. For more information on newsgroups, see *The Internet For Dummies,* 3rd Edition.

Find mailing lists of interest to you and subscribe. Don't limit yourself to lists you think pertain to your business. Check out all the lists that interest you. But add only a few at a time because some lists are so prolific that you'll be drowning in e-mail faster than you can say unsubscribe. Chapter 21 tells you all about mailing lists — how to subscribe and unsubscribe. As you find lists to your liking and you become comfortable, you can begin to participate actively in the groups, offering your particular expertise.

In the mailing lists, real interactions can lead to real business. You can respond to people privately — you don't always have to respond to the group. You'll likely find people actually looking for what you have to offer. Complete international deals have been formed and cemented using nothing but e-mail. Snail mail was used for invoicing, and electronic funds transfers were used for payment.

Be careful not to advertise, explicitly or implicitly. If you're a travel agent and subscribe to the Travel-L mailing list, for example, don't try to publish fares or specials to the list. And tacking things onto your signature is considered inappropriate. Make sure your signature is short, sweet, and professional — don't think you can get away with a long trailer and pretend you're just a sky writer drifting by. You'll get booted off the list.

Getting help from the outside

Another good reason to read mailing lists is to find people who know about what you want to know. You can often query an expert in your field if you know her e-mail address. If your request isn't inordinate, you'll probably get a response in a timely fashion. Most people don't mind an occasional, reasonable request for help. We get them all the time. As long as someone isn't asking us to do her homework, we generally try to help. But, in turn, learn one important motto: *Give back to the Net.* When someone queries you, be generous in your response. Try to keep the Net a cordial, responsive environment.

E-mail doesn't replace the need for phone, fax, video-conferencing, and letters, but it does have its strengths and can change how you do business. It won't eliminate meetings, but it can make them much more productive if you take the time to circulate an agenda via e-mail and agree to take some discussions "offline." Well, maybe you'll even handle it "online" — with e-mail.

E-Mail at the Office

We here at *Internet For Dummies* Central have some expertise all our own. We're among those who have been using e-mail since it was two days old, we've already been responsible for six other books that at least mention e-mail and at least thirteen more that cover it in depth, and we like to hear ourselves talk. Here's what we'd like to add:

E-mail and the corporate culture

If your office doesn't have e-mail yet, you are probably in the minority. If e-mail has made your organization palpably more efficient and a better place to work, you are probably in the minority, too. In a lot of work places, e-mail is just another office tool, like electric pencil sharpeners. Everyone finds that e-mail is a great way to communicate with remote field offices, or to send out those company memoranda that everybody circular-files anyway. But it can be much, much more.

The success of e-mail in an organization depends a lot on the organization's corporate culture. A friend of ours works for a large corporation that recently installed Lotus Notes, a premier groupware product that combines e-mail with user-friendly databases to promote efficient information sharing in organizations. The problem is that workers at our friend's company don't share information freely. That is part of their corporate culture. Employees are not even permitted to read their own job descriptions. Information is power. Can you guess how much people at this company are using Notes?

Many managers and consultants claim expertise in changing corporate cultures, but it is a task few are ever able to accomplish. E-mail itself can be useful in this endeavor, but never underestimate the resistance that office bureaucrats can throw up.

Making e-mail fly

Here are a few tips on what is needed for e-mail to really have an impact in your place of work:

Make e-mail universal

A big difference exists between 85 percent of employees being on e-mail and 100 percent being on e-mail. Getting to 100 percent might require public e-mail terminals so that the people who don't sit at desks can check their mail, or it might even require printing out messages for those who can't get to a terminal. But once everyone knows that they can reach anyone in the company, from the day they start work, e-mail will become the preferred way to communicate.

Get folks to check their e-mail daily

Getting everyone to check their e-mail at least once per day is vital for e-mail to succeed. Employees will do this naturally once e-mail takes off in your organization. Until then, make sure information is put out frequently enough to encourage daily checking. It might even be worthwhile to have an online contest or a recipe of the week. Anything's fair to get people to check their e-mail.

Another idea is to post a good company story every few days. This can be a thank you letter from a customer, an employee suggestion that worked out, or a problem that was successfully fixed.

Yes, you can try to force participation by diktat: "Effective immediately, all Nimbus employees must check their e-mail twice a day." After a few weeks of "No new messages," this rule will be forgotten along with any number of "Effective immediately" pronouncements.

The boss has to use it

The boss's having an e-mail address is not enough. Employees have to know that their supervisor will *read* their mail on a regular basis. They also have to believe that their boss understands how to use e-mail properly. In a recent Dilbert cartoon, the pointy-haired boss hands his secretary a piece of paper and says, "Send this by e-mail. Fax it too in case he doesn't check his e-mail. And mail the original so he has a clean copy." As usual, Scott Adams is on target.

As for messages that jump over boxes in the organization chart, tolerance will vary from company to company. Those that have an "open door" policy, at least on paper, should welcome an open e-mail policy. Remember the story in Chapter 1 about the head of a semiconductor plant who sent e-mail to all his subordinates, asking, "What are we doing that is keeping you from doing your job to the best of your ability?"

We do not recommend that you send e-mail over your boss's head in most companies. You would do better spending the time working on your résumé.

Encourage business partners to use e-mail

If you are big enough to have leverage, require all your suppliers to have e-mail. If you are a small operation, at least ask potential vendors if they use e-mail. Eventually they will get the message. E-mail can reduce errors from misunderstood phone calls and illegible faxes.

Some years ago, a few of us were working at a manufacturing company. One day, while walking through the stockroom, we noticed a shelf full of an unusual software documentation set that cost $900 a set. We knew that one particular customer had put in a special order for *one* set of those books, but we couldn't imagine why so many had been purchased. After relentlessly questioning our inventory control people, they finally produced a copy of the original purchase requisition. The multi-part form must have slipped askew a bit because a clerk's initials, "JS," appeared in the adjacent order quantity box on this copy. Someone had read "JS" as "15."

Your customers can be enticed to get online by your providing e-mail access to the people in your company they want to reach. A particularly valuable use of e-mail is online customer service. Most people are fed up with waiting forever for 800 (or worse, 900) numbers to answer. Your customers will love you if you provide an e-mail address for customer service and can achieve a fast — under two hours — response time. See *Customer Service For Dummies* (IDG Books Worldwide, Inc.).

Make finding people easy

A good, up-to-date, e-mail address directory must be available, preferably online. It should list people by name and by function. It should also have useful e-mail addresses external to your company, such as the key business partners, the online help desks for the software packages your company uses, the local public library, and so on.

Allow personal use

Employees should be allowed reasonable personal use of e-mail. Many companies have a "no personal use" policy for their e-mail. This is counter-productive and as likely to be respected as similar policies on personal telephone use. Often a fine line exists between personal and professional, in any case. The friend I call today to find out if she can go to the movies is the same person I'll call next week to help me with a tricky problem at work. Companies that try to regulate this level of behavior are usually cutting off their noses.

Reasonable personal e-mail use is a fringe benefit that is highly valued by employees and costs employers almost nothing. Remember that most systems have no per message charge for e-mail. Personal use will also encourage employees to check their e-mail regularly, helping e-mail to succeed as a corporate tool.

What is unreasonable use? We think companies can fairly prohibit usage that violates the law, reveals confidential company information, supports an employee's side business or political activities, or requires more than a few minutes of time during normal working hours.

Today, many employees are part of the sandwich generation — they are responsible for small children and infirm parents. To the extent that e-mail lets them handle their personal responsibilities more efficiently, it will improve productivity and reduce absenteeism.

Arrange for remote access

Being able to read e-mail at work is not enough. On any given day in most companies, someone key is on the road. These people need their e-mail. A worker with a sick kid can still get a lot done at home via e-mail. While you're at it, make sure you have an e-mail address on the Internet that reads info@yourcompanyname.com. And have a mailbot (a program that automatically sends a response) all set up to answer.

Respect employee privacy

Monitoring employees' e-mail may be legal in some places, but we do not think it is ethical anywhere. If you *do* choose to snoop in the company e-mail system, at least let your employees know that is your policy.

Case study: EKMS, Inc.

EKMS, Inc. is a small firm in Cambridge, Massachusetts that specializes in managing patent portfolios and licensing inventions to industry. Its fast-growing practice keeps its staff hopping. Dozens of ideas need to be evaluated to find one with real potential. License negotiations can be long, tedious, and complex. The payoff on a successful deal can be years down the road, so EKMS President Ed Kahn keeps a tight rein on expenses. A half-dozen employees work out of a spartan two-room suite in an industrial building. Each has a Macintosh computer with cc:Mail installed (see Chapter 19 for more about cc:Mail).

Why use e-mail when everyone sits in the same room? Kahn says, "My staff is on the road a good part of the time. E-mail helps them stay in touch with each other. And even when they are in the office together, they have their own work to do. It's hard to get much done if someone asks you a question every few minutes. E-mail keeps interruptions to a minimum."

With hundreds of hard copy patent documents to work with, Kahn isn't throwing out his fax machine any time soon, but he finds e-mail an important backup when faxes just won't go through, a real problem in some parts of Europe.

Building teams

Every few years, a new hot management buzz word comes along. Right now it is *team building*. The notion that a group of workers dedicated to a single goal can get a lot done is hardly new, however. Whether you think teams are hype or hope, e-mail can do a lot to make a small group more effective. The first step, of course, is to make sure that all team members have an e-mail account and know each other's address. The next step is a team mailing list. Encourage team members to copy fellow members on all important mail. Make replying promptly to other team member's mail a team value. Make sure that each team member has a common set of applications on her computer. Make sure that they all know how to attach and read all the document types they need to use.

Dealing with incompatible programs

E-mail works great when you are sending simple text messages. When you try to send anything more complex, such as a word processing file or a picture, problems can arise. That likelihood is directly proportional to the urgency of the document.

Actually, a simple explanation exists for this commonly observed phenomenon. Every personal computer made today has an anxiety sensor in its keyboard that measures how hard you are typing and how often you have to backspace. When the detected anxiety level is high enough, a message is sent to your mailer using USP, the User Stress Protocol, and nothing can go through.

A different explanation, popular with techies, points out that today we have

- ✔ Five major operating systems — Windows, Macintosh, MS-DOS, OS/2, and UNIX

- ✔ Variants within them — Windows 95 versus Windows 3.1, Berkeley UNIX versus System V

- ✔ Dozens of different types of applications — word processors, spread-sheets, graphics, page layout . . .

- ✔ Different brands with different file formats within each application category — Word versus WordPerfect versus WordPro in word processors

- ✔ Different versions within each brand — Word 6 versus Word 5.1 versus . . .

- ✔ Different encoding schemes use by mailers — MIME, uuencode, BinHex . . .

- ✔ Different compression programs — zip, gzip, Stuffit, compress . . .

Think of the above list as a giant combination lock. You can easily understand why sending a spreadsheet across the hall is sometimes hard, let alone around the world, if you don't use the same combination as your recipient.

Here are a couple of ways to avoid these headaches:

Agree on a lingua franca

Make up a list for your organization of the preferred format for sending files in each category, including compression and mailer transfer format.

The Macintosh versus PC religious debate used to be a big source of file transfer conflict. It is no longer any excuse. Mac software is available that can read just about any file format available for the PC. And all Macs sold in the last five years can read, write, and format PC disks.

Rehearse

Think about what types of documents you will need on a regular basis and try sending sample documents of each type to your colleagues before crunch time.

Send a test file with all combinations

If you are having trouble sending an important document to someone with a different mailer program, make up a short sample file in that format — for example, the first page of your document. Then send it out a number of times using all the different encoding formats your mailer can muster. One of them may work.

Don't forget sneaker net

Putting a document on a disk and carrying it to another computer is sometimes called *sneaker net*. It usually works. Also, if you are struggling with an important transmission some afternoon, be aware of the deadline for your overnight delivery service's pickup. Once a disk with your files on it is in the hands of FedEx, UPS, Airborne, or DHL, your keyboard will know that the jig is up and you transmission will work mysteriously. If not, at least the recipient will get the disk the next morning.

When all else fails, remember ASCII always works

Well, almost always. Some mailers have trouble with messages longer than 20,000 to 30,000 characters. Also end-of-line characters vary among Windows, Macintosh, and UNIX. Still, plain ASCII text is your best bet in a pinch.

When making a disk for sneaker net, always save the file you want to send in several formats. Include text or ASCII as one of those formats.

The legal status of e-mail signatures

Is a signature on a piece of e-mail legally valid? We are not lawyers, but as we understand things in the United States, the law takes a pretty broad view of what constitutes a valid signature. If someone has a piece of e-mail that appears to be signed by you, you will likely have to prove you did not send it. This applies equally to ordinary e-mail and e-mail that has been signed using public key cryptography (see Chapter 22) — though the American Bar Association has developed a draft guideline giving special recognition to cryptographic digital signatures, and the state of Utah recently passed a law based on those guidelines (Web users can see `http://www.state.ut.us/ccjj/digsig/default.htm`).

E-Mail on the Road

More and more workers are taking their computers with them when they travel. A major reason these road warriors lug their seven-pound laptops, spare batteries, charger, and modem down endless airport corridors is to be able to stay in touch.

Large companies often have local network access numbers in the various cities and countries where they do business. If you don't work for one of these e-mail-savvy firms, you may want to consider finding an e-mail provider that offers local access service in the places you are likely to visit, or that has an 800 number you can use when you're out of town. At *Internet For Dummies* Central, we find having our own 800 number worthwhile for e-mail pickup, even though only one person travels much.

Accessing your e-mail from overseas

Getting your mail when you are in a foreign country can involve more than finding a local service provider. You may not find a jack in your hotel room that will take your modem cable. Modem standards can vary in different countries as well. One possibility is to visit a cybercafe. These trendy establishments serve Internet with their coffee. If you haven't been to one, imagine a hippie-dippy coffee shop with Internet terminals at every table. Cybercafes exist in many major cities. You pay for terminal use by the hour. Because many Internet service providers will allow telnet access, you may be able to walk in, rent a terminal, and use telnet to check your e-mail (see *More Internet For Dummies*, Chapter 19, for information on how to use telnet). Most cybercafes have network-knowledgeable wait staff that can help you figure it all out, even in English. You can even transfer files to your laptop using sneaker net.

We were able to use this method of getting e-mail on a recent trip to Paris. A cybercafe called Cyberia (`cyberia@easynet.fr`) is in the center of Paris at the Pompidou Center. It's was easy and fun. The biggest problem was typing with a French keyboard, which is just different enough to cause lots of typos.

If you do access your e-mail service provider account from overseas, we recommend that you change your password when you get home. Also, variations in world keyboards make it a good idea to avoid special characters in e-mail account passwords. You may have a hard time finding the character you need in time to log in.

Can I really be busted for taking Netscape abroad?

Until recently, if you had the North American version of Netscape Navigator 2.0 on your laptop and traveled from the U.S. to a country other than Canada without a license, you violated U.S. export laws. The same goes for a wide variety of software packages with "U.S. Only" labels. (See "Why are there domestic and foreign versions of software?" in Chapter 22.)

The U.S. recently changed its regulations to let you travel with encryption software to most countries as long as you don't give the software to anyone else and your laptop remains in your personal possession or under lock and key the entire time you are abroad. You also must keep a record of each trip for five years.

Minitel: The Internet comes home

We're writing this sidebar in Paris. Stylish 220 volt electrons energize our Powerbook laptop computer. France is where the e-mail revolution first took hold.

In the 1970s, the French telephone monopoly, France Telecom, decided it wanted to do away with the phone book; they were expensive to print, clumsy to use, and always out of date. Instead, every French household would be offered a small green computer screen and keyboard. To find someone's phone number, you would just type in the name, and the phone company's computer would look it up for you in a central database. You would also be able to type in names of goods and services and see advertisements from companies, thereby replacing the yellow pages. They called it *Minitel.*

The one thing France Telecom did not intend Minitel to do was to let subscribers send electronic messages. After all, they were selling phone service!

But the programmers who built Minitel wrote in a rudimentary messaging capability, saying they would need it while they wrung out the bugs in the complex new software. Somehow they neglected to turn the messaging off when the first public trials of Minitel were held in Alsace, and word leaked out. The programmers and some sympathetic managers looked the other way as thousands of French men and women discovered this hidden feature of Minitel until it became just too popular to turn off.

Today, le Minitel is a French institution, successful beyond even the secret dreams of its developers, except in one little area — the French still use phonebooks.

While we were in Paris, France Telecom made a startling announcement: it was going Internet. In the not-too-distant future, every French household will enjoy Internet access for the price of a local phone call, which, as it turns out, is pretty expensive. France may become the most road-warrior-hospitable country on earth. We like the food, too.

French-born Philippe Le Roux serves on the national board of The Information Technology Watching Network and is the North American correspondent for Planete Internet. *His article, "Virtual Intimacy" can be found in* Internet Secrets (IDG Books Worldwide, Inc.). *You can send e-mail to him at* leroux@dummies.com.

Chapter 7
E-Mail in Our Lives

E-mail is already a way of life for some of us — we can't imagine a day without it. Well, on occasion we've actually gone several days without it, but you have to be someplace exotic to make its absence worth your while. You may take a long time before showing signs of addiction, but once you connect with someone you love using e-mail, you'll start to understand what the hoopla's all about.

E-Mail at Home

Electronic mail can help around the home in many ways. Sure, it is a way to get messages when you are not home or don't want to answer the phone. Big deal, an answering machine can do that, too. E-mail can do a lot more for your life.

Keeping in touch with the family mailing list

In our highly mobile society, family members tend to be scattered around the globe. E-mail is a great way to stay in touch. Remember the movie *Starting Over* where a guy is having an anxiety attack in Bloomingdale's and his brother asks if anyone has a Valium — and a dozen people offer him some? Well, bring up e-mail at the next family gathering. We'll bet you'll be surprised who has it. Get an e-mail address from everyone in the room who has one. After you get home, send a message to all the people on the list, just saying "Hi!" and asking for any other addresses.

In fact, some of us have seen our family grow this year as a direct result of e-mail. A long-lost cousin of Carol's found her on the Travel-L mailing list and sent e-mail to see if they were related. And her cousin-the-doctor in Texas helped her via e-mail when her dad was sick last year. Her brother's online at work in Vermont, and now she's finding Baroudis all over the place. It's amazing what a little e-mail can do.

Kids at college

E-mail is a particularly good way to communicate with your offspring who are away at college. Nowadays, almost all colleges give computer accounts with e-mail to their students (considering the price of tuition, it's not a lot to ask). Assuming your e-mail provider doesn't charge for messages (most don't), the savings in collect phone calls alone can pay for your e-mail account.

Even more importantly, e-mail lets you stay in touch with your favorite college students without crowding their space. They can read your mail when they want and respond when they want. This takes some of the angst and guilt away and saves the embarrassment of talking to you in front of their roommates.

The younger generation has adopted e-mail as their own. With e-mail, you're meeting them on their own turf. It lets them keep their feeling of independence. After all, letting them learn to be on their own is why you took out that second mortgage, isn't it?

E-Mail for Kids

If you have children or are planning to have children, a wide variety of resources out there can be reached by e-mail. Here we talk mostly about school age kids. College kids these days are heavily into e-mail and the Internet, anyway.

K–12 is the label that's given to all the education that happens in the United States between preschool (nursery school or day care) and college. It's a broad category. We use it here because many mailing lists and newsgroups use the K–12 designation, and it seems to be common ground for many people. Obviously, text e-mail is more appropriate for somewhat older children, but mailers that allow graphics can let even small kids exchange messages in the form of drawings.

E-mail can put the whole world at a kid's fingertips. She can make friends anywhere, practice her French or Spanish or Portuguese or Russian or Japanese, search databases for her term paper, and even let her political leaders know what a future voter thinks.

The Internet for young children

We have to say up front that we are strong advocates of allowing children to be children, and we believe that children are better teachers than computers are. Neither John nor Carol owns a television set, and none of our kids watch TV. Now that you know our predisposition, maybe you can guess what we're going to say next: We are not in favor of sticking a young child in front of a screen. How young is young? We feel that younger than age 7 is young. Many educators feel that unstructured computer time under age 11 is inappropriate. We recommend that children get as much human attention as possible and believe that computers make lousy babysitters. At that age, children benefit more from playing with trees, balls, clay, crayons, paint, mud, monkey bars, bicycles, and other kids.

Frankly, even if you do want to let your small kids use the Internet, there isn't much for the pre-reading set, anyway.

Schools are actively debating e-mail and Internet access for their students. Teachers and parents go round and round, and ignorance seems to prevail. Find out as much as you can and get involved. The more you know, the more you can advocate for appropriate access.

A wonderful book called *The Internet For Teachers,* by David Clark (published by IDG Books Worldwide, Inc.), can help you understand all that can be gained from e-mail and the Internet, and it can arm you with the information you'll need to face hordes of cynics, including school administrators, teachers, and other parents. The book focuses on the Internet from an educator's perspective, including why the Internet is important, how to use it, and where to find education-specific resources. Though it's aimed at teachers, it's a great find for parents.

What about all that bad stuff I've been hearing?

Parents, educators, and free-speech advocates alike agree that nothing substitutes for parental guidance when it comes to the subject of e-mail and Internet access. Just as we parents want our children to read good books and see quality films, we also want them to find the *good* stuff on the Internet. If you take the time to learn with your children, you have the opportunity to share the experience and to impart critical values and a sense of discrimination that your children need in all areas of their lives.

Remember that the good stuff on the Net far outweighs the bad. Sexually explicit material does exist, but it's a minuscule percentage of all that's out there (it represents a much smaller percentage of what's on the Net than the material you find in an average bookstore), and *it's not easily available.* You have to work to get it, and, more and more frequently, you have to *pay* to get to most of it.

Perhaps highest on the list of parents' concerns about e-mail access for children is the question of their kids corresponding with unsavory adults and older kids. We say *perhaps* because parents who have taken the time to learn about access issues understand that the threat is not so great as some would have us believe and that, with reasonable attention, this concern can become a non-issue.

Children can develop inappropriate associations in many places, particularly as they grow older and become more independent. Developing a relationship with your child based on trust, openness, and a willingness to listen is your best long-term defense against these risks. Your child talks to her e-mail friends from your home where you can better exercise gentle supervision. Your child's use of e-mail can be a valuable avenue to developing the skills that will protect her in the future.

Mailing lists for kids and parents

Mailing lists are a great source of fun, education, and help for kids and parents alike. Chapter 21 tells you how to subscribe to mailing lists. Throughout this chapter, we provide just the list name and its description. Many more lists are available where these come from, so if none of them strikes your fancy, don't despair.

kidmedia

This mailing list is a professional-level discussion group for people interested in children's media (television, radio, print, and data). To subscribe, send mail to kidmedia-request@airwaves.chi.il.us for individual articles or to kidmedia-d-request@airwaves.chi.il.us for daily digests. On the subject line, enter SUBSCRIBE, UNSUBSCRIBE, or HELP (to receive the charter and info file).

kidsphere

The kidsphere list was established in 1989, to stimulate the development of an international computer network for use by children and their teachers. Send subscription requests to kidsphere-request@vms.cis.pitt.edu.

kid

On this list, children post messages to other children. Send subscription requests to kids-request@vms.cis.pitt.edu.

dinosaur

For subscription requests to this low-volume list about dinosaurs, send a message to `listproc@lepomis.psych.upenn.edu` in the following format:

```
SUBSCRIBE DINOSAUR <yourname>
```

pen-pals

This list provides a forum in which children correspond electronically with each other. The list is not moderated, but it is monitored for content. Send subscription requests to `pen-pals-request@mainstream.com`.

y-rights

This group, open to everyone, discusses the rights of kids and teens. Send an e-mail message to `LISTSERV@sjuvm.bitnet`. In the text of the message, include one of these lines:

- To subscribe to the list: `SUB Y-RIGHTS` *firstname lastname* (substitute your own first and last name)
- To receive the daily digest of the list: `SET Y-RIGHTS DIGEST` *firstname lastname*
- To receive the list of previous discussions: `GET Y-RIGHTS FILELIST` *firstname lastname*

kid cafes

Kid cafes are mailing lists that exist for kids aged 10 to 15 to have conversations with other kids — kids in general and kids in specific. Kids can find "keypals" with similar interests and exchange messages with them.

Several different kid cafes are available, depending on whether one is joining as an individual or part of a school class. The kid cafes listed in Table 7-1 are all LISTSERV lists managed at `LISTSERV@vm1.nodak.edu`. See Chapter 21 for details on how to subscribe.

Table 7-1	Kid Cafes
Name of list	**Description**
KIDCAFE-INDIVIDUAL	For individual participants looking for keypals
KIDCAFE-SCHOOL	For classroom groups looking for keypals
KIDCAFE-TOPICS	Open discussion of any appropriate topic
KIDCAFE-QUERY	Asking questions of other kidcafe participants

Lists for parents of kids with problems

One of the most profound and heartening human experiences available on the Internet has to do with the help that total strangers freely offer one another. The incredible bonds that form among people sharing their experiences, struggles, strengths, and hopes redefine what it means to reach out and touch someone. We encourage everyone who has a concern to look for people who share that concern. Our experience of participating in mailing lists and newsgroups related to our own problems compels us to enthusiastically encourage you to check things out online. You can do so with complete anonymity. You can watch and learn for a long time, or you can jump into the fray and ask for help.

We caution you that everyone who gives advice is not a medical expert. You have to involve your own practitioners in your process. Many people have found enormous help, however, from people who have gone down similar paths before them. For many of us, it has made all the difference in the world.

We list in this chapter a few of the available online mailing lists and discussion groups. Almost certainly you'll find a mailing list or group specific to your needs, regardless of whether we list it here, and new groups are added every day. If you're using a commercial provider such as America Online, Prodigy, or MSN, or CompuServe, your provider has special forums that may interest you as well.

In Chapter 21, we describe how to use e-mail mailing lists. If you find something of interest in the rest of this chapter, you'll have a reason to learn how to do it.

Notice that some lists are *talk* lists, which feature free-flow discussion; some lists have very focused discussions, and some lists are almost purely academic. (Table 7-2 provides the names of several of parents' lists.) You can't always tell from the name. If it looks interesting, subscribe and see what sort of discussion is going on there. You can always unsubscribe if you don't like it.

Table 7-2	Self-Help Mailing Lists for Parents	
Resource Name	*Description*	*To Contact*
add-parents	Support and information for parents of children with attention deficit/hyperactivity disorder	Send e-mail to `add-parents-request @mv.mv.com`
our-kids	Support for parents and others regarding the care, diagnosis, and therapy for young children with developmental delays	Send the e-mail message *subscribe our-kids* to `majordomo@tbag.osc.edu`

Resource Name	Description	To Contact
behavior	Support for behavioral and emotional disorders in children	Send the message *subscribe behavior* to `listserv @astuvm.inre.asu.edu`
deafkids	Support for deaf children	Send the message *subscribe deafkids* to `listservs juvm.stjohns.edu`
cshcn-l	Support for children with special health care needs	Send the message *subscribe cshcn-l* to `listserv @nervm.nerdc.ufl.edu`
dadvocat	Support for dads of children with disabilities	Send the message *subscribe dadvocat* to `listserv @ukcc.uky.edu`
ddline	Children's disability list	Send the message *subscribe ddline* to `listserv @uicvm.uic.edu`
ds-c-imp	Overview of childhood impairment issues	Send the message *subscribe ds-c-imp* to `listserv @list.nih.gov`
ds-c-sb1	Support for spina bifida	Send the message *subscribe ds-c-sb1* to `listserv @list.nih.gov`
ds-c-00	Discussion of major childhood measures issues	Send the message *suscribe ds-c-00* to `listserv @list.nih.gov`

Ze E-mail for ze Lovers

You may not believe that the hottest e-mail comes from the French, but don't knock it 'til you try it.

Whether you're looking for love or you have already found it, e-mail can add a little spice to your life. For an in-depth treatise on the affair, we highly recommend the article "Virtual Intimacy" by Philippe Le Roux, in *Internet Secrets*. Meanwhile, we've rounded up the tips from experienced e-mail lovers, Dionysos and Chica, who have each fallen in love many times in virtual worlds.

✔ If you have a love in your life, ask him, her, or it for an e-mail address. E-mail is a wonderful way to share sweet words. Discovering loving messages in your Inbox is always a nice surprise and can help you through a hard day at the office. And, sometimes talking about things in e-mail is easier than talking face to face, as long as it's not the only way you communicate.

✔ If you want to meet someone, find mailing lists that interest you. Don' t go to the singles ads. Look for someone who shares your passions.

✔ When you haven't heard from that special someone in several days, suspect the technology first. E-mail is seductively reliable. You begin to count on its being there, and all of the sudden, it's not. But more often than not, what's suddenly gone wrong in an e-mail relationship is that mail isn't getting through or someone's connection is down.

✔ Likewise, if your friend seems to be ignoring something you said, or is saying things that seem odd to you or out of context, suspect missing messages. It may happen once in two hundred times, but messages do get lost, or get out of sync, or get delayed (sometimes for days) in some black hole in the Net.

✔ Be slow to anger, quick to forgive. Remember, you can't see the person's face, can't hear his or her tone of voice. Before you take offense, try reading a message over several times. Look for what might have been a typo that could alter the meaning. Try to read it as ironic, sarcastic, or funny before you take it seriously.

✔ Read your own messages carefully — hard to do in fits of passion, we understand, but you're probably not polysyllabic then, anyway. In ordinary conversation, be careful what you type.

✔ If you start to fall for somebody over the Net, get his or her phone number. Call and talk even if for just a few minutes. Often this telephone call will break any serious illusions you have or help you with another level of trust. Besides, when you suddenly can't get to your e-mail, it'll be too late to ask for the number. Then what will you do?

✔ Be aware of what you type. Be especially careful of addresses. Make sure that the mail you send is going where you intend and understand the consequences for you if someone else were to read it by mistake. For example, if you send your e-mail from work, how would you feel about your boss or coworkers seeing it?

✔ Know that e-mail lands several places in its route. If you compose your mail on your personal computer and you download all your mail to your personal computer, you minimize the chances of someone else reading your mail, but you don't eliminate them. If you leave your messages on your computer at work or on your account at your service provider, people (system administrators, for example) can read your mail, and often your entire disk is backed up, your mail included.

✔ Have a good time. E-mail has sparked many wonderful romances, even marriages.

✔ "Take care of yourself. The electronic dating is virtual. Discovering somebody by his words is very exciting and interesting. We're all looking for a way to discover people without being influenced by the appearance, the look, and all this artificial stuff. But we, as humans, have developed ways of reading people using a lot of tools and signals (like feelings), and the electronic talks make us miss those tools. As our brains don't like the empty, they try to fill it with what we're looking for. Virtual intimacy can be false in two ways: because the correspondent is lying or because you're lying to yourself, just exaggerating the good feelings you have reading the messages from the other party. Virtual Intimacy can make you discover intensity in yourself you never suspected, but can make you live some high deceptions. If the safety of your emotions is more important than your living, be very careful. If you're able to take some risks for living intense things and discover new worlds of emotion, this virtual world of encounters is yours." —Dionysos

✔ If you don't meet your life's partner by e-mail, we're sure you'll discover a lot of interesting people with whom you can form very special friendships.

You can write to Chica at `chica@dummies.com` and to Dionysus at `dionysus@dummies.com`.

E-Mail for People with Disabilities

Electronic mail can be a both a boon and a bane for people with disabilities. It is a boon for disabled people who can type at a keyboard and read a CRT screen. It gives those people access to a whole new world of computer networking. For those who cannot read a screen or use a keyboard, it can seem one more barrier to integrating with an increasingly networked world. But adaptive technologies exist that can help them make e-mail a plus in their lives.

E-mail and the hearing impaired

For people who are deaf or hard of hearing but can use a computer, e-mail is a natural aid. It gives them direct access to a mainstream communications tool.

A few problems make e-mail not quite natural for the Deaf:

✔ Lack of integration with TTY, the primary means of telecommunication for the Deaf and hard of hearing. A TTY is a simple and cheap computer terminal popular among the Deaf but is, unfortunately, not compatible with all the e-mail systems we know of.

✔ Language problems. English is a second language for many deaf people. Their primary language (at least in the U.S.) is ASL, American Sign Language. Many hearing people believe that ASL is just English expressed as hand movements. Nope. ASL has a unique grammar and vocabulary and is no more like English than French is. Many deaf people write impeccable English just as many French people do. However, for others, communicating in written English is not that easy.

If you are communicating with a deaf person via e-mail, show the same patience and courtesy as you would when speaking to a guest from a non-English-speaking country.

E-mail and the vision impaired

For people who have difficulty reading a computer display or who simply cannot do so, e-mail may seem a step backward. Most vision impaired people would be happier just talking on the telephone. E-mail is as unnatural for them as it is natural for the Deaf. But technologies exist that help vision impaired people read their e-mail. And e-mail does offer some benefits, particularly at work. To the extent that corporate communications flow on e-mail, it is more accessible to people with vision impairment than older paper memoranda. So in some ways, e-mail is the glass that is half full.

The main adaptive technologies that allow people with vision impairments to read e-mail are

✔ Extra Large Type. In some cases, this requires nothing more than adjusting the font size in your mailer program. Also, screen magnification programs are available for DOS, Macintosh, and Windows. The Macintosh program, CloseView, is included for free on the MacOS System disks.

✔ Voice To Speech. All Macintosh and most Windows machines sold today include sound output capability. Older PCs can be upgraded by adding a sound card or multimedia package. A variety of speech synthesis software is available that will allow you to have your e-mail "read" to you.

✔ Braille printers. A couple of these devices, also called embossers, are on the market. They tend to cost as much as a computer, however.

People with other disabilities

Disabilities vary widely in their nature and severity. Many people have multiple disabilities. Finding a way for severely or multiply disabled people to use e-mail often requires developing solutions on a case-by-case basis, drawing on assistive technologies that already exist, or, in some cases, developing new ones. E-mail and mailing lists are a great way for those who are trying to help to stay in touch and learn about what's new, what works, and what doesn't work.

Resources for people with disabilities

A large number of mailing lists deal with disability issues. See Chapter 21 for information on how to use mailing lists. Table 7-3 contains a few useful lists.

Table 7-3	Mailing Lists Dealing with Disability Issues
Resource Name	**Description**
L-HCAP	A LISTSERV list about all disabilities (moderated)
BLINDNEWS	A LISTSERV list about blindness (moderated)
DEAF-L	A LISTSERV list for the deaf

For additional information on e-mail and Internet resources for the disabled, see "Internet Access for People with Disabilities," by Jim Allan, K.C. Dignan, and Dave Kinnaman in *Internet Secrets* (IDG Books Worldwide, Inc.).

E-Mail for Seniors

While senior citizens are not generally known for their rapid adoption of advanced technology, e-mail may be an exception. Here are some of e-mail's benefits for seniors:

- E-mail lets you stay in touch with family and friends.
- E-mail is a great way to make new friends, particularly if you have limited mobility.
- E-mail costs are relatively low compared to long-distance telephone calls.
- Many seniors have adopted a peripatetic life style. With e-mail, you can check your mail from just about anywhere.
- Many seniors have difficulty hearing and understanding speech. E-mail lets you read your messages.
- Many seniors also have difficulty reading. Computers with large type display can help.
- An increasing number of mailing lists and other support services are available for seniors via e-mail.

Preventing E-mail Injuries

As more people earn their livelihood sitting at a computer, more and more people are suffering from a variety of discomforts and disabilities associated with keyboard usage. We can't cover all the issues and recommendations in this book, but here are a few tips in case you become a heavy user of e-mail:

- ✔ Sit comfortably. When you are sitting at your computer, your thighs should be horizontal and your feet should be flat on the floor. If you cannot sit this way in your present chair, try a different chair or buy an adjustable chair.

- ✔ Your keyboard should be at a level so that your forearm and upper arm roughly form a 90-degree angle. Standard desks are too high for most users, unless you have a high chair with a foot rest.

- ✔ Your mouse should be at the same level as your keyboard. Give your mouse room to roam. A mouse pad helps the mouse work with less effort on your part and reserves space for the mouse on your desk.

- ✔ Place your computer screen so that you can look at it comfortably. The top of the usable screen window should be at or slightly below eye level. We invariably need to raise it up from the desk (on top of a pile of otherwise useless computer manuals).

- ✔ Turn your monitor from side to side until you find a usable position that minimizes glare and reflections from your room. If necessary, move lights that shine on your monitor screen to a location where you cannot see their glare or reflection on the screen.

- ✔ Take frequent, short breaks. Look at a tree at least twice a day.

Part II
The Two Big E-Mail Programs

The 5th Wave   By Rich Tennant

Now take your time and see if you can identify the person who attacked you on e-mail.

In this part . . .

Lots and lots of e-mail programs exist. We take a look at two of the most widely available ones. They're easy to get, and they're *free!*

Chapter 8

Eudora Light E-Mail

In This Chapter

▶ Understanding Eudora Light

▶ Sending and receiving mail with Eudora

▶ Replying to and forwarding messages

▶ Saving money with Eudora

*E*udora is an easy-to-use mail-reading program from QualComm, Inc., that works with WinSock and dial-up SLIP or PPP Internet accounts. Eudora runs under Windows and on the Mac and lets you write mail messages, read your mail, and reply to and store your messages in folders. It lets you define a standard signature, deals beautifully with all kinds of attachments, and has a good address book. And you can download a freeware version named *Eudora Light*, or you can load it from the CD-ROM in the back of this book. What more could you want?

TIP

So who is Eudora, anyway?

According to the Eudora manual, the program's author was reading Eudora Welty's short story "Why I Live at the P.O.," and he was inspired. It's nice to know that even nerds read some real books from time to time.

Light Up Eudora Light

Eudora was written by QualComm, Inc. — or actually by its QUEST (QualComm Enterprise Software Technologies) group.

The Eudora program requires the following:

✔ An Internet connection that supports WinSock or MacTCP programs — for example, if you are connected to the Internet via Trumpet Winsock or Internet Chameleon software

✔ At least 1MB of free disk space

Telling Eudora about you

Before you can use Eudora, you have to tell it about yourself:

1. **Double-click the Eudora icon to run the program if it's not already running.**

    You see the Eudora Light window with the Settings dialog box on top of it (see Figure 8-1).

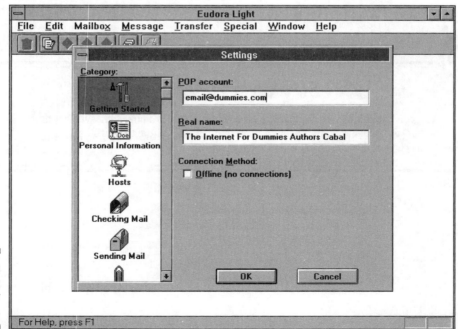

Figure 8-1:
Telling Eudora your life's story.

2. **In the <u>P</u>OP Account box, enter your e-mail address.**

   This is usually your login account on your Internet provider's computer, but it doesn't have to be — it's wherever you receive mail.

3. **In the <u>R</u>eal name box, enter your real name as you want it to appear in parentheses next to your e-mail address.**

4. **Click the Hosts icon in the list of icons on the left side of the Settings dialog box.**

   A new bunch of boxes appears in the Settings dialog box.

5. **In the <u>S</u>MTP box, enter the name of the Internet host computer to which you send your mail (your mail *gateway*).**

   If you're not sure, ask your Internet provider.

6. **Click the Checking Mail icon on the left side of the Settings dialog box.**

7. **Click the Sa<u>v</u>e password box so that an × appears in its box.**

   This setting tells Eudora to ask you for your Internet password the first time it checks your mail and to store your password for future mail checks. If this setting isn't selected, you have to type your password each time you check your mail.

   Skip this step if someone might sneak up to your computer and secretly check your mail when you are off refilling your coffee mug.

8. **Click the Sending Mail icon on the left side of the Settings dialog box.**

   Yet more settings appear.

9. **Click the <u>I</u>mmediate send box to remove the ×.**

   You just told Eudora not to send each message as you write it. Instead, you plan to write a few messages and then send them in a batch. This arrangement saves on Internet connect-time.

10. **Click the Attachments icon on the left side of the dialog box.**

11. **Click the <u>A</u>ttachment directory button (which is currently blank), choose the directory in which you would like to store attached files, and click the Use Directory button.**

    The directory name you just chose appears on the <u>A</u>ttachment directory button.

12. **Leave everything else as it is (for now).**

    You may want to change some settings later, but these should do for now.

13. **Click OK to save these settings.**

    The Settings dialog box disappears, leaving you with a rather blank-looking Eudora Light window.

Eudora now knows enough about you to send and retrieve your e-mail messages from the Internet. If you need to change your settings later, choose Special⇨Settings from the menu bar.

Eusing Eudora

Before we get into the details, we have a few words about how to use Eudora: Eudora displays lots of windows, including mailboxes that show lists of messages, message windows that show the text of one message, composition windows for writing your own messages, and other windows. Eudora happily lets you display lots of windows at a time, and you can switch among them.

In Windows, you close a window by double-clicking the little horizontal bar in its upper-left corner. To temporarily minimize (iconize) a window, click the downward-pointing triangle in its upper-right corner. To turn an iconized window back into a regular window, double-click it.

On a Macintosh, you close a window by clicking once in the little box in the upper-left corner of the window.

This is all standard Windows and Mac stuff — we just thought that we would point out that these gizmos work in Eudora, too.

To leave Eudora, choose File⇨Exit. If you have composed any messages that haven't been sent yet, Eudora asks whether to send them now. You can choose Send them and then quit (if you want to get those messages out the door) or Just QUIT (to quit the Eudora program without sending the messages).

Eudora Light for Windows has a cute row of icons on its toolbar. If you can't guess what a button does, position the mouse pointer on the button and keep it there for a few seconds. A label appears telling you the name of the button.

When you run Eudora, you should also run the program (such as InterSLIP or Chameleon Custon) that you use to connect to the Internet unless your software is set up to connect automatically. When you tell Eudora to send a message or get your mail, it is going to ask your Internet connection program to try to send or receive mail. Eudora can get confused if the connection software isn't running already.

Hello, World!

To try Eudora out, send yourself a message. It's the fastest way to find out whether things are working.

Here's how to send a message:

1. **Click the New Message icon on the toolbar, or choose Message⟿New Message from the menu bar, or press Ctrl+N.**

   The New Message button is the one that looks like two pieces of paper and a pencil. You see a window that looks like the one in Figure 8-2.

2. **Click to the right of the To label in the window. Then type the e-mail address to which you want to send a message.**

   To send a test message to yourself, enter your own e-mail address.

   If you want to send the message to more than one person, you can enter more than one Internet address. Just separate the addresses by commas. We'll talk about using an address book to address your messages in Chapter 9 in the section "Quick Ways to Address Your Mail."

3. **Click to the right of the Subject label and type the subject of your message.**

   You can also press the Tab key to move from the To line to the Subject line. As always, make the subject as specific as possible.

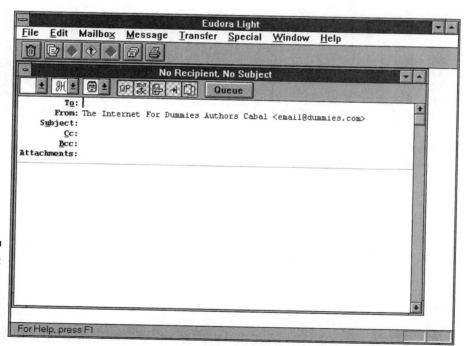

Figure 8-2:
Composing
a message
for Eudora
to send.

What are all those buttons?

At the top of the message window, Eudora displays a row of interesting-looking buttons. You can use them to control a bunch of cool things about your messages:

✔ **Priority:** Controls the priority of the message. Purely for decoration; all messages are delivered in the same way.

✔ **Signature:** Controls whether your signature file is automatically stuck at the end of the message. You usually see *JH* in cursive, indicating that a signature will be used in the message. Click the button to the right of the box to switch to *None*. See the section "Kilroy Was Here" later in this chapter for information on how to create your own signature.

✔ **Attachment Method:** Controls the way Eudora attaches files to your message if the file contains something other than text. See the section "Pass Me That File" in Chapter 9 for information on attaching files to a message.

✔ **QP (Quoted-Printable):** Usually pressed (selected); controls the way Eudora attaches text files to your message. Just leave it pressed.

✔ **Text as Documents (TEXT/DOC):** Tells Eudora more about how to handle attached text files. When this button is pressed, attached text files are sent as separate files. When this button isn't pressed, the text in the file is stuck at the end of the message.

✔ **Word Wrap (a page with a curving arrow):** Tells Eudora to word-wrap so that you don't have to press Enter at the end of every line.

✔ **Tab (a right-pointing arrow):** Tells Eudora to type spaces when you press the Tab key. If this button isn't pressed, the Tab key moves you to the next field in the window (usually the To field). Leave it pressed.

✔ **Keep Copy (two sheets of paper, one dog-eared):** Tells Eudora to keep a copy of your messages in your outbox.

✔ **Queue or Send:** Click this button when you are done composing your message. (The next section describes how you control which button you see.)

---

4. **If you want to send anyone copies or *blind* copies, enter the address (or addresses) in the C̲c and B̲cc fields.**

   Blind copies are copies of a message that are sent to someone without the other recipients knowing it. Blind copies are especially useful in industrial espionage. We get to attachments in a minute.

5. **Below the gray line, type the text of your message.**

   You don't have to press Enter at the end of every line — Eudora word-wraps to make your message look nice.

6. **To send your message, click the Queue or Send button, whichever button appears.**

If you set up Eudora to send all messages immediately (using the Immediate send option on the Settings dialog box), Eudora shows a Send button rather than a Queue button at the right end of the toolbar for the message.

Now you know how to send e-mail!

When Does Eudora Send the Message?

Eudora can hold your messages in a *queue* (just imagine all those messages standing patiently in line) and send them on your signal. Or Eudora can send your messages as soon as you finish writing them — it's your choice. Use the Immediate send option in the Settings dialog box to control when Eudora sends out messages that you compose.

Queue up my messages

You can save connect-time with your Internet provider if you do as much message reading and writing as possible when you are not connected; and then you can connect to the Internet and send your messages in a group. If sending a message ties up your PC for a minute or two, you may prefer to keep your messages in a queue and send them every few hours.

When we told you how to set up Eudora in the "Telling Eudora about you" section earlier in this chapter, you turned off the Immediate send option in the Settings dialog box. Turning the setting off tells Eudora to hold your messages in a queue.

If Eudora is set up to hold outgoing messages in a queue, nothing seems to happen when you click the Queue button. To send the messages in the queue, press Ctrl+T (or choose File⇨Send Queued Messages from the menu bar). If you chose the Send on check option in the Settings dialog box (you probably did — it's the default), Eudora sends your queued messages whenever you check your incoming mail, too.

What if you want to see your queue? Easy — choose Mailbox⇨Out from the menu bar. You see a list of the messages in the queue. Messages that have already been sent have an *S* in the leftmost column, while those waiting in the queue have a *Q* (see Figure 8-3).

If you want to save a message and send it later, choose File⇨Save from the menu bar. Then close the window. The message is saved in your outbox but not queued for sending, so you can edit and send it later.

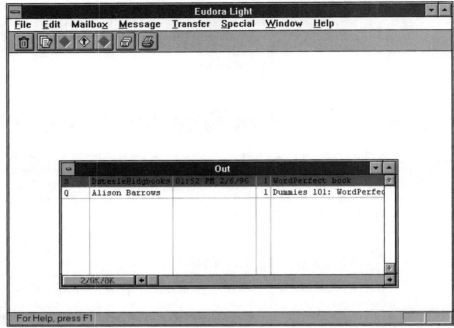

Figure 8-3:
The Out
mailbox
is your
electronic
outbox.

Here Comes Your Mail!

Well, you've sent mail, but how about getting the mail that's coming to you? How about the test message you sent earlier, for example?

Getting the mail

Here's how to get your incoming messages from your mail server:

1. **Press Ctrl+M (or choose File⇨Check Mail from the menu bar) to get your mail.**

   The first time you check your mail, Eudora asks for your password.

2. **Type the password to the computer where you get your mail (your mail server). Press Enter or click the OK button.**

   The password appears as a row of asterisks when you type it, so type carefully.

Eudora connects to your mail server, grabs your mail, and copies it to your PC. You see a Progress window showing a series of messages as it does this.

When Eudora is done downloading your incoming messages, you see a message saying that you have new mail and you may hear a cute tune. If you don't have any messages, you get an apologetic message telling you so.

3. Click OK to make the message go away.

You see a new window called *In* with a list of your incoming messages, if any (see Figure 8-4).

If the In window doesn't appear automatically, you can open the In window at any time by choosing Mailbox⇨In from the menu bar (or by pressing Ctrl+I).

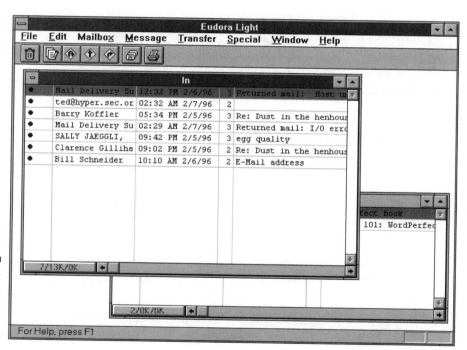

Figure 8-4:
Sorting
through the
day's mail.

Testing, testing

If you are testing Eudora and you're not yet sure that you plan to use it, you can tell Eudora *not* to delete the messages after it downloads them to your computer. Then you can use another mail program to download the messages again. Of course, once you start using Eudora, we're sure that you'll love it!

To tell Eudora to leave incoming messages on your mail server, choose Special⇨Settings from the menu bar, click the Checking Mail icon, click the Leave mail on server setting so that an × appears, and click OK. Now Eudora retrieves your mail as usual, but it doesn't delete it from

your mailbox at your mail server, where your mail is held. The good thing about this arrangement is that if you screw up retrieving your mail, you can download it again. When you get Eudora working as you would like, be sure to turn the Leave mail on server setting off.

If your provider has an extremely old mail server program, each time you check your mail you may get all the old messages in your mailbox as well as the new ones. If this happens to you, tell your provider to get a newer mail server. (QualComm, the people who wrote Eudora, give away a nice one called qpopper.)

Checking mail automatically

Wouldn't it be nice if Eudora could automagically check your mail every half hour? It can!

Choose Special⇨Settings from the menu bar, click the Checking Mail icon, and type a number of minutes in the Check for mail every box. Then click OK. Eudora checks your mail automatically at the interval you entered.

If you are not always connected to the Internet, automatic mail-checking can be annoying. If Eudora can't connect to your mail server, it displays a panicked message about the problem, like this: `Error getting network address for iecc.com`. Don't worry when you see such a message — it just means that you are not connected to the Net. Even worse, if your computer is set to "dial on demand," every half hour, it'll dial up your provider, check the mail, and hang up.

Reading the mail

The In window shows the contents of your In mailbox — messages you haven't read yet. You see one message per line with the name of the person who sent it (you, in the case of your test message), when it was sent, the number of pages, and the subject. In the leftmost column, you see a black dot or bullet for messages you haven't yet read. The leftmost column is blank for messages that you have read but haven't replied to or deleted.

To read a message, double-click it in the In window. You see a message window like the one shown in Figure 8-5. It shows the message's priority (usually Normal), subject, and text.

When you are looking at a message, you can easily reply to the message, delete it, forward it to someone else with your comments, or redirect it to someone else, as described in the sections "Sending your response," "Getting rid of messages," and "Sharing a message with friends" later in this chapter — just read on.

Sending your response

To reply to a message, follow these steps:

1. **Select the message in the In mailbox (or any mailbox, for that matter) by clicking it once, or display the message by double-clicking it.**

2. **Click the Reply button on the toolbar (the one with the U-turn sign), choose Message⇨Reply from the menu bar, or press Ctrl+R.**

   Eudora shows you a message window so that you can compose your reply. Eudora fills in the address of the person you are replying to and copies the subject from the original message. The text of the message you are replying to appears in the body of the message with each line preceded by a >.

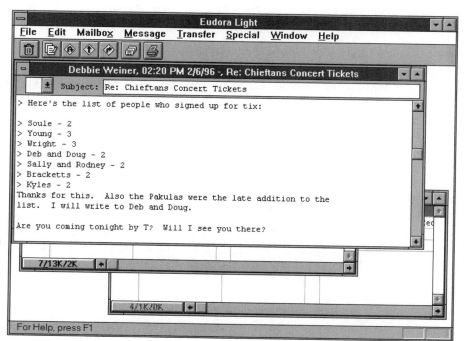

Figure 8-5:
A message
from the
outside
world.

3. **Delete all but the important parts of the quoted original message.**

   If you are responding to a particular point in the original message, leave just that point. Be sure to delete the most boring parts of the original message — headers and the signature.

4. **Write and send the message as usual.**

After you reply to a message, an *R* appears in the leftmost column of the In window, so you know that you have already dealt with the message.

Getting rid of messages

You can delete a message that you have already read. With a message on-screen or selected from a mailbox, click the Delete button on the toolbar (the trash can), choose <u>M</u>essage⇨<u>D</u>elete from the menu bar, or press Ctrl+D.

If you delete a message by accident, you can dig it out of the trash. Choose Mailbo<u>x</u>⇨<u>T</u>rash from the menu bar to see the Trash mailbox with all your deleted messages.

To get rid of the messages in your Trash mailbox (so they don't fester there forever), choose <u>S</u>pecial⇨<u>E</u>mpty Trash from the menu bar. Or choose <u>S</u>pecial⇨<u>S</u>ettings from the menu bar, click the Miscellaneous icon, click the <u>E</u>mpty Trash when exiting setting so that you see an × in its box, and click OK. Now when you choose <u>F</u>ile⇨E<u>x</u>it, Eudora takes out the trash.

Moving along to the next message

When you have read a message, you can close the message window to see the In window again. Then double-click another message to read it.

You can also press Alt+Down-arrow key to move to the next message.

Committing a message to paper

To print a message on your PC's printer, select the message from the mailbox or display the message on the screen. Then click the Print button on the toolbar, press Ctrl+P, or choose <u>F</u>ile⇨<u>P</u>rint from the menu bar. You see a Print dialog box that lets you choose which pages to print and how many copies. Click OK when you have made your choices.

Sharing a message with friends

Here's how you forward a message to someone else:

1. **Select the message in the In mailbox (or any mailbox, for that matter) by clicking it once, or display the message by double-clicking it.**

2. **Click the Forward button on the toolbar (the straight arrow) or choose Message➪Forward from the menu bar.**

   Eudora shows you a new message window. The text of the original message appears, indented by the > character (this character shows that you are repeating information you received from someone else). You can delete the part that won't be interesting to the person to whom you are forwarding the message, and you can add your own comments at the end (or anywhere).

3. **Type the address of the person to whom you want to forward the message just to the right of the To label.**

   If you want to forward the message to more than one person, you can enter more than one Internet address separated by commas.

4. **Then send the message as usual by clicking the Queue or Send button.**

   After you forward a message, an *F* appears in the leftmost column of the mailbox window by the message you forwarded.

Oops! This message isn't for me!

If you feel that you got a piece of mail in error and you want to pass it along to its proper recipient, you can redirect it:

1. **Select the message in the In mailbox (or any mailbox, for that matter) by clicking it once, or display the message by double-clicking it.**

2. **Click the Redirect button (the right-turn arrow) or choose Message➪Redirect from the menu bar.**

   Eudora displays the message in a new message window, but redirecting doesn't indent the text the way forwarding does. Also, the message is from the person who originally sent it, not from you.

3. **Enter the address to which you want to redirect the message.**

4. **Send it as usual.**

   After you redirect a message, a *D* (for reDirected) appears in the leftmost column of the mailbox containing the original message.

Saving Money with Eudora

You can use Eudora when you are not connected to the Internet. This is a great advantage because it enables you to read your mail and concoct responses at your leisure, without worrying about how much money you are spending on connect-time to your Internet provider.

Getting set to save money

Here is how to set up Eudora to minimize your connect time:

1. **Choose Special⇨Settings from the menu bar to see the Settings dialog box.**

2. **Click the Checking Mail icon. Don't enter any number (or enter zero) in the Check for mail every box.**

   This tells Eudora not to check for mail except when you tell it to.

3. **Click the Sending Mail icon. Don't choose Immediate send.**

   That is, click the little box to remove the ×. This setting tells Eudora not to send each message as soon as you have written it. Instead, Eudora waits until you give the word.

4. **Select the Send on check box so that an × appears in it.**

   This setting tells Eudora that while it is checking for new mail, it can send any mail that is waiting to be sent.

Now Eudora is configured to let you read and write your e-mail when you are not connected to your Internet account.

Checking your mail frugally

When you want to read and respond to your e-mail, follow these steps:

1. **Run Eudora.**

2. **In Eudora, take a look at your In mailbox to see whether you want to respond to any messages. Also compose any new messages you want to send (by clicking the New Message button on the toolbar, pressing Ctrl+N, or choosing the Message⇨New Message command).**

3. **Connect to the Internet.**

   For example, if you use Internet Chameleon, run Custom and choose Connect.

4. **Back in Eudora, choose File⇨Check Mail from the menu bar (or press Ctrl+M).**

   A Progress window tells you as Eudora gets your new messages and sends your messages that are queued up, waiting to be sent.

5. **Click OK to clear any box that tells you about new mail (or that you don't have any).**

6. **Disconnect from the Internet.**

   If you use Internet Chameleon, switch back to Custom and choose Disconnect.

7. **In Eudora, read your new messages.**

   They appear at the bottom of your In mailbox with a bullet in the leftmost column. Read them, compose replies, delete boring ones, move good ones into other mailboxes, or whatever.

8. **When you are finished with your messages and ready to send them, connect to the Internet again.**

9. **In Eudora, choose File⇨Check Mail from the menu bar again or press Ctrl+M.**

   If you chose the Send on check box in the Settings dialog box as we suggested, this step both checks for new mail and sends your queued outgoing mail.

10. **Disconnect from the Internet.**

Kilroy Was Here

You can make a *signature* that Eudora can automatically add to the end of messages you send. A signature usually consists of your full name, e-mail address, perhaps your mailing address or phone number, and maybe some pithy saying.

Creating your own personal signature

To make a signature, follow these steps:

1. **Choose Window⇨Signature to open the Signature window (logically enough).**

   You see a totally blank window, unless you've created a signature before (in which case you see your existing signature).

2. **Type the text of your signature in the window, as shown in Figure 8-6.**

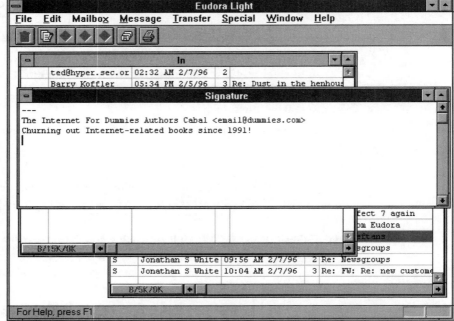

Figure 8-6:
A signature
appears at
the bottom
of messages
you send so
that you
don't have
to type this
stuff over
and over.

3. **Double-click the Control-menu box in the upper-left corner of the window to close it.**

   Eudora asks whether you want to save the changes to your signature.

4. **Click Yes.**

   Eudora remembers this signature forever or until you change it.

Signing with a flourish

To add your signature to a message, take a look at the window in which you are composing the message. Make sure that the Signature box (the second thingy from the left on the icon bar) says *JH* for John Hancock — put it right here.

If you don't want to include your signature with a message, click the arrow button to the right of the Signature box and choose None from the list.

That's not all Eudora Light can do — read Chapter 9 for more!

Chapter 9

Fancy Moves with Eudora Light

● ●

In This Chapter

▶ Sending and receiving files with Eudora

▶ Using Eudora's address book

▶ Keeping important messages in mailboxes and folders

▶ Getting Eudora Pro

● ●

*C*hapter 8 explained how to install Eudora and start using it as your e-mail program. We think you'll agree that it's easy and pleasant to use — we've been using Eudora for several years and still love her. This chapter explains more fun things that you can do with Eudora.

Pass Me That File

When you send a message, you may want to include a file that you have stored on your PC. Such a file is called an *attachment* (not an emotional attachment, just an attachment). You can attach a word-processing document, a graphics file, or anything that can be stored in a file on your computer.

When you attach a file, think about the person who will receive the file. What is this person going to do with it? If you send a Microsoft Word for Windows 6.0 document, the person on the other end must have the same program or a program that can read that type of document. If you correspond with folks on different types of computers — especially UNIX and mainframe folks — they may be out of luck. You may want to find out beforehand which types of files your correspondents can deal with.

There are three different methods you can use to attach a file, known as MIME, uuencode, and BinHex. See "I'm So Attached to You" in Chapter 5 for details on how they differ. In most cases, MIME's the one you want.

Attaching a file

To attach a file to a message, follow these steps:

1. **Compose the message as usual.**

   You can compose a new message using the New Message button on the toolbar, or you can reply to or forward a message. You can attach a file to any message you send with Eudora.

2. **Choose Message⬂Attach File from the menu bar (or press Ctrl+H).**

   You see the Attach File dialog box, which lets you indicate the exact file you have in mind.

3. **Choose the directory and filename of the file to attach and click OK.**

   The directory and filename appear in the header of the message on the Attachments line.

   On the toolbar for the message, the third box from the left shows which kind of encoding Eudora plans to use. The box usually shows a clown face, indicating that the file will be sent as a MIME attachment.

4. **To change the encoding, click the arrow button to its right and choose a different type (MIME or BinHex).**

5. **Send your message as usual.**

The contents of the attached file don't appear as part of the message. The file is "stapled" to the message but remains separate.

If you drag a file from the Windows File Manager into Eudora, the file is attached to the message you're composing.

If you change your mind about attaching the document, click the filename in the message header and press the Del key to delete it.

You might think that rather than use the Message⬂Attach Document command, you can just type the directory and filename of the file you want to attach right into the header of your message. But no! Eudora doesn't let you do this (we don't know why not).

Including information from a document

Another way to send information from a word-processing document as an e-mail message is to copy the text from your word-processing program into Eudora. When you copy text into a message, the text appears as part of the text of the message, not as an attachment.

In your word processor, highlight the text you want and copy it to the Clipboard (by choosing Edit⇨Copy from the menu bar). In Eudora, start a new message and put your cursor where you want the text to appear. Choose Edit⇨Paste from the Eudora menu (or press Ctrl+V) to copy it from the Clipboard.

Getting an attached file

When Eudora retrieves your mail from your mail server, it notices immediately whether an incoming message has an attachment. If you previously told Eudora where to store all attachments, it will store the attached file there. If you have never told Eudora where to put attached files, Eudora stops in its tracks and displays a Save Attachment dialog box. This dialog box lets you decide in which directory to put the incoming file. Of course, because you can't see the message yet, you may not know what the file contains, so it can be hard to decide where it should go. You may be able to guess by its original filename, which Eudora shows you.

Eudora automatically decodes the attached file, by using BinHex or MIME as appropriate, so it appears just as it did when it left the sender's computer.

If you don't want to be bothered every time Eudora gets an attached file, you can tell Eudora in advance which directory to put attachments in. Choose Special⇨Settings from the menu bar so that you see the Settings dialog box. Click the Attachments icon and then click the big Attachment Directory button. Eudora displays a dialog box that lets you choose the directory. Click the Use Directory button after you have chosen it. The directory name now appears right in the big button (strangely enough). Click OK.

From now on, all attachments are filed in that directory. You are still notified when attachments arrive because the messages to which they are attached show up in your In mailbox.

When you open a message to which a file is attached, you see a line like this:

```
Attachment Converted: C:\DOWNLOAD\DAG32.TRE
```

This line says that the message has an attachment, that the attachment was successfully downloaded, decoded, and stored, and where the resulting file is and what it's called.

Eudora Light can't deal with uuencoded files. If someone sends you a file attachment with uuencoding, Eudora Light doesn't know what to do with it, so it just displays the uuencoded file as part of the e-mail message. The text of the uuencoded file looks like a 15-month-old has been pounding on the keyboard with the Caps Lock key on (we know this from direct experience with a 15-month-old), except that each line begins with an *M*. If you get a uuencoded file, either tell the person who sent you the file to send it again using BinHex or MIME, or upgrade to Eudora Pro.

Macintosh users might want to get a copy of Jeff Strobel's shareware utility UULite. Contact jstrobel@world.std.com. It saved our you-know-whats when we were writting this book!

Quick Ways to Address Your Mail

Typing Internet addresses can be annoying with all the strange punctuation. Even more annoying is having to type lists of addresses when you want to send a message to a bunch of people. To avoid this annoyance, you can use Eudora's *nickname* feature.

What's in a nickname?

A nickname is a short name you can use instead of typing an entire Internet address. If you intend to send a great deal of mail to *Internet For Dummies* Central, for example, it can be a pain to type email@dummies.com over and over. It's much nicer to type Dum instead.

No problem! Eudora lets you make up as many nicknames as you want, and it stores them forever. A nickname can be short for one Internet address or for a whole list of them. To fool with nicknames, click the Nicknames button on the toolbar (the little stack of address cards), choose Window⇨Nicknames from the menu bar, or press Ctrl+L. You see the Nicknames window (see Figure 9-1).

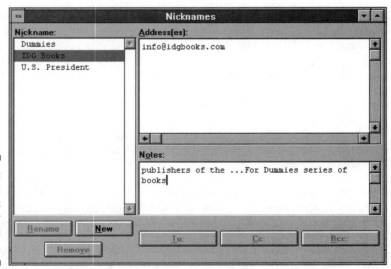

Figure 9-1: Making nicknames for your friends and associates.

The Nickname box lists all the nicknames you have created. The Address(es) box shows the actual Internet address (or addresses) for the nickname you have chosen. And the Notes box contains any notes you want to enter about the person or group of people.

When you are done using the Nicknames window, double-click the Control-menu box in the upper-left corner of the window (the button with the little gray hyphen). If you made any changes to your nicknames list, Eudora asks whether it should save the changes. Click Yes.

Making a nickname

To make a nickname, follow these steps:

1. **Click the New button in the Nicknames window.**

   You see the New Nickname dialog box, as shown in Figure 9-2.

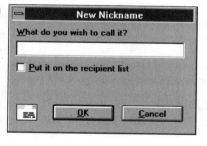

Figure 9-2:
Creating
a new
nickname
for one
person or
for a group.

2. **Type the nickname you want to create. For example, type** Dummies.

3. **Click OK.**

   The New Nickname dialog box goes away and you return to the Nicknames window. The new nickname appears on the Nickname list.

4. **In the Address(es) box, type the actual Internet address to use for this nickname.**

   If this nickname is for a group, enter a list of addresses separated by commas, or press Enter after each entry.

5. **Press Tab to move to the Notes box and enter any notes about the nickname.**

   If you know which mail program the person (or people) use, note it here because you might need to know this when you're sending attached files. You might also want to enter any alternative e-mail addresses that people might have (many folks have several).

6. **Repeat these steps for all the nicknames you want to create.**

It is okay to separate the addresses for a list of people by pressing Enter after each address when you type in the Address(es) box in the Nickname dialog box. But you cannot do this anywhere else in Eudora. Instead, you have to separate the addresses by commas.

When you are reading a message from someone you correspond with, it's easy to make a nickname. Choose Special⇨Make Nickname from the menu bar or press Ctrl+K. Eudora asks what you want to call the nickname. When you enter a name and click OK, Eudora creates a nickname for the person who sent you the message and you never have to type the address again.

Using a nickname

We like to keep the Nicknames window open in our Eudora Light window so that we can use nicknames whenever we want. When you are composing a message and you want to send it to someone with a nickname, choose the person from the Nickname list in the Nicknames window and click the To button. The nickname appears in the To field in the message that you are composing.

You can start a new message even more easily, in fact: In the Nicknames window, choose the person to send the message to and click the To button. Eudora figures that you want to start a new message to that person and opens a new message window with the nickname in the To field.

You can choose more than one nickname from the Nickname list if you want. Click one of the nicknames and then Ctrl+click each name you want to use.

No more mail for you!

To get rid of a nickname for someone you never, ever plan to write to again, choose the nickname from the Nickname list in the Nicknames window and click the Remove button. Sayonara, buddy!

Who did you say you were?

You can also rename a nickname. Renaming a nickname changes the nickname, but it doesn't change the real e-mail address for the nickname. For example, if you created the nickname *Bill Clinton* for the President of the United States and if a new president were elected, you could rename the nickname. The nickname would continue to use the same e-mail address, president@whitehouse.gov.

To rename a nickname, choose the nickname from the Nickname list in the Nicknames window and click the Rename button. Type the replacement name and click OK. The name of the nickname changes in the Nickname list.

File It, Eudora

If you are like us, you want to save a certain number of your messages. To keep them organized, we like to save them in different groups, which Eudora calls *mailboxes*. Eudora comes with three mailboxes:

- ✔ **In:** Stores incoming mail until you move it or delete it.
- ✔ **Out:** Stores outgoing mail.
- ✔ **Trash:** Provides a place for deleted messages to die; Eudora doesn't delete them until you choose Special⇨Empty Trash from the menu bar.

You can create your own mailboxes (for example, one for personal messages, one for a discussion of your department's budget, one for project planning messages, and one for messages about the football pool). After you have made a mailbox and put messages in it, you can read the messages, reply to them, delete them, or move them to other mailboxes exactly as you would if they were in your In mailbox.

Opening a mailbox

To look at a mailbox, choose Mailbox from the menu bar. The menu that appears contains all your mailboxes, including those you have created. Choose a mailbox, and a window for that mailbox opens. For example, to look at the trash, choose Mailbox⇨Trash.

When you open your Out mailbox, messages that have already been sent appear with an *S* in the leftmost column. Those that are queued for sending are marked with a *Q*.

What are those funky-looking numbers?

In the lower-left corner of a mailbox window, you see a box that says something like *5/10K/135K*. This is Eudora's cryptic way of telling you that five messages are in the mailbox (the first number), they take up 10K of disk space (the second number), and that junk lying around in the mailbox takes 135K of disk space (the third number). To tell Eudora to get rid of the junk, click the box (it's really a button). Eudora takes out the trash, and the third number shrinks to zero.

Make me a mailbox

To create a new mailbox and move a message into it, follow these steps:

1. **In the In window or any other mailbox window, select the message you want to put in the new mailbox by clicking it.**

   Alternatively, you can display the message by double-clicking it.

2. **Choose Transfer⇨New from the menu bar.**

   You see the New Mailbox dialog box, as shown in Figure 9-3.

Figure 9-3: Making a new mailbox to hold your fascinating messages.

3. **Type the mailbox name in the box.**

   The name can contain spaces. Capitalize it nicely so that it will look good on your menus and windows.

4. **Click OK.**

   Eudora makes the new mailbox and moves the chosen message into it.

Your new mailbox now appears on both the Mailbox and Transfer menus. To see the new mailbox, choose Mailbox from the menu bar and then choose the mailbox name. To move a message into the new mailbox, select or view the message, choose Transfer from the menu bar, and choose the mailbox name. What a convenient system!

If you want to set up a bunch of mailboxes without moving messages into them, choose Mailbox⇨New from the menu bar.

Saving a message in a text file

What if you want to use a message in a document that you are writing? Saving a message from Eudora into a text file is easy. Either view the message or choose it from the mailbox where it lives. Then choose File⇨Save As from the menu bar. You see a Save As dialog box that lets you decide which directory to put the file in and which filename to use. When you click OK, Eudora makes the file.

Alternatively, run your word processor. Display the message in Eudora, highlight the part of the text that you want to use in your document, and choose Edit⇨Copy from the Eudora menu (or press Ctrl+C) to copy it to the Clipboard. Switch to your word processor and paste the Clipboard text into your document by choosing Edit⇨Paste from the menu bar.

For organizing lots of mail, use folders

We really like mailboxes. Mailboxes are great for saving all your interesting mail by topic or by sender. However, if you set up more than 12 mailboxes, the Mailbox and Transfer menus get rather long. What to do? Organize your mailboxes into folders.

A *folder* is a collection of mailboxes with a name. For example, if you have mail about three different projects that you are accepting bids on, you could make a folder named *Bids* containing one mailbox for each project. We've got a folder named *Books* with a mailbox for each book we've written containing e-mail messages about writing arrangements, corrections to be made, and so on. (No complaint messages, of course.)

To create folders, move mailboxes into folders, get rid of mailboxes you don't use any more, and rename mailboxes, choose Window⇨Mailboxes from the menu bar. You see the Mailboxes window (not too surprisingly), shown in Figure 9-4. You see all of your mailboxes listed in both lists. Both lists are entitled *Top Level,* that is, mailboxes that are not contained in folders.

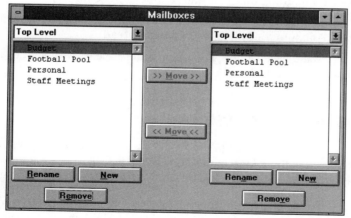

Figure 9-4:
Get your
mailboxes
organized!

You can use the Mailboxes window to do lots of things, including deleting and renaming mailboxes, creating folders, and moving mailboxes into and out of folders. The next few sections tell you all about these tasks. When you are done using the Mailboxes window, double-click the Control-menu box in its upper-left corner (the button with the little hyphen in it). A Close button on this window would have been nice!

Fold me a folder

You can create mailboxes from the Mailboxes window by clicking the New button; you see the same dialog box you used in the section "Make me a mailbox" earlier in this chapter. You use the same dialog box for making folders. Here's how to make a folder and put some mailboxes into it.

1. **Display the Mailboxes window by choosing Window⇨Mailboxes from the menu bar.**

2. **Click the New button.**

   You see the New Mailbox dialog box.

3. **Type the name for the new folder in the box.**

   Use capitalization and spaces so that the folder name will look nice on the Mailbox and Transfer menus.

4. **Click the Make it a folder box so that it contains an ×.**

5. **Click OK.**

   Eudora makes the folder and then displays the New Mailbox dialog box again so that you can create a mailbox in your new folder.

6. **Create a mailbox that you want to put into the folder.**

   Type the mailbox name and click OK. If you've already got a mailbox or two to put into the folder, click Cancel instead.

   In the Mailboxes window, the folder name appears with a little (what else!) folder icon to its left.

What is in this folder?

You can use the Mailboxes window to see what mailboxes are in a folder. Just double-click the folder name in one of the lists. It doesn't matter whether you double-click the folder name in the left-hand or right-hand list.

When you double-click the folder, the folder name appears at the top of the list and the mailboxes it contains are listed below it. The other list in the Mailboxes window continues to say *Top Level* above it, indicating that it lists mailboxes that aren't in any folder. Figure 9-5 shows the Mailboxes window with a folder named *Bids*.

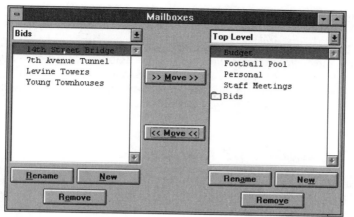

Figure 9-5:
The Bids
folder
contains a
mailbox for
each of your
important
construction
projects.

Stuff that mailbox into a folder

Observant readers noticed that when one of the lists in the Mailboxes window displays the contents of a folder, the two Move buttons (>>Move>> and <<Move<<) are no longer gray. When the two lists in the Mailboxes window display different mailboxes (like the *Top Level* mailboxes in one list and the *Bids* mailboxes in the other list), you can move mailboxes into or out of a folder.

To move a mailbox into a folder, follow these steps:

1. **Display the contents of the folder in one of the lists in the Mailboxes window.**

2. **Select the mailbox you want to move from the *Top Level* list.**

3. **Click the >>Move>> or <<Move<< button to move the mailbox from one list to the other.**

   If the folder is listed in the left-hand list, click the <<Move<< button. If the folder contents appear in the right-hand list, click the >>Move>> button.

   The mailbox jumps from one list to the other, landing in the folder.

You can use the same method to move a mailbox from one folder to another. Display the contents of one folder in one list in the Mailboxes window and display the contents of the other folder in the other list. Use the Move buttons to move mailboxes from one folder to the other.

When you create a folder that contains mailboxes, the folder appears on the Mailbox and Transfer menus. When you choose the folder name from one of these menus, you see a menu of the mailboxes in the folder.

Get this mailbox outta here

If you find that you no longer want to use a mailbox, you can delete it. First look at all the messages in the mailbox to be sure that you want to delete them all. Use the Transfer command to move any messages you want to save into other mailboxes. Then delete the mailbox from the Mailboxes window by selecting the mailbox name and clicking the Remove button.

Who named this mailbox?

You can change the name of a mailbox or a folder. In the Mailboxes window, select the mailbox or folder you want to rename, click the Rename button, type the new name into the dialog box that appears, and click the Rename button again.

You'll Love Her Big Sister, Eudora Pro

The commercial version of Eudora, Eudora Pro, has other features, including these:

- More icons appear on the toolbar, like an icon to click for checking your mail.

- You can send attached files using uuencoding. If you need to send files to folks whose e-mail programs can't deal with MIME or BinHex attachments, this feature is worth the price of the program.

- You can define two different signatures so that you can use one for friends and the other for business.

- Eudora Pro can automatically *filter* your incoming messages so that you can deal with e-mail automatically according to rules you set up (deleting all messages from someone you don't like, for example, or storing all messages from a mailing list into a separate mailbox).

- A built-in spell checker makes it easier to send literate-looking messages. Just click the Check Spelling button on the toolbar.

If you find that you like Eudora Light and use it frequently, think about buying Eudora Pro. It's not very expensive. After all, if everyone uses the shareware version and nobody buys the real thing, the software division of QualComm (who wrote it) will go down the tubes and the program will never be updated. Be a good citizen of the Internet and buy the software you use. (End of commercial announcement.)

Chapter 10

Netscape Mail: It's a Breath Mint AND a Floor Wax!

In This Chapter

▶ Sending mail with Netscape

▶ Receiving mail with Netscape

*Y*es, this is the same Netscape that everyone uses to surf the World Wide Web (WWW). The newest version (2.0) of Netscape is an adequate — if not superb — mail program as well as a Web browser. Like Eudora, Netscape runs on your PC or Mac and downloads and uploads mail from and to your mail server.

We strongly prefer Eudora for mail, but because some people are stuck with Netscape, we'll discuss it here.

Setting up Netscape Mail

We'll assume that you already have Netscape installed as a WWW browser.

Getting Netscape set up for use as a mail program is a little more complicated because, while you can go Web surfing without any further setup, to make Netscape a useful mail program you have to fill it in on little details like your e-mail address. Fortunately, the setup is straightforward, though tedious.

1. **Start Netscape.**

2. **Choose Window▷Netscape Mail.**

   Netscape will probably pop up an incomprehensible complaint about not being able to use a POP3 server. Yeah, we know, that's why we're here. Ignore it and click OK. You should see a screen like the one shown in Figure 10-1, with one sample welcome message waiting.

3. **Choose Options⇨Mail and News Preferences. Select the tab called Servers.**

   You should see a screen like the one shown in Figure 10-2.

4. **In the Outgoing Mail (SMTP) and Incoming Mail (POP) servers fields, enter the names of the computers that your Internet provider uses for outgoing and incoming mail.**

   Your Internet provider should have given you the names when you signed up. Most likely, both names will be the same.

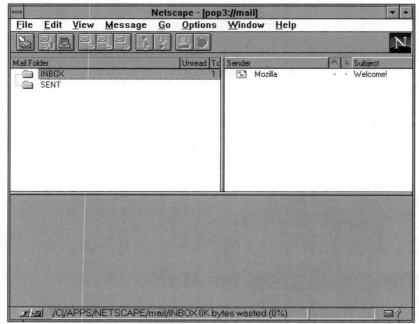

Figure 10-1:
Netscape
Mail ready
and waiting.

5. **Under POP User Name, enter your user name.**

   This is the name your provider assigned to you when you signed up.

   You can leave the rest of the fields alone in this window. The fields may not be exactly the same as in the figure here; that's okay.

6. **Select the Identity tab.**

   You should see a screen like the one shown in Figure 10-3.

7. **After Your Name, enter the name you'd like to have shown in the return address on outgoing mail.**

   This is your actual name, like John Q. Public, not your e-mail address, which we discuss next.

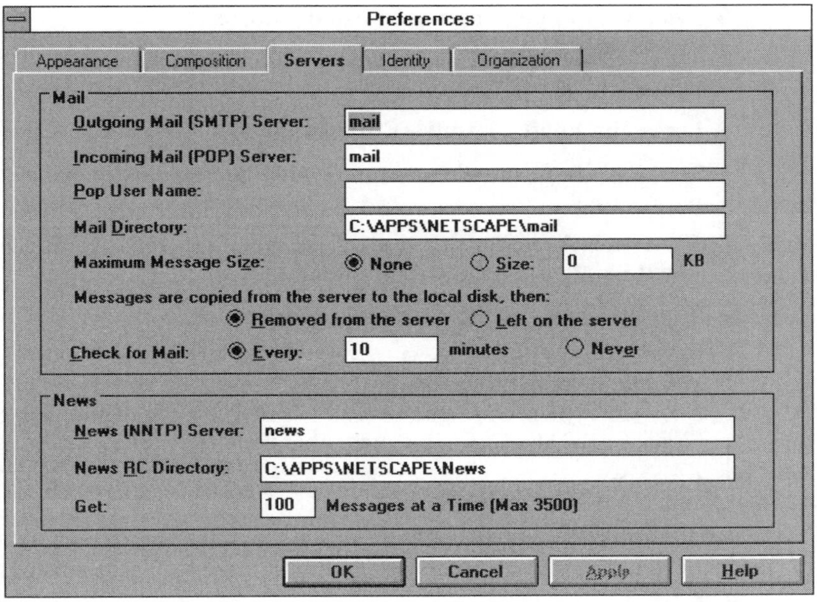

```
┌─────────────────────────────────────────────────────────────────┐
│ ─                          Preferences                            │
├─────────────────────────────────────────────────────────────────┤
│  Appearance │ Composition │ Servers │ Identity │ Organization │   │
│  ┌─Mail──────────────────────────────────────────────────────┐   │
│  │  Outgoing Mail (SMTP) Server:    [mail                   ] │   │
│  │  Incoming Mail (POP) Server:     [mail                   ] │   │
│  │  Pop User Name:                  [                       ] │   │
│  │  Mail Directory:                 [C:\APPS\NETSCAPE\mail   ] │   │
│  │  Maximum Message Size:      ● None    ○ Size: [0    ] KB   │   │
│  │  Messages are copied from the server to the local disk, then: │
│  │           ● Removed from the server  ○ Left on the server │   │
│  │  Check for Mail:  ● Every: [10      ] minutes  ○ Never    │   │
│  └───────────────────────────────────────────────────────────┘   │
│  ┌─News──────────────────────────────────────────────────────┐   │
│  │  News (NNTP) Server:   [news                             ] │   │
│  │  News RC Directory:    [C:\APPS\NETSCAPE\News            ] │   │
│  │  Get:   [100   ]  Messages at a Time (Max 3500)           │   │
│  └───────────────────────────────────────────────────────────┘   │
│        [   OK   ]   [ Cancel ]   [ Apply ]   [ Help ]             │
└─────────────────────────────────────────────────────────────────┘
```

Figure 10-2:
Ready to set up your servers.

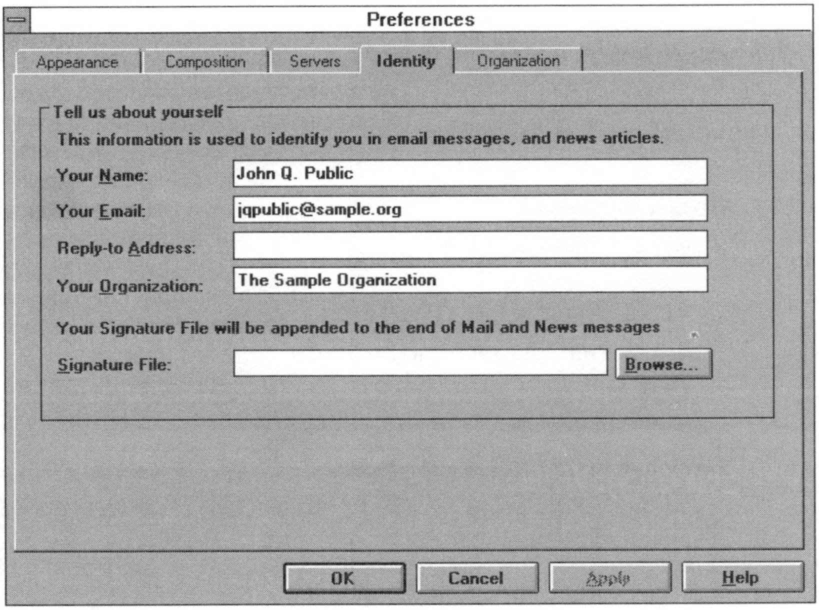

```
┌─────────────────────────────────────────────────────────────────┐
│ ─                          Preferences                            │
├─────────────────────────────────────────────────────────────────┤
│  Appearance │ Composition │ Servers │ Identity │ Organization │   │
│  ┌─Tell us about yourself────────────────────────────────────┐   │
│  │  This information is used to identify you in email messages, and news articles. │
│  │  Your Name:          [John Q. Public                    ] │   │
│  │  Your Email:         [jqpublic@sample.org               ] │   │
│  │  Reply-to Address:   [                                  ] │   │
│  │  Your Organization:  [The Sample Organization           ] │   │
│  │  Your Signature File will be appended to the end of Mail and News messages │
│  │  Signature File:  [                          ] [Browse...] │   │
│  │                                                           │   │
│  └───────────────────────────────────────────────────────────┘   │
│        [   OK   ]   [ Cancel ]   [ Apply ]   [ Help ]             │
└─────────────────────────────────────────────────────────────────┘
```

Figure 10-3:
Who the heck are you?

8. **After Your Email, enter your e-mail address.**

   This is generally your user name, the @ sign, and your provider's system name.

9. **Leave the Reply-to Address blank.**

   The Reply-to Address defaults to your e-mail address, which is almost always right.

10. **(Optional) After Your Organization, enter any organization name that you'd like to have appear on outgoing mail.**

11. **You can leave the Signature File blank for now.**

   If you'd like to have a short (no more than four lines, please) signature automatically added to the end of each message, run the Windows Notepad, type in the signature, and save it to a file named something like \NETSCAPE\SIG.TXT. Then enter that filename in the Signature File field.

12. **Click OK.**

That's all the setup you need to do. You can twiddle with some of the other parameters later if you're feeling bored, but nothing else important needs to be changed.

Sending Mail with Netscape

The steps for sending mail from Netscape are almost identical to those for sending mail from Eudora (you are doing the same thing, after all):

1. **Start Netscape.**

2. **Choose File⇨New Mail Message.**

   This step opens a mail composing window. If you're already looking at the Netscape mail window, you can also press the New Mail button on the icon bar (the third button from the left).

3. **Fill in the recipient's address (or addresses), indicate the subject, and type the message.**

4. **Click Send to send the message.**

   That's the little flying envelope at the left end of the icon bar.

Netscape gives you the choice of sending mail immediately or stashing your mail in the Outbox and sending it later. If you have a dial-up account where you pay by the hour, composing all your mail and then connecting to your provider to send all the mail at once is invariably more economical.

You can switch between immediate and deferred mail sending in any message composition window. In that window, you can choose Immediate or Deferred from the Options menu. If you use deferred sending, outgoing mail is placed in a folder called *Outbox* until it's sent. You send your mail by choosing File⇨Send Mail in Outbox on the menu bar or by pressing Ctrl+H.

Receiving Mail with Netscape

The Netscape Mail window has three parts. The upper-left part shows your list of mail folders. The upper-right shows the messages in the current folder, and the bottom part shows the current message. (This three-part window was introduced in the Agent and Free Agent net news programs and is becoming a standard.) You can adjust the sizes of the three parts of the windows by dragging the separating bars with the mouse.

To receive and read mail, follow these steps:

1. **Start Netscape.**

2. **Choose Window⇨Netscape Mail.**

   This step opens the Netscape mail window, which you saw in Figure 10-1. Netscape may try to retrieve any waiting mail immediately. If it doesn't, click the Get Mail button, the leftmost button on the icon bar. Incoming mail is filed in your INBOX folder. If you've never retrieved mail before, it asks you for your mailbox password on the mail server, which is generally the same password you use to connect to your Internet provider.

3. **Click the INBOX icon in the left column of the screen to see the messages in your Inbox.**

   The upper-right part of your screen shows the subject lines for incoming mail.

4. **Click each message to read it or click Next or Previous to read messages in order.**

After you have a message on the screen, you can click the Print, Delete, and other buttons to handle messages. We discuss the other functions, such as replying to and forwarding messages, a little later in this chapter.

In the list of messages, two columns of inscrutable little icons are between the name of the message's author and the message's subject. The first column is a *flag* which lets you flag a bunch of messages and then do something with all of them, like move them all to another folder. (As of Netscape 2.0b6, you can turn the flags on, but the group operations don't work reliably.) The second column is a little green hockey puck, which means that the message hasn't been read yet. Click the flag or puck column to turn the flag or puck on or off. Netscape shows a little dot that you can use as a target for your clicking. Marking a message as unread is a handy way to remind yourself that you still need to do something with a particular message.

Replying to Messages

First, click the desired message. Then choose Message⇨Reply, click the Reply button (it has an envelope with a bent arrow under it), or for the lazy, press Ctrl+R. Netscape opens a message composition window with the To: and Subject: fields all set and the original message loaded into the message body. Compose your reply and edit down the quoted material to the minimum needed to remind your correspondent what the discussion is about. Then click the Send button.

You can also use Message⇨Reply to All or the Reply All button (the envelope with two bent arrows) to address the reply to all recipients of the original message, not just the sender.

Forwarding with Netscape

When a message is on-screen, choose Message⇨Forward or click the Forward button, and Netscape opens a new window for your message. Netscape treats the old message as an attached file. You can't edit your old message, although you can add comments of your own to send along with it.

If you want to edit a message as you forward it, click Reply and then edit the To: field to address the message to the person to whom you wish to send the edited version.

Filing with Netscape

Netscape lets you have as many mail folders as you want. To create a new mail folder, choose File⇨New Folder. Once you've created your folder, you can use the mouse to drag messages from the current folder to other folders. Hold down the Ctrl key while dragging to move rather than copy.

You can also move and copy messages by using the Message menu, but dragging is much more convenient.

Netscape Attachments

In Netscape, you click the Attach button to send an attachment. Unlike most other mail programs, Netscape lets you attach any file or document you can describe with a *URL (Uniform Resource Locator,* the naming scheme used on the World Wide Web). Netscape gives you your choice of attaching a document by default (the last message or page you were looking at) or attaching a file. In the window that the Attach button opens, click Attach Location (URL) to attach a document, or click Attach File to attach a file. If you attach a file, you can click the Browse button to choose the file to attach. When you've decided what to attach, click OK to attach the file or document to the outgoing message and close the Attach window.

For incoming mail, Netscape displays any attachments that it knows how to display (Web pages and image files in the popular GIF and JPG formats). For other kinds of attachments, it displays a little description of the file, which you click. After you click the file description, Netscape runs an appropriate display program if it knows of one, or Netscape asks you whether it should save the attachment to a file or configure a display program, which Netscape can then run to display it.

The Address Book

With Netscape, you can keep an address book of your favorite addresses. The easiest way to add an entry is to select a message from someone you want to add to the address book and then choose Message⇨Add to Address Book. Netscape opens an Address Book Properties window. Adjust the entry if needed and then click OK to add the entry to your address book. (You can leave the nickname field blank because it's not very useful.)

Using your address book

Whenever you're creating a message, you can open the address book by clicking the Mail To: or Cc: buttons in the message composition window. You'll see a list of all of the entries in your address book. Click the one you want; then click one of the three buttons at the bottom of the address book, To:, Cc:, or Bcc:; and then click OK. The selected address is added to your message.

Editing and adding entries in the address book

You can edit entries in the address book by opening the address book window using Window⇨Address Book. To change an item, click the item and then choose Item⇨Properties.

To add a new entry, choose Item⇨Add User. This opens an empty Address Book Properties window into which you have to type the person's real name and e-mail address. Then click OK to add it.

If you double-click an entry, Netscape opens a message composition window addressed to that person.

Creating address lists

Netscape makes it possible — if not exactly easy — to make address lists. First, you have to have entries in your address book for everyone who you want to have on your list. Create the entries using Item⇨Add User. Then create the list using Item⇨Add List. This opens an Address Book Properties window, suggesting the not-exactly-inspired list name of New Folder. Change the name to something better and click OK. (Don't enter any e-mail addresses yet.)

Now your list appears in the Address Book window as an empty folder. Drag in the addresses you want to have in the list. (*Note:* The addresses remain as independent entries as well.) If you have other lists, you can drag names from one list to another. Dragging a name off a list removes it from that list. Don't drag one list into another because that just messes up both lists. (A future version of Netscape may fix this.) Once you're happy with your addresses and lists, choose File⇨Close to close the address book window.

Part III
Using Online Services for E-Mail

"IT HAPPENED AROUND THE TIME WE SUBSCRIBED TO AN ONLINE SERVICE."

In this part . . .

Many people find that the easiest way to get started with e-mail is to sign up for an account with an online service provider. We show you how to get started sending mail from the most popular commercial providers and from traditional UNIX shell providers.

Chapter 11
America Online Mail

In This Chapter

▶ Reading e-mail from AOL
▶ Creating your own messages
▶ Using FlashSessions to read your mail off-line
▶ A quick look at GNN

America Online (AOL, to its friends) is a widely used online service that includes Internet access and an easy-to-use e-mail system that can get your message to AOL members or any Internet account. This chapter describes AOL software version 2.5. AOL updates its software and the graphics that appear in its dialog boxes all the time, so your screen may not exactly match the figures in this chapter.

Mail It, AOL

America Online has a mail system through which AOL members can send messages to each other, as well as to the rest of the Internet.

Your Internet address is your screen name (omitting any spaces) plus @aol.com. If your screen name is John Smith, for example, your Internet address is JohnSmith@aol.com.

Checking for New Mail

When you sign on to AOL, it tells you whether you have any mail. On the left side of the Welcome! window you see either the message "No New Mail" or the message "You Have Mail." Another way to tell whether mail is waiting for you is to look at the List Unread Mail icon on the Flashbar — it's the far left one, a picture of a little mailbox. If the little red flag is *up*, you have mail.

Reading Your Mail

To read your unread mail, follow these steps:

1. **Click the leftmost icon on the Flashbar, the one just below the word *File*.**

   This is the Read New Mail icon. Alternatively, you can choose Mail⇨Read New Mail from the menu or press Ctrl+R.

   You see the New Mail dialog box, as shown in Figure 11-1. Each line on the list describes one incoming mail message with the date it was sent, the sender's e-mail address, and the subject.

2. **To read a message, highlight it on the list and click Read or press Enter.**

   The text of your message appears in another cute little dialog box.

3. **To reply to the message or forward it, see "Sending a reply" or "Forwarding a message" in this chapter.**

4. **To see the next message, click the Next button.**

   If you are looking at the last message in your inbox, the Next button doesn't appear. (Makes sense!)

5. **When you finish, double-click the little box in the upper-left corner of each window you're finished with.**

From the Welcome window, you can click the You Have Mail icon to see your new mail.

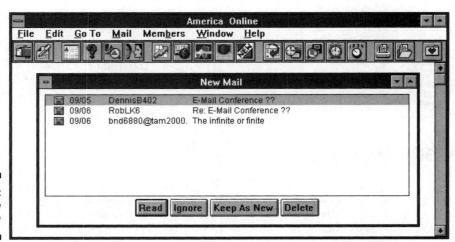

Figure 11-1:
Any new
mail?

Keeping messages

After you have read your mail, AOL keeps each message for a few days and then throws it away. If you want to keep a message around, select it from your list of mail and click the Keep As New button.

Don't reply to really annoying messages right away. You may have to get some information, or you may have to cool off after reading the brainless message some jerk sent you.

Sending a reply

To reply to a message you have received, display it as described in "Reading Your Mail" earlier in this chapter. To reply, follow these steps:

1. Click the Reply button.

You see a dialog box like the one in Figure 11-2. The To address is already filled in with the address from which the original message came, and AOL suggests a subject line.

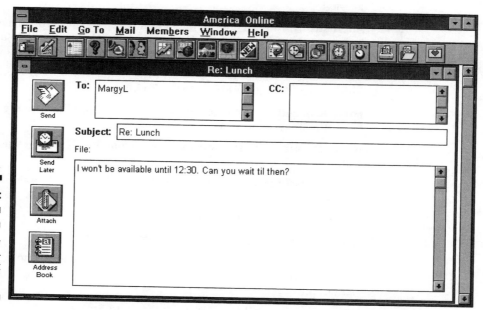

Figure 11-2:
When you reply to a message, AOL addresses it for you.

2. **Type the text of your message in the box in the lower part of the dialog box.**

3. **To send the message, click the Send icon.**

Forwarding a message

To forward a message to someone else, display it as described in "Reading Your Mail" earlier in this chapter. Then click the Forward button, address the message, add any text you want (like *I thought you might want to see this* or *Get a load of this idiotic idea!*) and click Send.

Composing a New Message

You don't have to reply to other messages; you can start an exchange of messages, assuming that you know the e-mail address of the person you want to contact:

1. **Click the second icon from the left on the toolbar, the picture of a pen at an angle.**

   Alternatively, you can choose Mail⇨Compose Mail from the menu bar. Or just press Ctrl+M. You see the Compose Mail dialog box, which looks very much like the one you used when replying to or forwarding a message — see Figure 11-2.

2. **Enter the recipient's address in the To box.**

   For AOL members, just enter the screen name. For others on the Net, type the entire Internet address.

3. **In the CC box, enter the addresses of anyone to whom you want to send a copy.**

   You don't have to send a copy to yourself — AOL keeps copies of mail you have sent.

4. **Enter a brief subject line in the Subject box.**

5. **In the box with no name, type the text of your message.**

   Don't use the Tab key because it moves your cursor from one box to the next in the dialog box. You can press Enter, though, to begin a new paragraph.

6. **When you like what you see, click the Send button.**

   AOL confirms that the mail is winging on its way.

7. **Click OK to make the message go away.**

Attaching a File to Your Message

If you want to send a file on your PC to someone as an e-mail message, AOL makes the process easy. When you are writing the message in the Compose Mail window, click the Attach button. The Attach File dialog box is displayed, which lets you choose any file from your PC. Select a file and click OK. The file is included as a MIME attachment. Attachments work great for sending files to other AOL members and to anyone who can deal with MIME.

If you want to send a message to someone who can't handle MIME attachments, here's a way to include a text file with a mail message to anyone:

1. **Run Windows Notepad, your word processor, or any other program that can display the text you want to send.**

2. **Using that program, copy the text to the Clipboard.**

   In most programs, you copy by highlighting the text and choosing Edit⇨Copy from the menu. Most Windows programs let you copy high-lighted text by pressing Ctrl+Ins or Ctrl+C.

3. **In America Online, begin a new message by replying to a message or by composing a new message.**

   (See "Sending a reply," "Forwarding a message," or "Composing a New Message" earlier in this chapter.)

4. **Place your cursor in the text box where you type the text of the message.**

5. **Choose Edit⇨Paste (or press Ctrl+V).**

   The text appears.

6. **Send your message as usual.**

You *are* limited as to how much text you can copy at a time into the Clipboard, but it's big. If you have trouble, copy the text one piece at a time. This method works only for text, not for pictures or data files.

Saving a Message on Your PC

If you get a message on AOL that you want to download to your PC, display it on the screen as described in the section "Reading Your Mail" earlier in this chapter. Then choose File⇨Save As from the menu bar. AOL lets you choose the directory and filename in which to save the file on your computer. When you click OK, it saves the e-mail message as a text file. Nice and easy!

The AOL Address Book

AOL lets you make an address book of the e-mail addresses of your friends and coworkers. When you are composing a message, click the Address Book button on the Compose Mail window. You see the Address Book window shown in Figure 11-3.

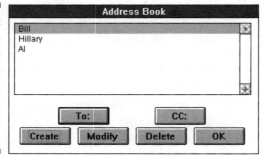

Figure 11-3: The address book contains a list of the folks to whom you like to send mail.

In your address book, you can store addresses of your correspondents along with the nicknames you'd like to use for them — that is, what you'd like to type when you address mail to each person. For example, instead of typing *president@whitehous.gov*, you can use the nickname *Bill*.

To add an address to your address book, click the Create button in the Address Book window. The Address Group window opens (a mysterious name for this window, unless you realize that you can use the address book for creating small mailing lists, too). You see the Address Group window in Figure 11-4.

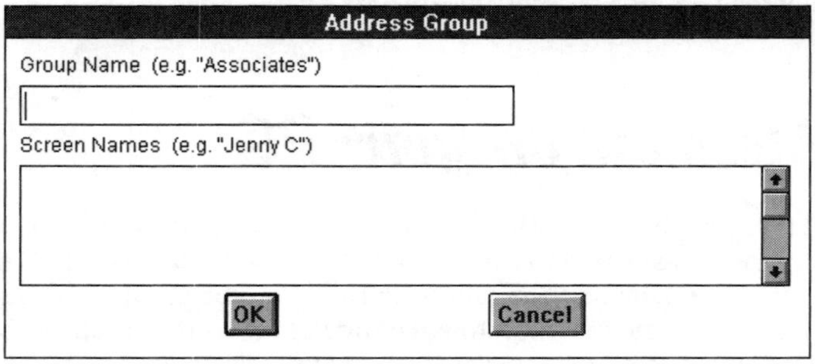

Figure 11-4: When you add someone to your address book, you enter the Group Name (nickname) and Screen Names (actual address).

In the Group Name box, type the person's real name or the name you'd like to type when addressing e-mail to the person. In the Screen Names box, type the person's AOL screen name or Internet address. To create a mailing list with one group name, enter a list of AOL screen names or Internet addresses in the Screen Names box. Click OK when you are done.

Using your address book to address a message is easy:

1. **Click the Address Book button in the Compose Mail window.**

   You see the address book, shown in Figure 11-3.

2. **Select the person to whom you want to send the message and click the To button.**

   The person's e-mail address appears in the To box in the Compose Mail window.

3. **Click OK in the Address Book window to make it go away.**

A Cheaper Way to Use AOL

AOL has a nice feature that lets you read your e-mail and newsgroup messages offline (when you are not connected to AOL). This feature, called *FlashSessions,* can save you big bucks in connect-time.

FlashSessions enable you to tell AOL to log into your account, send e-mail messages you have composed, get the new mail, and log off as fast as it can. You can also tell AOL to perform this series of steps at a preset time each day, such as in the middle of the night when your computer and telephone aren't doing anything else.

Setting up FlashSessions

Here's how to tell AOL that you want to use FlashSessions:

1. **Choose Mail⇨FlashSessions from the menu bar.**

   You see the FlashSessions dialog box.

2. **If each of the boxes in this dialog box do not already contain check marks, click in the boxes.**

   These boxes control what AOL does during FlashSessions. Make sure that all the boxes have an × in them so that AOL will upload and download all the e-mail messages, files, and Usenet articles that are waiting to be transmitted.

If you want AOL to run FlashSessions automatically on a schedule, continue with step 3. If you want to perform FlashSessions only when you give the command, skip to step 9 and read "Flashing on AOL" later in this chapter.

3. **Click the Schedule FlashSession button.**

   You see the Schedule FlashSessions dialog box. Now you have to tell AOL how often to log on and get your e-mail.

4. **Choose which days you want AOL to get your mail.**

   Click the boxes for days you want to skip to remove the × from the box. If you use AOL at work, for example, you might want to skip getting your mail on Saturday and Sunday.

5. **Click the How Often box to choose how often during the day you want AOL to get your mail.**

   To get your mail during the night, for example, choose Once each day.

6. **Click the up and down arrows for the Starting Time to choose the time you want the downloads to begin.**

   If you choose Once each day for How Often, the Starting Time is the time that the download begins each day. To get your mail at 5:00 a.m. every day before you get to work, for example, set the first Starting Time (the hours) to 5 and the second number (the minutes) to zero. Notice that AOL uses a 24-hour clock: To get your mail at 2 o'clock each afternoon, set the hours to 14.

7. **Click the Enable Scheduler box so that it contains an ×.**

8. **Click OK.**

   You return to the FlashSessions dialog box.

9. **Double-click the Control-menu box in the upper-left corner of the FlashSessions dialog box to close it.**

Now your AOL software will log on to AOL following the schedule you set. It will send any e-mail you composed, get any incoming e-mail for you, get any articles in Usenet newsgroups to which you subscribe, and post any Usenet newsgroup articles you've written.

Composing e-mail offline

If you use FlashSessions, you can compose your e-mail when you are not connected to AOL. Choose Mail⇨Compose Mail from the menu bar or press Ctrl+M. You see the Compose Mail dialog box, which looks a lot like Figure 11-2. Address and write your e-mail message as usual. When you finish, click the Send Later button. AOL saves the message to be sent the next time you run a FlashSession.

Flashing on AOL

To run a FlashSession any time, just choose Mail⇨Activate FlashSession Now. You see the Activate FlashSession Now dialog box. Click Begin to start the FlashSession. Now AOL works like a player piano, or a program being controlled by an invisible robot. It logs on, transmits to AOL the e-mail you composed, downloads your incoming e-mail, downloads articles in the Usenet newsgroups you selected, and logs off, recording its actions in a FlashSession Status dialog box so that you can see what it has done.

Reading flashed mail

After you have used a FlashSession to download your e-mail, read it by choosing Mail⇨Read New Mail (or press Ctrl+R). To see a list of all the mail you've downloaded, not just your new mail, choose Mail⇨Read Incoming Mail. You can reply to mail and forward messages — click the Send Later icon when you finish editing the messages.

What about GNN?

GNN is an Internet service owned and operated by AOL. It's similar to AOL in several ways: the sign-up process is similar, both come with nicely packaged, easy-to-install software, and neither is particularly cheap. And both can do e-mail.

If you have a GNN account, you use a program called GNNmessenger to read and write e-mail. Using GNNmessenger, you can send and receive e-mail to and from other GNN users in addition to folks on the rest of the Internet. To read your mail and compose new messages offline, you can run GNNmessenger when you aren't connected to GNN.

Your Internet address is your username (omitting any spaces) plus @gnn.com. If your username is John Smith, for example, your Internet address is JohnSmith@gnn.com.

The top part of the GNNmessenger window (see the following figure) shows the list of messages, and one of the messages is highlighted. The bottom part of the window shows the text of the highlighted message. To read a message, just highlight it in your list of messages. Once you've read a message, you can

✔ Print the message by clicking the Print button on the toolbar, pressing Ctrl+P, or choosing File⇨Print from the menu.

✔ Delete the message by clicking the Delete button on the toolbar, pressing d, or choosing Edit⇨Delete Selection from the menu.

✔ Reply to the message by clicking the Reply button on the toolbar, choosing Send⇨Reply from the menu, or pressing Ctrl+R. If the message was addressed to other people too, you can click Reply All if you want your reply to be addressed to everyone who got the original message.

✔ Forward the message by clicking the Forward button on the toolbar or choosing Send⇨Forward from the menu.

(continued)

(continued)

✔ Save the message in a text file by choosing File⇨Save Message from the menu. GNN asks for the directory and filename in which to save the message.

To create a new e-mail message from scratch, click the New button on the toolbar, press Ctrl+N, or choose Send⇨New Message from the menu.

If you want to send a file to someone as an e-mail message, you can. GNNmessenger can handle all three methods of attaching files (uuencoding, MIME, and BinHex). To attach a file to your message, compose it as usual. You can start a message from scratch, reply to a message, or forward one: it doesn't matter. When you see the Send Mail window, choose Attachment⇨Browse from the menu.

Choose the directory and filename of the file you want to send along with the e-mail message.

If you don't tell it otherwise, GNNmessenger attaches the file using MIME. If the person who will receive the file has an e-mail program that can't handle MIME attachments, you can change the attachment method to uuencoding by choosing Attachment⇨Uuencode from the menu.

What if someone sends you a message with a file attached? If the file was attached using MIME or uuencoding, GNN stores the file in the DOWNLOAD subdirectory of the GNN program directory (on most systems, this is C:\GNN\DOWNLOAD).

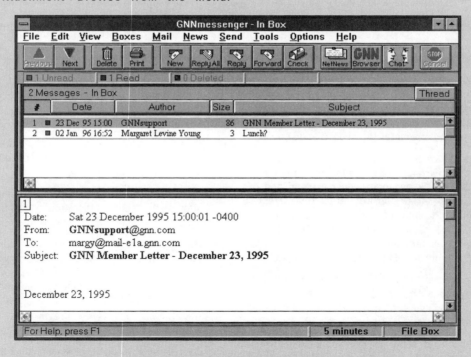

Chapter 12
CompuServe Mail

· ·

In This Chapter

▶ Using WinCIM to get your CompuServe Mail

▶ Sending and receiving e-mail from the Internet

▶ Attaching files to CompuServe messages

· ·

Introduction to CompuServe Mail

CompuServe is a very successful online service that caters to business and professional users. It has a mail service for exchanging messages with other CompuServe users. The same mail service works for sending and receiving e-mail to and from Internet addresses. This chapter describes how to use CompuServe's mail.

Note that CompuServe makes it easy to send attached files to other CompuServe users, but it's inconvenient and cumbersome to send attached files to the Internet. Also, CompuServe charges extra (about ten cents a message) when you receive messages from the Internet.

This chapter describes how to use CompuServe with its Windows software: the CompuServe Information Manager (CIM) for Windows, better known as WinCIM (version 2.01). If you are using CompuServe's Macintosh software, MacCIM, or a different version of WinCIM, your screens will look a little different from those shown in this chapter.

WinCim and MacCim are on the CD-ROM that comes with this book. See Appendix C for information on how to install the software and sign up for a CompuServe account.

My user ID is what?!

Unlike most other online services and Internet providers, CompuServe assigns a number to each user. Rather than an easy-to-remember username (such as ElvisLives or HeartThrob117), you get a number that looks like 77777,7777.

The exact number of digits varies, but your user ID is always a number with a bunch of digits and a comma somewhere in the middle. Users in the U.S. and Canada usually have numbers that begin with a 7, and overseas users usually have numbers that begin with 1 (this numbering scheme dates back to the stone age of computing, in the late 1960s. The numbers are base 8, by the way).

Your Internet e-mail address is not the same as your CompuServe ID — you have to modify it to include the fact that it is a CompuServe account number. To figure out your e-mail address, change the comma in your user ID to a period, and add @compuserve.com to the end. If your CompuServe ID is 77777,7777, for example, your Internet e-mail address is 77777.7777@compuserve.com. In 1996, CompuServe will allow users to have real names, with letters in them, instead of these funky-looking numbers. Click the Go button on the toolbar and type REGISTER to find out how to register for a name for your account.

Do I Have Mail?

When you start WinCIM and connect to CompuServe, the status bar at the bottom of the WinCIM window tells you how many messages you have waiting for you. If any messages are waiting, the number of messages appears on the Get New Mail icon on your toolbar (the one with a picture of an envelope). Click the icon to see your mail.

Reading Your Mail the Cheap and Easy Way

The most efficient way to read your mail is offline, that is, while you're not connected to CompuServe. You don't have to pay for connect time while you are reading and composing messages. Here's how it works:

- ✔ You use the Mail⇨Send/Receive All Mail command on the menu. This command grabs all your mail and downloads it (copies it) from CompuServe into your In Basket, a storage area on your hard disk.

- ✔ You disconnect from CompuServe.

✔ While you're disconnected (and therefore not paying connect-time charges), you read your e-mail at a leisurely pace. You can even write replies or compose messages to other people. Messages you write are stored in your Out Basket, which is also on your hard disk.

✔ When you finish reading your mail, you use the Mail⇨Send/Receive Mail command again to send the messages in your Out Basket and pick up any additional messages in your In Basket.

The result is that you are online only long enough to download your incoming mail and upload your outgoing mail.

Ready to try it? Follow these steps:

1. In WinCIM, choose Mail⇨Send/Receive All Mail from the menu.

WinCIM asks whether you want it to hang up when it finishes getting your mail.

2. Click the Disconnect when Done box so that it has an × in it and then click OK.

WinCIM dials CompuServe, logs on, grabs your mail, stores it in the In Basket on your hard disk, and hangs up. There! You stop paying connect charges. WinCIM tells you how many messages it sent (messages you have composed since the last time you connected to CompuServe) and how many incoming messages it received.

3. To read your messages, choose Mail⇨In-Basket from the menu.

You see your In Basket, which looks like Figure 12-1.

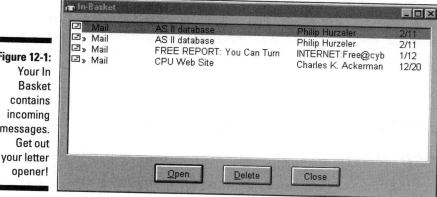

Figure 12-1:
Your In Basket contains incoming messages. Get out your letter opener!

4. **To read a message in your In Basket, double-click it (or select it and click Open).**

5. **To reply to a message, click the Reply button, compose a response, and click Send Now (if you want to connect to CompuServe and send it right now) or Out-Basket (to put the message in your Out Basket to be sent the next time you connect to CompuServe).**

   When you reply to a message, WinCIM addresses the message for you. All you have to do is type your response.

6. **To forward a message to someone else, click Forward, address the message, and click Send Now or Out-Basket.**

   See the section "Using Your Little Black Book" later in this chapter to learn how to use the Recipient List dialog box to address a CompuServe message.

7. **To see the next message in your In Basket, click Next.**

8. **Compose any new messages by choosing Mail⇨Create/Send Mail from the menu.**

9. **After you finish reading and composing mail, choose Mail⇨Send/ Receive All Mail from the menu.**

   WinCIM calls CompuServe again, sends all the mail in your Out Basket, and checks for any mail that has arrived since you last checked it.

You can see the messages in your Out Basket by choosing Mail⇨Out-Basket from the menu. You see a list of the messages you have written but that have not yet been sent to CompuServe. If you want to change a message (perhaps you thought better of that snappy retort in a message to your boss), you can edit the message by highlighting it and clicking Open. To send all the messages in your Out Basket right away, click Send All.

In addition to your In Basket and Out Basket, WinCIM provides you with a filing cabinet in which to file your messages. After you read a message, you can click File It to store it in your filing cabinet. See that little filing cabinet icon on the toolbar? Click it to see what's in your filing cabinet.

Reading Your Mail the Expensive and Easy Way

If you don't feel like dialing in twice to get and send your mail, you can read it while you're online. Go ahead, waste your money — we don't care! Use any of these methods:

> ✓ Choose the Mail⇨Get New Mail command from the WinCIM menu bar.

> ✓ Click the Go icon on the toolbar (the one with the green traffic light), type **mail**, and click OK.

> ✓ Click the Get New Mail icon (an envelope) on the toolbar.

You see the Get New Mail window (see Figure 12-2).

If you have messages waiting to be read, they appear in the Get New Mail dialog box. For each message, you see the subject of the message, the sender, and the number of characters in the message.

Figure 12-2:
The Get
New Mail
dialog box
lists your
unread mail.
Better read
fast
because
you're
online!

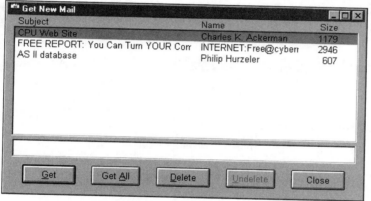

To read a message, double-click it or click it and click the Get button. Here are some things you can do when you're looking at a message online:

> ✓ Copy it to your In Basket on your computer by clicking the In-Basket button on the toolbar.

> ✓ Forward the message to someone else (maybe they want to deal with it!) by clicking Forward. See the section "Using Your Little Black Book" later in this chapter to learn how to address the message.

> ✓ Respond to the message by clicking Reply.

> ✓ Save the message in the WinCIM filing cabinet on your hard disk by clicking File It.

Using Your Little Black Book

When you send mail to another CompuServe user, you address a message to that person's CompuServe ID (the one that looks like 77777,7777). When you send mail to someone on the Internet, you address the message to INTERNET:username@host.

For example, you can send a test message to us authors here at *Internet For Dummies* Central by addressing it to INTERNET:email@dummies.com.

When you create a new e-mail message or forward a message to someone, you have to address it. Whether you are connected to CompuServe or not, choose Mail⇨Create/Send Mail. You see the Recipient List dialog box, shown in Figure 12-3.

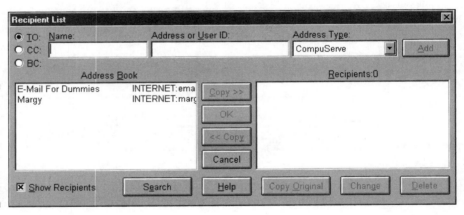

Figure 12-3:
WinCIM
maintains
an address
book of your
favorite
addresses.

The Recipient List dialog box in Figure 12-3 shows two lists of addresses: On the left are the addresses in your address book, and on the right are the addresses to which this particular message is addressed. At the top are boxes for you to enter the recipient's Name and Address.

Here are some things you can do:

- To address the message to someone in your address book, choose the name from the Address Book list and click the Copy>> button. The address appears in the list on the right side.

- To address the message to someone who isn't in your address book, type the person's name in the Name box and her e-mail address in the Address box. Set the Address Type to the type of account you are mailing the message to. Click the Add button to move the name and address into the list on the right so that the message will go to her. If you want to add the name to your address book too, for use in addressing other messages, choose the name in the list on the right side and click the <<Cop_y button. WinCIM lets you enter comments about the person (remember, if you don't have anything nice to say . . .). Do so, if you want, and then click OK.

✔ If you decide that you don't want to send the message to someone after all, choose her name from the list on the right and click _Delete.

✔ If you want to send a copy of the message to someone (or a blind copy), click the CC (or BCC) option. Then either choose an address from your address book or enter the person's information in the _Name and Address boxes. In the list on the right side, each address is preceded by To:, CC:, or BC:, to show how the message will be addressed to that person.

When you finish addressing the message, click OK. The Create Mail dialog box opens. Enter the subject in the Subject box and the text of the message in the big box. When you finish, click _Out-Basket to park the message in your Out Basket until the next time you send messages to CompuServe, or click _Send Now to connect to CompuServe and send it right away.

To add or edit the addresses in your address book, choose _Mail⇨Address Book from the menu bar or press Ctrl+A. You see your address book with all the names and addresses you have entered. You can add new names, change existing ones, or delete names you don't write to any more.

You can use the Clipboard to copy text from another program into a mail message. To include text from a word processing document, for example, select the text in your word processor, copy it to the Clipboard (in most programs you use the _Edit⇨_Copy command), place your cursor where you want the text to appear in your message in WinCIM, and choose _Edit⇨_Paste from the menu.

Send Along This File, Too

The Create Mail dialog box enables you to attach a file to a message. If it's a text file, you can send it to anyone. If it's not text, you can send it only to other CompuServe users. (This limitation may change when CompuServe supports one of the standard methods of attaching nontext files to e-mail, such as uuencoding or MIME.)

To attach a file to a message, just click the A_ttach button. You see the File Attachment dialog box.

Click the _File button to choose the file you want to send along with the message. When you select it, the pathname of the file appears in the box next to the _File button. Set the File_Type to the type of file you're sending:

- **Binary:** Any file other than text
- **Text:** Text only with no formatting or special characters (the only kind of file you can send to Internet addresses)
- **GIF:** Graphics file in Graphics Interchange Format
- **JPEG:** Graphics file in Joint Photographic Experts Group format

Type any other information you want to send along with the file and then click OK. Send the e-mail message as usual.

When you receive a file attached to an e-mail message, you receive a separate message with the same subject line as the message to which it was attached. (It sounds like attached text files get detached, but as long they arrive, it sounds good to us.) The message announces that a file awaits your attention. After WinCIM asks you where to store the file, click Retrieve to download it to your computer.

If you want to practice mailing messages, go to the Practice Forum (click the Go icon, type **practice**, and click OK). Connect time is free while you're using this service, and the forum gives you someone to write to while you practice.

CompuServe has Internet accounts, too!

SPRYNET is CompuServe's entry into the Internet market. If you want a plain Internet account instead of a CompuServe account, SPRYNET gives you unlimited Internet access for $19.95 (as of early 1996, anyway). To find out more about SPRYNET, click the Internet icon (the globe) on the WinCIM toolbar. When you see the CompuServe Mosiac window, type the following URL (Web address) into the Web Page box:

`http://www.sprynet.com/`

Click on the underlined links or icon that describe SPRYNET.

Chapter 13

Prodigy Mail

· ·

In This Chapter

▶ Signing up for a Prodigy account

▶ Using the new Prodigy Mail program

▶ Sending and reading e-mail

▶ Using Prodigy's address book to address your mail

· ·

*W*hen Prodigy was the first of the big commercial online services to offer World Wide Web browsers, people signed up for Prodigy accounts in droves. Prodigy's e-mail commands work both for sending messages to other Prodigy users and for sending e-mail to the Internet. This chapter tells you how. The instructions apply to Prodigy's Windows software, using version 1.1. Your version of the software may not look exactly the same — Prodigy updates its software all the time!

Who am us, anyway?

Each prodigy user has an ID, an unmemorable combination of letters and numbers that's used for logging in as well as the e-mail address. As many as five other people can use your account. Each gets a separate user ID. You, as the person who signed up for the account, have a user ID that ends with an *A:* You are the account owner. The other folks who can use your account have user IDs that are the same as yours but that end with a different letter (*B* through *F,* if you were wondering). You can prevent the other users (kids, for example) from using Prodigy's extra-

charge services and certain uncensored Internet services.

Each of the five IDs has its own e-mail mailbox, and people can't read each other's mail. You see only the mail for the ID you used when signing on.

If other members of your family want their own accounts so that they can have their own e-mail inboxes, press Ctrl+J and enter the Jumpword household access.

Take a Letter

Prodigy lets you exchange e-mail with both other Prodigy users and anyone with an Internet address. Prodigy comes with a separate e-mail program, called Prodigy Mail (another creative name).

To send and receive e-mail, you run the Prodigy Mail program. While you are using Prodigy Mail, you have to use the Prodigy Mail menu and the Prodigy Mail toolbar. You can *see* the Prodigy menu and the Prodigy toolbar, but you can't use 'em! This means that while Prodigy Mail is running, you can't do anything else with Prodigy (if this seems like a strange way to run a mail program, you understand the situation).

To use Prodigy's e-mail program, click the Mail button on the toolbar at the bottom left of the Prodigy window. If you have new mail waiting, an envelope icon appears near the right end of the toolbar — click the button. You see the Prodigy Mail window in Figure 13-1. Any e-mail messages you have received appear in the upper half of the Mail window.

After you finish reading and sending messages and you want to do something else with Prodigy, choose File⇨Exit from the menu or press Alt+F4 to exit from the Prodigy Mail program. You return to the Prodigy window, which displays a message suggesting that you use "your favorite navigation techniques" to see more information from Prodigy. For example, press F5 or click the Menu button on the toolbar to return to the Highlights window.

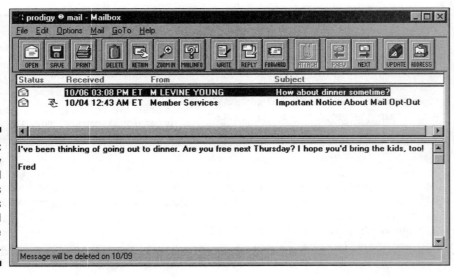

Figure 13-1: The Prodigy Mail program lets you (guess what?) send and receive e-mail.

Addressing Your Mail

To send a message to another Prodigy user, address the message to her user ID (ABCD123A, for example). To send a message to someone on the Internet, use her Internet address.

Your own Internet e-mail address is your user ID followed by @prodigy.com. If your user ID is ABCD123A, for example, your e-mail address is ABCD123A@ prodigy.com.

Reading Your Mail

Each message you have received appears in the top half of the Prodigy mail window with the date received and subject line. To read a message, double-click it or select the message and click the Open icon on the Prodigy Mail window's toolbar. (This toolbar is displayed in the usual Windows location, just below the menu bar, rather than at the bottom of the window.)

Peculiarly, some messages appear in the lower half of the Mail window, and other messages make the entire Prodigy Mail window shrink to an icon, revealing the Prodigy Highlights window, which displays the mail message. Why? We're not sure. It looks alarming when this happens, but stay calm. A Return to Mail button appears in the lower-right corner of the window: Click it and the Prodigy Mail window reappears, looking none the worse for wear.

When you double-click an e-mail message, the text is displayed in the lower half of the Prodigy Mail window.

After you read a message, here are some things you might want to do with it:

- To reply to the message, click the Reply icon on the Prodigy Mail toolbar or press Ctrl+R. See the section "Writing a Message" later in this chapter to learn how to compose and send the message.

- To forward the message to someone else, click the Forward button on the Prodigy Mail toolbar or press Ctrl+F. See the section "Writing a Message" later in this chapter to learn how to compose and send the message.

- If you get a particularly juicy message, you may want to save it on your hard disk. After opening the message, click the Save icon on the toolbar or choose File⇨Save Message from the Prodigy Mail menu and tell Prodigy where to put the file.

- You can print the message by clicking the Print icon on the toolbar, choosing File⇨Print from the Prodigy Mail menu, or pressing Ctrl+P.

- ✔ If the message bores you, delete it by pressing Ctrl+D or clicking the Delete icon on the toolbar. The message doesn't actually go away until you exit from the Prodigy Mail program; instead, it hides in the trash can icon, which appears next to the message in the list of messages.

- ✔ Prodigy normally deletes your mail after about two weeks. If you want to keep it in your inbox longer than that, click the Retain icon on the Prodigy Mail toolbar or press Ctrl+E. Prodigy then keeps the message hanging around for an extra 14 days.

- ✔ To see the next message on your list, press Ctrl+PgDn. To return to the previous message, press Ctrl+PgUp.

If mail arrives while you're using Prodigy Mail, the Update icon near the right end of the toolbar turns into a NewMail icon. Click it to retrieve the new messages: they appear in your list of messages.

Writing a Message

To compose a brand new message, click the Write button on the toolbar or press Ctrl+W. The Prodigy Mail Write window appears.

Two other ways to see this window are to reply to a message you're reading (by clicking the Reply icon or pressing Ctrl+R) or to forward a message you're reading (by clicking the Forward icon or pressing Ctrl+F).

Here's how to compose your message:

1. **In the To box, enter the user ID of another Prodigy user (or your own, if you like to talk to yourself) or an Internet address and press Enter.**

   When you press Enter, the address appears in the list below the To box. You can keep typing addresses and pressing Enter if you want to send your missive to a number of people.

   If you're replying to a message, your message is already addressed to the person who sent the message to which you are replying.

2. **In the Subject box, type a subject line for the message.**

   Remember to make it specific!

   If you are replying to or forwarding a message, the subject of the original message appears in the Subject box.

3. **In the large box, type the text of the message.**

   If you are using Windows, you can use the Cut and Paste commands to copy information to the text of the message. For example, you can copy information from a word processing document to the Windows Clipboard (using the Edit⇨Copy command or Ctrl+C) and paste it in your e-mail message by pressing Ctrl+V.

4. **Check the spelling of your e-mail message by clicking the Spell button on the Prodigy Mail toolbar.**

   Sending e-mail with speling errers is so tacky! Prodigy Mail offers such a nice feature by including a built-in spell checker!

5. **If you want to attach a file to the message, click the Attach button on the Prodigy Mail toolbar or choose File⇨Attach from the menu.**

   Choose the file you want to attach and click OK. You can attach as many as three files to each e-mail message.

   Attachments can be sent only to other Prodigy users, not to folks on the Internet or other online services. Prodigy will doubtless change this limitation sooner or later because the other online services (particularly AOL) allow you to attach files sent to Internet users.

6. **To send the message, click the Send button on the Prodigy Mail toolbar or press Ctrl+S.**

   Prodigy Mail sends the message, but it continues to be displayed in your window. To compose another message, click the Clear icon to clear away the entries for the last message.

7. **To return to the Prodigy Mail inbox, press Ctrl+M or click the Mailbox icon.**

   Prodigy asks whether you want to discard your unsent message. Yes, your message *was* sent when you clicked the Send button. Prodigy is wondering about that *next* message you *might* have been thinking about writing.

If you want to test your ability to send an e-mail message, send one to this address: email@dummies.com.

You'll get a personalized response from our mail robot.

Working Offline

Prodigy doesn't make it easy to read or write e-mail messages while you are not connected to your account. However, here are a couple of tricks you can use:

> ✔ You can include in a mail message a text file from your hard disk. If you create a text file with a list of things you want for your birthday, for example, you can send it to your mother without retyping the list. Click the Import button on the Prodigy Mail toolbar or choose File⇨Import from the menu when you are composing the message.

> ✔ When you are reading your e-mail messages in Prodigy Mail, you can save the current message on the hard disk by clicking the Save icon on the toolbar or choosing File⇨Save Message from the Prodigy Mail menu and telling Prodigy where to put the file.

Prodigy's Address Book

Prodigy keeps an address book of the addresses you plan to use frequently. You can add the e-mail addresses of your friends and coworkers and type their names instead of their yucky addresses when you address your mail. You can store both Prodigy user IDs and Internet addresses, and you can assign a *nickname* to each address to make it easier to type. If your best friend has a CompuServe account, for example, it's tough to remember the string of numbers that make up her account number. Assign her a nickname in the address book so that you can type the nickname, not her Internet address. You can also create a list of addresses if you frequently send messages to the same group of people.

To see your address book, click the Address button on the Prodigy Mail toolbar (see Figure 13-2). Prodigy downloads your address book from your Prodigy account (interesting — most online services store your address book on your own hard disk). You can create a new entry in your address book by clicking the Add Entry button. In the Address Entry window that appears, type the person's name (or whatever you want to type to address mail to the person) in the Nickname box. Then type the person's Prodigy account ID (like ABCD123A) or

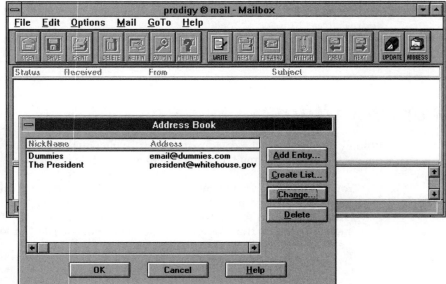

Figure 13-2: Your address book is your little black book of Internet and Prodigy addresses.

Internet address in the ID/Address box. Click OK to enter this person in your address book. Then click OK in your address book to leave and save your changes.

Once you have someone in your address book, you can use the address in a message. When you are composing a message, you can click on the Address button on the toolbar. Because you have a message in the works, an additional button appears in your Address Book window: the Select From button. When you click it, you see the Select From Address Book window. Select an address from the list on the left and click the Send To button to include that address in the To box for your e-mail message. Click the Send CC button if you want to "cc" (send a copy to) the person. When you've selected the addresses you want to use, click OK to make the Select From Address Book window disappear. The addresses you chose appear in the window for the message you are writing.

You can't use any other Prodigy services while Prodigy Mail is running. To leave the Prodigy Mail program, choose File⇨Exit from the menu or press Alt+F4.

Stuff Prodigy Won't Do

Prodigy Mail works well, but a few things that it doesn't do (as of this writing, anyway) would be awfully convenient. They include

- **Forwarding your mail automatically.** Let's say you have two accounts, one with Prodigy and one with CompuServe. Wouldn't it be nice if you could get all your mail on just one of the accounts? UNIX shell accounts and some online services let you leave a forwarding address so that all mail to that account is forwarded automatically to another account. Prodigy doesn't (and neither does CompuServe, if you were wondering).

- **Adding a signature to your mail.** Eudora, all UNIX e-mail programs, and many other e-mail programs let you create a standard signature that you can add to all your mail. This saves you having to type your name, e-mail address, and a snappy one-liner at the end of each e-mail message. Prodigy doesn't do signatures.

On the other hand, Prodigy can send a greeting card for you by e-mail. Choose Goto⇨Greeting Cards (Ctrl+T) from the Prodigy Mail menu, and you'll jump to the American Greetings screen that helps you choose among birthday, holiday, or other cards, address your card, and send it— for a modest charge, of course.

Chapter 14

Microsoft Exchange and Microsoft Network

In This Chapter

▶ Reading e-mail

▶ Sending e-mail

*M*SN, or the Microsoft Network, is the new kid on the block, online service-wise. It debuted on the same day that Windows 95 was shipped. Windows 95 also comes with Microsoft Exchange, an e-mail program that works with MSN as well as with other online services and your local area network. This chapter describes how to use Exchange with MSN.

Hey, Mr. Postman

When you connect to MSN, if you have unread mail, MSN asks whether you want to run Microsoft Exchange (the Windows 95 mail program) to read it.

You can run Microsoft Exchange while you are using MSN, or you can run it any time to read and compose mail while you are offline, that is, not connected to MSN. Working offline is a good way to save on connect time.

To run Microsoft Exchange, click the Start button on the Windows 95 taskbar and then choose Programs⇨Microsoft Exchange. Or double-click the Inbox icon on your desktop. The Microsoft Exchange window looks like Figure 14-1.

You can use Microsoft Exchange to handle e-mail from many different sources, including CompuServe, AOL, other online services, and even faxes. You have to refer to the Windows 95 documentation to set up this program, and you may want to get a friendly computer nerd to help you, because the setup can be confusing.

Figure 14-1:
Microsoft
Exchange, a
program
that comes
with
Windows 95,
handles
your MSN
e-mail.

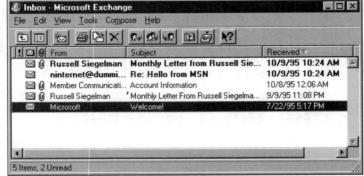

Reading Your Mail

The Microsoft Exchange window lists your incoming mail. If you haven't read it yet, the line of information about the message appears in bold. To read a message, just double-click it.

Here are some things you can do when you are looking at an e-mail message:

- ✔ **Reply to the message:** Click the Reply to Sender icon (a person's head with a left-pointing arrow), press Ctrl+R, or choose Compose⇨Reply from the menu. If you want to address the message to everyone who received the original message (including people who were cc'd on the original message), click the Reply to All icon on the toolbar (the next icon to the right), press Ctrl+Shift+R, or choose Compose⇨Reply to All from the menu. See the section "Take a Letter!" for info on how to type the text of the reply and send it.

- ✔ **Forward the message:** Click the Forward icon on the toolbar (a right-pointing arrow with a person's head).

- ✔ **Delete the message:** Click the Delete icon on the toolbar (an X), press Ctrl+D, or choose File⇨Delete from the menu.

- ✔ **Print the message:** Click the Print icon on the toolbar, press Ctrl+P, or choose File⇨Print from the menu.

- ✔ **File the message:** Choose File⇨Save As from the menu.

- ✔ **Display the next message in your Inbox:** Click the Next button on the toolbar (the down arrow) or press Ctrl+>. To see the preceding message, click the Previous button (the up arrow) or press Ctrl+<.

After you finish looking at the message, close the window by clicking the Close button in the upper-right corner of the window.

Take a Letter!

So you're ready to write a love letter to Bill Gates? Click the New Message icon on the toolbar of the Microsoft Exchange window, press Ctrl+N, or choose Compose⊏>New Message from the menu. You see the New Message window, which looks like Figure 14-2. You also use the New Message window when you reply to or forward an e-mail message (as described in the section "Reading Your Mail" earlier in this chapter).

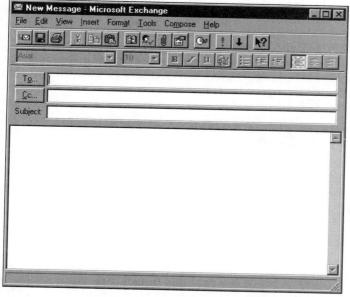

Figure 14-2:
You use this window to create a new e-mail message with Microsoft Exchange.

Here's how to use the New Message window to send an e-mail message:

1. **Type in the To box the address to which you want to send the message.**

   When you reply to a message, Microsoft Exchange fills in the address of the person whose message you are responding to.

   You can enter several addresses, separated by commas. To send a message to another MSN user, type the member ID. To send a message to someone on another commercial online service or with an Internet account, type the person's Internet address.

   If you want to use your address book to enter the address for the message, see the section "Using the Address Book" later in this chapter.

2. **If you want to send a copy of this message to someone, type the person's address in the Cc box.**

   To send copies to several people, separate the addresses with commas.

3. **Type the subject of the message in the Subject box.**

   When you reply to or forward a message, Microsoft Exchange fills in the subject of the original message.

4. **Type the text of your message in the big text box.**

   If you are replying to or forwarding a message, the text of the original message appears in the message text box so that you can quote parts of it in your response. Be sure to delete the boring parts.

   If you are sending a message to another MSN user, you can dress up the text with all kinds of formatting. Use the icons on the second toolbar to make text boldface or italicized or to change the font. Don't bother using fancy formatting in messages to be sent to the Internet, however, because the formatting will be lost.

   If you are forwarding a message, the text of the original message appears, including the headers that show its original author. You can add your own notes at the beginning of the message, perhaps explaining why you are forwarding it.

5. **Check the spelling of your message by pressing F7 or choosing Tools➪Spelling from the menu.**

   The spell checker works just like the one in Microsoft Word (must be a coincidence). When the spell checker finds a word it doesn't recognize, you can ignore it for this message only, add it to your dictionary (so that it isn't flagged ever again), or correct it. When the spell checker is done, it tells you so.

6. **Click OK to thank the spell checker.**

   Politeness never hurts!

7. **Send your message by clicking the Send icon on the toolbar (the leftmost icon), pressing Ctrl+Enter, or choosing File➪Send from the menu.**

   Exchange sends the message to MSN and onward to its destination. The New Message window is displayed.

If you decide not to send the message after all, just close the window without sending the message.

Here's a File, Too

You can attach a file to a message so that the person receives the file in addition to the message. If you are sending the file to an MSN user, the process works great and you don't have to know anything about how attachments work behind the scenes. To send a file to an Internet user, however, or a user on another commercial online service, attachments use an obsolete but still popular system called *uuencoding* (see Chapter 16 for a description of uuencoding). Before you send a file, check with the people you want to send the file to and ask whether uuencoding works for them.

As of this writing, MSN doesn't allow e-mail messages to Internet addresses to contain attachments, but Microsoft plans to support uuencoding, and eventually it may also add support for the standard method of attaching files, called MIME. Try sending an attachment to an Internet address and see whether it works!

To attach a file to an e-mail message, click the Attach File icon on the toolbar (the one that looks like a paper clip) or choose Insert⇨File from the menu. Either way, you see the Insert File dialog box in which you choose the file to insert. When you click OK, an icon for the file appears in the text of your e-mail message. Then send the message as usual.

What's This Icon Doing in My Message?

Someday you'll receive a message with an icon in it, like the one in Figure 14-3. An icon in a message is an attached file — a document, a picture, or even a program. The icon in Figure 14-3 is a shortcut to an MSN window. When you double-click it, MSN displays the MSN Accounts and Billing Information window.

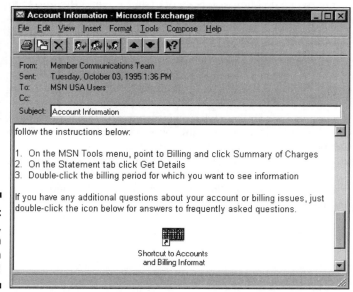

Figure 14-3: Waiter, there's an icon in my soup!

If someone you don't know sends you e-mail with an icon, don't be in a big hurry to double-click it. How do you know what the icon does? In the worst case (unpleasant but entirely possible), it could be a virus that attacks your machine and leaves your hard disk in shreds. Just a word of caution — don't double-click with strangers!

Using the Address Book

When you are addressing a message, you can click the T̲o or C̲c button to see your personal address book. Or you can click the Address Book icon on the toolbar or choose T̲ools⇨A̲ddress Book from the menu, or press Ctrl+Shift+B whenever you want to refer to the address book. The Personal Address Book window appears.

To add a name to your address book, do the following:

1. **Click N̲ew on the Address Book dialog box.**

   You see the New Entry dialog box, like the one in Figure 14-4.

2. **For the entry type, choose the way in which messages can reach this person.**

   For people with MSN accounts, for example, choose The Microsoft Network Member. For other people with Internet addresses, choose Internet over The Microsoft Network (that is, send the message to MSN for delivery over the Internet).

3. **Click OK.**

   You see the New Properties dialog box next. The exact name of the dialog box, and the entries it contains, depend on the entry type.

4. **Fill in the blanks.**

   For an entry for someone with an Internet address, for example, fill in the person's e-mail address, domain name, and real name. For E-mail address, it wants the part of the e-mail address that comes before the @. (In the address email@dummies.com, for example, it's email.) For Domain name, type the part of the e-mail address that comes after the @ (such as dummies.com). We don't know why Microsoft Exchange makes you split up e-mail addresses this way.

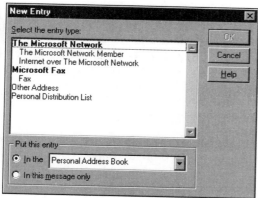

Figure 14-4:
How do
you send
messages to
people? Add
them to your
Address
Book in the
New Entry
dialog box.

If you want to enter other information about the person, you can click the Business, Phone Numbers, or Notes tab to see the other parts of the dialog box.

5. To add this person to your address book, click OK.

To address a message to someone who's in your address book, in the New Message window, select the name and press the To button. When the Address Book dialog box appears, choose the name of the person you want to send the message to and click the To button to add the person to the list of people in the To box. Click OK to make the address book disappear, and you return to the message you are composing.

Working Offline

You can read and compose e-mail even when you're not connected to MSN (giving you the luxury of being able to think without the meter running).

Just run Microsoft Exchange and compose and read your messages as usual. The messages you create are stored in your Outbox. You can send them the next time you're connected to MSN.

In Microsoft Exchange, to see the messages in your Outbox, click the Show/Hide Folder List icon on the toolbar (the second from the left). The Microsoft Exchange window splits so that the left side lists your folders and the right side lists the messages in the chosen folder.

Aha! Unbeknownst to you, you have been looking at the messages in your Inbox all this time. To see the messages in your Outbox, choose it from the list.

To send the messages in your Outbox, choose Tools➪Deliver Now Using➪All Services (or press Ctrl+M). If you have defined other services for delivering your mail, you can choose Tools➪Deliver Now Using➪The Microsoft Network. Quick as a bunny, Microsoft Exchange logs you into MSN, sends your mail, checks for incoming mail, and logs you off.

To make the list of folders in your Microsoft Exchange window go away, click the Show/Hide Folder List icon on the toolbar again.

Chapter 15
Netcom E-Mail: NetCruiser

• •

• •

*N*etcom is a large, fast-growing, national Internet access provider based in San Jose, California. It offers the full range of Internet services at rates that are very reasonable for the frequent user. Netcom provides a free software package, NetCruiser, which includes an e-mail program that can send messages both to other Netcom users and to the rest of the Internet.

This chapter describes NetCruiser 2.1. Netcom updates its software from time to time, so if you have a later version, it may behave slightly differently. We describe how to use Netcom's software running under Windows 95. It also works fine with Windows 3.1. By the way, you can install NetCruiser from the CD-ROM included with this book. See Appendix C for all the details.

Launching NetCruiser

Once you have the Netcom software set up, NetCruiser appears in a Netcom folder on your Program menu (in Windows 95) or in the Netcom program group under Program Manager (in Windows 3.1). Double-clicking the NetCruiser icon gives you a NetCruiser Login dialog box. Your user name is already on the screen. Type your password into the password box and press the Enter key.

The blue bar at the top of the Login dialog box shows you the progress of your login request. Several things have to happen between typing your password and doing anything useful or interesting: NetCruiser has to find your modem, dial the access number, and get an answer. Then Netcom's login computers have to check your user name and password and find a host computer that has the time to deal with you. Any of these steps can fail. But if you just keep trying, you'll get through.

Cruising with NetCruiser

When you log in, NetCruiser starts you off in the Web-browsing tool — specifically, at the Netcom Homeport (shown in Figure 15-1). All of NetCruiser's various applications are available from the icon bar just below the menu.

The help that you get by clicking the question mark icon isn't very helpful — it's just installation and registration help. Helpful help comes from the NetCruiser button at the bottom of the Homeport page.

Reading Your Mail

Check your mail by following these steps:

1. **Either click the inbox icon (the second from left on the toolbar) or select Internet⇨Read Mail-In from the menu.**

2. **Double-click on Inbox in the dialog box that appears.**

    The screen splits into two windows, as you see in Figure 15-2.

3. **From the list of messages in the top window, double-click on the name of the message you want to read.**

    The text of the message appears in the bottom window.

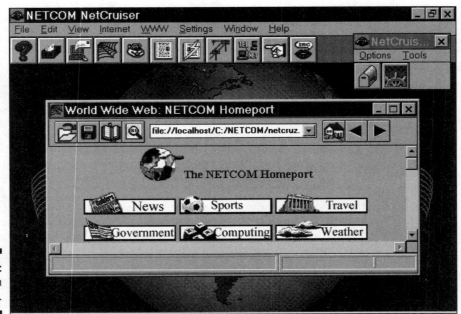

Figure 15-1:
The Netcom
Homeport.

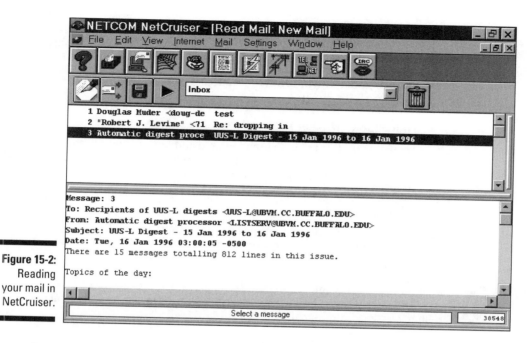

Figure 15-2:
Reading
your mail in
NetCruiser.

Writing a New Message

To send a message to another Netcom user, address the message to your friend's user name (*newuser*, for example). To send a message to someone on the Internet, use the person's Internet address.

Your own Internet e-mail address is your user name followed by @ix.netcom.com. If your user ID is *newuser*, for example, your e-mail address is newuser@ix.netcom.com.

To send e-mail to someone, follow these steps:

1. **Click the computer icon on the toolbar (third from the left on the top row), or select Internet⇨Send Mail-Out from the menu.**

   A Send Mail window opens (see Figure 15-3), along with an Address Mail To dialog box.

2. **To address the message, type the address of a person you want to send mail to on the left side of the Address Mail To box, or select an address from your address book.**

   We talk more about the address book in "Keeping an Address Book" later in this chapter.

3. **Click the Use button.**

   The address shifts to the right side of the screen. When the right side of the box lists all the recipients you want, click OK.

4. **In the Send Mail window, type a subject in the Subject box.**

5. **Write the message.**

6. **Think about whether you really want to send it.**

   An awful lot of e-mail is written in haste and anger. Unlike with snail mail, you don't have all that cooling-off time while you look for a stamp and walk to the mailbox. If you decide the world is better off without this message, click the torn letter icon to cancel.

7. **Send the message.**

   Click the computer icon on the Send Mail toolbar. Just to confuse you, this icon is identical to the icon you clicked in step 1 and sits right below it. Be sure you click the lower one.

If you want to test your command of e-mail, send a message to us at email@dummies.com. You'll get a message back from our friendly mail robot, telling you what your e-mail address is.

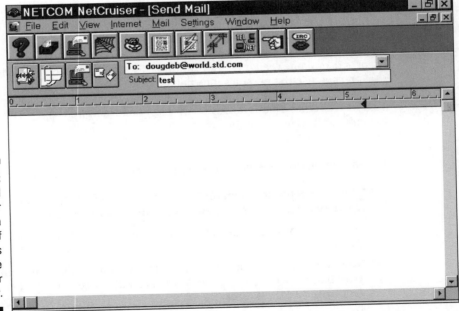

Figure 15-3:
The Send Mail toolbar is an extra row of buttons below the regular toolbar.

Take That Message and . . .

The icons at the top of the Read Mail window (shown in Figure 15-2) spell out all the things you can do with a message. Once you have a message displayed in the bottom half of the window, you can

- **Reply to it.** Clicking the fountain pen icon opens up a Send Mail window, with a new message addressed to the sender of the original message. Learn more about the powers of the Send Mail window in "Writing a New Message" in this chapter.

- **Forward it to somebody else.** Similar to writing a new message, the letter-with-two-arrows icon opens an Address Mail To dialog box and then creates a Send Mail window — with the to-be-forwarded message and all the chosen addresses already in it.

- **Save it.** Clicking the disk icon saves the current message in the NETCOM\MAIL directory. Messages in this directory can be read offline by any word processor you might have, but it will be a bear to figure out which message is which. The first message you save is filed as 00000001.MSG, the second as 00000002.MSG, and so on. Your best bet is to resave them as word-processing documents with names and in directories or folders that give you a chance of finding what you want.

- **Get over it.** Selecting another message in the message list and clicking the arrow icon moves you to that message.

- **Trash it.** Clicking the trash can icon sends the open or highlighted message into oblivion.

Reading and Sending Attached Files

When the message you are reading has a file attached to it, two new icons appear in the Read Mail toolbar. Click on the eye icon to open the attached file. Click on the icon that shows a disk with a note paper clipped to it to save the attached file to your hard drive.

To attach a file to a message you send, do this:

1. **When the message is ready to go, click the paper clip icon on the Send Mail toolbar.**

   An Open window appears.

2. **In the Open window, find the file you want to attach.**

3. **Click OK.**

The location (on your machine) of the attached file appears in the Attachments window just below the subject line. Two extra icons appear in the Send Mail toolbar. Clicking the eye icon will open the attached file so that you can check that it is really the one you wanted. If it isn't, you can unattach it by clicking the icon with a paper-clipped trash can.

If you send an attached file to an Internet address, the file is attached using MIME. Make sure that the recipient's e-mail program can handle MIME attachments.

Keeping an Address Book

Nobody remembers all those crazy e-mail addresses. When you come across an address you think you will need to use again, store it:

1. **Open either the Send Mail or Read Mail window (by clicking the computer or Inbox icon in the top row).**

2. **Select Mail⇨Address Book from the menu.**

3. **Click the New Entry button.**

4. **Fill out the Edit Address Book Entry form.**

The form gives space not just for the person's name and e-mail address, but also for handy comments like "Bob's roommate's sister's husband."

Now whenever the Address Mail To window appears, the list of people in your address book appears as well (showing their real names, not their e-mail addresses). When you select a name from the address book and click the Use button, the corresponding e-mail address magically appears in the E-Mail Recipients window.

Stuff That NetCruiser Can't Do

NetCruiser certainly handles the basics — sending and receiving mail, forwarding, replying, and attaching files — but like most online services, it is short on fancier features. Netcom won't forward mail for you automatically or add a zippy signature to the end of each message. But hey, nobody's perfect!

(This chapter was contributed by Doug Muder)

Chapter 16

UNIX Mail: Pine

In This Chapter

▶ Dealing with UNIX, if you absolutely must

▶ Using Pine, the latest, greatest UNIX e-mail program

▶ Learning other UNIX mail features, like automatic mail forwarding

*W*e assume that you have a very good reason for choosing to use a UNIX shell provider. Either you had no choice at all, UNIX shell accounts are the only accounts available to you (either economically or geographically), or your perverse nature propels you toward the obscure, arcane, user-hostile environments where Men are Men but *Nerds are Kings.*

Getting Your Shell Account

One reason you might be using a UNIX system may be that you have access through school or work, and that's what's available. If that's the case, signing up, if not automatic, is probably pretty straightforward. Look for somebody with the title System Administrator.

If you have to pay for your shell account, try to find a service with real service. UNIX Internet providers are widely available, and most major cities have them now. If you're a first-time user, you probably will want to call the provider and talk to a live human being to get your account set up and learn the appropriate settings for your communications software. If the person on the other end of the phone is less than helpful, look for another service.

Shell Shock: Getting Connected

Unlike commercial online service providers that give you a disk with their software all configured and installed and ready to stick into your machine, UNIX shell providers tend to resemble secured posts with armed sentries waiting for you to provide the secret password before they blow your head off. Getting connected is not always that bad, but it can seem that way.

Shell providers assume that you have some kind of communications package installed and that you know how to set it up to dial in to an account. Maybe you do, and maybe you don't. If you're not an experienced computer user, we strongly suggest that you find a friend who is experienced or else get help from whomever sold you your computer. Even experienced computer users sometimes have difficulty with this part.

If you don't have any friends or if you're the first kid on your block to try to do this, we highly recommend *Modems For Dummies*, 2nd Edition, by Tina Rathbone (IDG Books Worldwide, Inc.). You don't need all 464 pages, but chances are that she'll answer most of your questions. The 464 pages attest to the fact that getting set up is not so easy, and because we have to stop writing this book at some point, we don't cover it all here.

Your modem probably came with some communications software, and that software probably came with a manual. Can you find it? We're not necessarily saying that it will help, but it probably won't hurt. Windows 3.1 users can use the Windows Terminal program that comes as a standard part of Windows (it's not great, but it'll do). Windows 95 users can fire up HyperTerminal (click the Start button and choose Programs➪Accessories➪HyperTerminal).

Using some combination of friends, sales support, manuals, and prayer, people really do manage to get themselves connected. You'll know you're there when

 ✔ You choose Phone➪Dial (or your package's equivalent) and you hear your modem dialing a number (if your modem has a speaker — not all of them do).

 ✔ You see intelligible text displayed on your screen.

 ✔ When you type your response, what you think you're typing appears on-screen as you type it — with a little tolerance for typos and hidden passwords.

That's it. Congratulations — the really hard part is over.

Yikes! It's UNIX

If you have a UNIX shell account, you have to deal, unfortunately, with UNIX. For the purpose of this chapter, we assume that you don't know how to use UNIX already. When you use the Internet through a UNIX shell provider, the more UNIX you know, the better. So if you want to make your Internet life more fun, learn more UNIX. Get a copy of *UNIX For Dummies*, 2nd Edition and *MORE UNIX For Dummies*, brought to you by people you know and trust (and published by IDG Books Worldwide, Inc.).

We'll assume that you know how to log in, up to the point that you are faced with one of the most daunting sights in all of computerdom: the UNIX prompt.

It's waiting for you

The UNIX prompt is UNIX's way of telling you that it is waiting breathlessly for you to type a command. UNIX prompts vary — in fact, you can change it to *Yes, oh great one?* if you are in the mood. Your UNIX prompt is usually a single character, like *$* or *%*. UNIX aficionados can tell a lot about what kind of UNIX you use just from the prompt, but you don't have to worry about varieties of UNIX if all you want to do is deal with your e-mail.

If you're a Mac or Windows user, put away your mouse. Dial-up UNIX is a mouse-free environment, and trying to use it will only frustrate you. When we talk about putting your cursor somewhere in a UNIX program, we mean use the arrow keys or navigation keys inside the program to move the cursor. Pointing and clicking your mouse won't move the cursor. Sorry.

Telling it what to do

To give UNIX a command, you wait until you see the UNIX prompt, type the command exactly right, and press the Return or Enter key (we call it Enter in this chapter). To type a command exactly right, you have to type the correct character, correctly capitalized — UNIX makes a big distinction between capital and small letters. If we tell you to type **pine** and you type **Pine**, it's not going to work. Hint: Most UNIX commands are in lowercase.

Here are some rules that apply to typing UNIX commands:

- ✔ If you make a typing mistake, press the Backspace key, or try Delete or Ctrl-H.

- ✔ To cancel the entire command before you have pressed Enter, press Ctrl-U, or try Ctrl-K. The command disappears.

✔ When you finish typing the command, press the Enter or Return key (okay, we said that already).

✔ If you type a command that UNIX doesn't know, or if you mistype a command, you see a message saying that UNIX couldn't find the command.

✔ Don't type any extra spaces in the middle of commands. Do, however, type a space *after* the command and any other information that we tell you to type on the command line.

✔ If you're stuck, type **help**. Not all UNIX systems have a help command, but it's worth a try. All UNIX systems have online manuals, accessible via the man command, but they are written in Afghani, so forget about them unless you're extremely desperate.

✔ Many UNIX shell account providers have created files with lots of useful information for new users. Make sure that you read everything your provider or system administrator suggests before you take the next step.

✔ If you're really stuck, send an e-mail message to staff. If you're even stucker than that, call your Internet provider or system administrator on the phone and pose your question as calmly as possible to a real person.

Pico? Vi? Emacs? What are they?

To write an e-mail message, you use a text-editing program. The most commonly used text editors in the world of UNIX are

✔ vi, a powerful but totally confusing editor that has been around forever. We hate it (but who asked us?).

✔ emacs, another powerful editor that is much less confusing. But it's still not exactly user-friendly.

✔ Pico, an easy, friendly, and all-around preferable text editor. Voted "best of breed" by the authors of this book.

If you're not sure whether your UNIX system has the Pico editor, type the following command when you see the UNIX prompt: pico.

Don't forget to press Enter. If you get an error message, Pico is not available. If you see a screen with a line that starts *UW PICO(tm)* at the top, you're in! Press Ctrl-X to leave Pico.

If you don't have Pico, maybe you have emacs. Type **emacs** at the UNIX prompt to find out. If you see a line at the bottom of the screen that says something like *Fundamental 100%,* you've got it. Press Ctrl-X and then Ctrl-C to leave.

As a last resort, you may have to use the dreaded vi editor. Type **vi** at the UNIX prompt. If your screen fills with lines that contain nothing but a tilde (~) at the beginning, you're running vi. Type the following and press Enter to quit (no, we're not kidding): :q!

You can tell your e-mail program which text editor you want to use. Naturally, we recommend Pico if you have it, emacs as a second choice, and vi as the editor of last resort. Pine always runs the Pico editor unless someone has changed its configuration.

We can't teach you everything you really need to know about the Pico, emacs, and vi editors, but the next three sections tell you the bare essentials.

Pico for dummies

When you are in Pico, you can just type along merrily, using the arrow keys to move around as needed. When you are done typing your message, press Ctrl-X to leave. If you haven't already saved your message, Pico asks you if you want to do so.

Table 16-1 lists some particularly useful Pico commands.

Table 16-1	Particular Pico Commands
Keystrokes	*What They Do*
Ctrl-A	Moves to the beginning of the line
Ctrl-D	Deletes the current character
Ctrl-E	Moves to the end of the line
Ctrl-G	Gets help
Ctrl-O	Saves your text
Ctrl-T	Checks your spelling
Ctrl-X	Exits

Emacs for dummies

When you find yourself in emacs, type your message, pressing Enter at the end of each line. If the line lengths are getting really uneven, move your cursor into a bad-looking paragraph and press Esc and then q. Emacs reformats the paragraph (a paragraph is defined as a bunch of lines of text followed by a blank line) to even up the line lengths.

When you are done composing your e-mail, press Ctrl-X and then Ctrl-S to save the message. Then press Ctrl-X, Ctrl-C to leave.

Table 16-2 lists our favorite emacs commands.

Table 16-2	Essential Emacs Commands
Keystrokes	*What They Do*
Ctrl-A	Moves the cursor to the beginning of the line
Ctrl-B	Moves back one character
Ctrl-D	Deletes the character the cursor is on
Ctrl-E	Moves the cursor to the end of the line
Ctrl-F	Moves to the next character
Ctrl-G	Cancels this command
Ctrl-N	Moves down to the next line
Ctrl-P	Moves up to the previous line
Ctrl-X, Ctrl-C	Exits from emacs
Ctrl-X, Ctrl-S	Saves the stuff you are working on
Del (or Backspace)	Deletes the preceding character
Esc q	Reformats the current paragraph and rewraps the lines

Vi for dummies

When you use vi, you are always in either *command mode* or *input mode* (we warned you about vi!). You start in command mode, but you enter text in input mode. To switch from command mode to input mode, move your cursor to the place where you want to insert text and press a. To switch from input mode back to command mode, press Esc.

To save your message and leave vi, get into command mode (by pressing Esc) and then type **ZZ** (make sure to capitalize them).

Table 16-3 lists some vital vi commands. Make sure that you are in command mode before typing these commands, and pay attention to capitalization.

Table 16-3	Vital Vi Commands
Keystrokes	*What They Do*
0 (zero)	Moves to the beginning of the line
a	Appends text after the current cursor position (switches to input mode)
A	Appends text at the end of the current line (switches to input mode)
b	Moves back one word
dd	Deletes the current line
h or left-arrow or Ctrl-H	Moves left one character. Some systems can't handle arrow keys, so you have some alternatives.
I (eye)	Inserts text before the current cursor position (switches to input mode)
l (el) or right-arrow or space	Moves right one character
u	Undoes the last command
w	Moves forward one word
ZZ or :x, Enter	Saves your file and quits vi
:w, Enter	Saves the current file
:q Enter	Quits vi
$	Moves to the end of the line

Using Pine to Read Your Mail

Way before the Internet became chic, folks used e-mail on networks of UNIX workstations, so UNIX e-mail lore runs deep. The easiest e-mail program you can find on a UNIX system (in our opinion) is Pine. The folks at the University of Washington in Seattle created Pine, which began as a mutant version of Elm, at the time the best available e-mail program, making it even easier to use than Elm. A particularly neat thing about Pine is that it can handle an extended version of mail called *MIME,* which lets you include all kinds of files with your messages.

If your system doesn't have Pine, complain to your Internet provider or system administrator (and tell her we sent you). Because Pine is available for free, it's available on lots of UNIX-based systems, including most Internet shell providers. Assure your Internet provider or system administrator that you will be back ten times per day with questions if you can't use Pine.

Pine originally stood for *Pine is nearly elm*, but now its authors, pumped up with self-esteem (not misplaced), proudly say that it stands for *Pine is NOT elm*.

Do you have mail?

You can tell whether you have messages in your mailbox because UNIX displays this message when you log in:

```
You have mail.
```

Running Pine

To run Pine, just type **pine** and press Enter. You see a screen like the one in Figure 16-1.

Figure 16-1 shows you Pine's *main menu* with a list of its favorite commands. Pine uses one-letter commands. Notice that one of the commands is high-lighted — you can also choose commands by moving the highlight (pressing the up and down arrow keys) and then pressing Enter. Toward the bottom of the screen, Pine tells you how many messages are in your inbox.

If you are using UNIX by way of a communications program, watch out for which terminal type your program is emulating. Pine works fine if your program emulates a VT100 terminal but not so well if it emulates an ANSI terminal. You can usually change which terminal type your program emulates.

```
PINE 3.89   MAIN MENU                          Folder: INBOX   0 Messages


        ?     HELP             -  Get help using Pine

        C     COMPOSE MESSAGE  -  Compose and send a message

        I     FOLDER INDEX     -  View messages in current folder

        L     FOLDER LIST      -  Select a folder to view

        A     ADDRESS BOOK     -  Update address book

        S     SETUP            -  Configure or update Pine

        Q     QUIT             -  Exit the Pine program



        Copyright 1989-1993.  PINE is a trademark of the University of Washington.
                         [Folder "INBOX" opened with 0 messages]
P Help                          P PrevCmd                    R RelNotes
O OTHER CMDS L [ListFldrs] N NextCmd                         K KBLock
```

Figure 16-1: Pine shows you a nice, simple menu.

Leaving Pine

After you finish using Pine, press q to quit. Pine asks whether you really, really want to quit (it's so sure that you just pressed q accidentally). Press y to leave. If you have left messages in your inbox that you have read but not deleted, Pine asks whether you want to move the messages to the read-messages folder — press y or n. If you deleted messages, it asks whether you want them to be expunged (really deleted) now — again, press y or n. Finally, you leave.

Sending messages

You're in Pine and you're ready to send some e-mail. No problem. Pine ordinarily runs the Pico text editor unless you or someone else has configured it otherwise. To send a message, follow these steps:

1. **Press c to compose a new message.**

   Pine displays a screen with prompts for To (the address to send the message to), Cc (addresses to send copies of the message to), Attchmnt (names of files to attach to the message), and Subject (the subject line).

   You can move from blank to blank by pressing the Tab key or the up- and down-arrow keys. You type the text of the message underneath the line that says — Message Text —.

   At the bottom of the screen is a list of the control keys you can use (the caret in front of a letter means that you press Ctrl with the letter — for example, ^G means that you press Ctrl-G).

2. **Enter the addresses on the To and Cc lines and the subject on the Subject line.**

   You can enter several addresses on the same line by separating them with commas.

3. **If you want to attach a file to the message, enter the filename in the Attchmnt (attachment) blank.**

   Alternatively, you can press Ctrl-J to tell Pine that you want to attach a file. It prompts you for the filename. The file has to be on your UNIX account. It can't be on the PC or Mac that you use to dial in to your UNIX account — you have to upload the file to your UNIX account before you can attach it to a message.

4. **Type the text of the message.**

5. **When you are ready to send the message, press Ctrl-X. Pine asks whether you really want to send it — just press y.**

   Pine sends the message and displays the main menu again.

   If you decide not to send the message after all, you can press Ctrl-C to cancel it.

This list shows you some cool things you can do while you are writing your message:

- ✔ For lots of helpful information about how to use Pine, you can press Ctrl-G. Pine has complete online help.

- ✔ You can even check the spelling of your message — just press Ctrl-T. Pine checks all the words in your message against its dictionary and highlights each word it can't find.

- ✔ You can include text from a text file. Move your cursor where you want the text to appear and press Ctrl-R. If you use Pine on a shell Internet provider, you have to upload the file from your own computer to the provider before you can include it.

Reading your messages

At the top of the main menu is a status line, and at the right end of it Pine tells you which folder you are viewing and how many messages it has (more on folders in a minute). Your *inbox* folder contains incoming messages you haven't read.

To read your incoming messages, follow these steps:

1. **Press i to see the messages in the current folder.**

   (This step assumes that you haven't changed to another folder — you learn how to change folders in "Looking in a folder" in this chapter.)

   Pine displays a list of messages (see Figure 16-2). You see one line of information per message, beginning with a + if the message was sent directly to you (not cc'd, for example). The next character is N for new messages you haven't read, D for messages you've deleted, and A for messages you have answered.

   You also see a message number, the date the message was sent, who sent it, how big it is (in characters), and the subject.

2. **To read a message, highlight it.**

   You can press the up- and down-arrow keys or p (for previous) and n (for next).

3. **When you've highlighted the message you want to read, press v to view it.**

   Pine displays the text of the message.

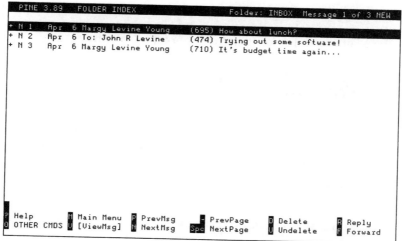

Figure 16-2:
Your
messages
are waiting
to be read.

When you are looking at a message, here are some things you can do:

✔ Forward the message to someone else by pressing f. You see the regular Pine screen for composing a message with the text of the original message included in the text of this message.

✔ Reply to the person who sent the message by pressing r. Pine automatically addresses the message to the person who sent the original one.

✔ Delete the message by pressing d. The message doesn't disappear right away, but it is marked with a D on the list of messages. When you exit from Pine, your deleted messages really get deleted. If you change your mind, you can undelete a message by pressing u.

✔ Move to the next message by pressing n. Or move back to the previous one by pressing p.

✔ Return to Pine's main menu by pressing m.

✔ Press ? to see Pine's online help.

Take a look at the list of commands at the bottom of the screen. Whenever you see O OTHER CMDS, more commands are available than can fit on the menu. Press o to see more commands.

Saving messages

Pine lets you create many folders in which to put your messages so that you can save them in an organized manner. To save a message in a folder, press s when you are looking at it or when it is highlighted on the list of messages.

If you save a message to a folder that doesn't exist, Pine asks whether you want to create that folder. Press y to do so. After you move a message to a folder, Pine automatically deletes it from your inbox. Very tidy.

Looking in a folder

After you've put messages in folders, you may want to look at them later. When you see Pine's main menu, you can press l (the lowercase letter *L*) to select which folder to view. Pine automatically makes several folders for you, including the ones in this list:

- ✔ **INBOX:** Your incoming messages; messages remain here until you delete or move them.
- ✔ **sent-mail:** Messages you've sent.
- ✔ **saved-messages:** A place to save messages before you send them.

Highlight the one you want and press Enter. Pine lists the messages in the folder.

You can make more folders by moving messages into them (as described in the previous section, "Saving messages").

Saving messages as text

If you want to use the text of a message elsewhere or download it to your own computer, save it in a text file first:

1. **View the message or highlight it on the list of messages.**

2. **Press e.**

   Pine asks for the filename in which to save the message (it puts the file in your home directory).

3. **Enter the filename and press Enter.**

That's it — Pine copies the text into a file.

Printing messages

To print a message, press y when you are viewing the message or when the message is highlighted on the list of messages.

What printer?

If you are dialing into a shell Internet provider to run Pine, pressing y to print your message usually doesn't work. The reason is that Pine is running on your provider's UNIX computer and the message would print on a printer connected to that computer, which is probably nowhere near where you are.

Here is the normal way to print a message on your own computer:

1. Save the message as a text file.

2. Download the file using whichever method works with your Internet provider.

3. Print it from your own computer.

What a drag — but wait! If you use ProComm or Kermit on a PC, or MacKermit or VersaTerm on a Macintosh, you are in luck. These programs are so smart that Pine can tell them to print directly on your computer's printer after you tell Pine to display the message. Ask a local Pine expert to set you up for direct printing on your PC.

Creating your own address book

It can certainly be annoying to type long, complicated Internet addresses. Let Pine do it for you: set up an address book.

When you press a at the Pine menu, you switch to *address book mode* (it even says ADDRESS BOOK at the top of the screen). If you have already entered some addresses, Pine lists them.

When you finish fooling with your address book, press m to return to Pine's main menu.

Take these steps to create an entry in your address book when you are in address book mode:

1. **Press a.**

   Pine asks for the full name of the person.

2. **Type the person's last name, a comma, and then the first name, and press Enter.**

   Pine asks for a nickname (the name you type when you address mail).

3. **Type the nickname (make it short but easy to remember).**

   Finally, Pine asks for the person's e-mail address.

4. **Enter it just as you would when you address a message.**

Pine stores the entry in your address book and lists it on the address book screen.

If you make a mistake, you can edit an entry later. Just highlight it on the list of addresses and press e to edit it.

You can also create an address book entry directory from the address of a message. If you are looking at a message from someone whose address you want to save, just press t. Pine prompts you for the person's full name (it might even suggest it, if it's part of the message header), nickname, and e-mail address. (Pine suggests the address of the sender of the current message.)

Attaching files to messages

You may want to send the following two types of files along with a message:

- ✔ Text files, composed entirely of ASCII text characters
- ✔ Other files, such as word processing documents, spreadsheets, or graphics files

E-mail can include only ASCII characters, so if you want to send something other than text, you have to convert it into text temporarily, send it, and have the recipient unconvert it. Luckily, Pine does most of this for you using a system called MIME (*M*ultipurpose *I*nternet *M*ail *E*xtension). MIME remembers not only the name of the attached file but also what type of file it is.

Before sending an attached file to someone, make sure that she can decode it at the other end. Not all mail readers can understand and decode MIME attachments. Windows and Mac mail programs, such as Eudora and Pine, can, but most versions of elm and the ancient UNIX `mail` program cannot. So ask your intended recipient first!

Including text in your message

If you want to send a text file to someone, you can include it as part of the text of the message. When you are composing the message, move the cursor to where you want the file to appear. Then press Ctrl-R and type the name of the file. The text appears in your message.

Attaching files

To attach one or more files to a message (using MIME), follow these steps:

1. **Compose a message as usual.**

    It contains any text you want to send along with the file (or files).

2. **Press Ctrl-J to tell Pine that you want to attach a file.**

3. **When Pine asks for the filename, type it.**

   If the file isn't in your home directory, type in the full pathname.

4. **When Pine asks for an attachment comment, enter a short description of the file.**

   Depending on the mail reading program that your recipient uses, this description will show up somewhere.

   Pine displays the filename and description on the `Attchmnt` line of the screen. Pine also numbers this attachment 1 (in case you want to attach other files, too).

5. **Repeat steps 2 through 4 for each file you want to attach.**

6. **Send the file as usual.**

Decoding attached messages

When you receive a message that contains MIME attachments, the message begins with a list of the attachments like the following:

```
Parts/attachments:
  1 Shown    5 lines Text
  2 OK     478 lines Text, "Table of contents"
  3 OK    1926 lines Text, "Draft of Chapter 2"
```

Then comes the text that was typed in the message. Following the text are instructions for viewing each attachment, similar to the following:

```
[Part 2, "Table of contents" Text 478 lines]
[Not Shown. Use the "V" command to view or save this part]
```

If the attached file consists of nothing but ASCII text, Pine can show it to you. To view an attachment, follow these steps:

1. **As Pine suggests, press v.**

   Pine asks which attachment you want to see. Actually, what it lists as attachment 1 is the text of the message. The first attached file is attachment 2.

2. **Type a number.**

   Pine asks whether you want to view the attachment or save it as a separate file.

3. **Press v or s.**

   If you pressed v to view the attachment, Pine displays it on the screen.

If you pressed s to save the attachment as a file, Pine asks for the filename to use. It suggests the name the file had when it was originally attached to the message.

4. **When you finish looking at the attachment, press e to exit from the viewer.**

If the attached file consists of other information, such as a word processing document or a graphics file, save it and then look at it using the appropriate program.

Other Cool Stuff about UNIX Mail

Here are some other UNIX mail tricks that you can use.

Sign here

You can make a *signature file,* a file that contains text for your mail program to include at the end of every message. The file must be called `.signature` and be in your home directory.

Use your text editor (remember Pico, emacs, and vi?) to make a signature file. Keep it short (no more than three lines long), and include your name, your e-mail address, other address information you want everyone to know, and (if there's room) a pithy or philosophical message that characterizes you.

To create or edit a file with a text editor, type the name of the file on the command line. For example, to create or edit the signature file using the Pico editor, type `pico .signature`.

After you've created a signature file, you don't have to type your signature at the end of every message. To test it, send a message to yourself and see how the signature looks. The signature appears at the bottom of the message when you compose it. To omit the signature information from a message, just delete it.

Forward, mail!

If you have several accounts, you may enjoy collecting all your incoming e-mail in one account and reading it all at the same time. UNIX makes this easy. To tell UNIX to forward all of your mail to another account, use a text editor to make a file named `.forward` in your home directory. (Yes, the name starts with a dot.) The file must contain one line of text: the e-mail address to which you want to forward your mail.

As soon as this file exists, your incoming mail starts bouncing along to the forwarding address. To turn off forwarding, delete the .forward file or rename it (as, say, forward without the dot).

Sorry, I'm gone

When you are on vacation, your e-mail can pile up alarmingly. And folks who have never met you in person may not realize that you are going to be gone for a week at your mountain-top meditation retreat. If you'd like to let everyone know that you are gone and when you'll be back, you can use the *vacation program.*

To run the vacation program, write a form letter that you'd like to be sent in response to any mail you receive. Store the message in a text file in your home directory called .vacation.msg. It might say something like

```
Thanks for your e-mail, but I'm meditating 16 hours a day
high atop Mt. Monadnock. I'll be back on Thursday the 8th, at
which time I'll sift through my mountains of e-mail and even-
tually get back to you.
```

Then, type

```
vacation -i
```

This initializes your *vacation database* that tracks who's sent you mail. Finally, you have to arrange to pass your mail to the vacation program. Create a file called .forward that contains:

```
\yourname, "|/usr/bin/vacation"
```

Instead of *yourname*, put your user name. This file tells the mail system to deliver incoming mail to your regular mailbox as normal and also to call the vacation program for each incoming message.

Each time a mail message arrives for you, the vacation program replies with your canned response. If the person's already received the canned response within the past week, it doesn't send it again.

When you get back from vacation, delete the .forward file to turn off the vacation program. Then start working your way through the messages stored in your incoming mailbox.

Your Automatic Secretary

If you get a lot of mail, you'll probably find that wading through all of your incoming mail starts to become a chore. One thing you can do is to arrange to sort your incoming mail into folders based on the sender and subject. This lets you deal with mail one category at a time and also lets you decide which incoming mailboxes to read.

 Before you try setting up mail sorting, ask your system administrator whether she has installed the widely used *procmail* mail sorting system as the standard mail delivery program. If not, the instructions that follow won't work. You can still arrange to sort mail, but setup is considerably harder. See our *Internet Secrets* for the gruesome details.

Setting up to sort incoming mail involves two steps:

- ✔ Creating the incoming mailboxes
- ✔ Defining the sorting criteria

You create the incoming mailboxes in Pine, and you create a file of "rules" for procmail to control the sorting criteria.

Making the mailboxes

To create the mailboxes, do this:

1. **Run Pine and press L to see the list of message folders.**

2. **Move the cursor to INBOX.**

3. **Press A to add a new mailbox.**

4. **Pine asks the name of the server to use.**

   Press Enter to tell it to use the very computer that you're logged into.

5. **Pine asks for the name of the folder to add.**

   This folder name is actually the name of the file to use. Generally, you want to put all of your mail folders in your mail directory, so if you want to call the folder *fred*, type `mail/fred` to put it in the mail directory.

   UNIX filenames should consist of lowercase letters, digits, and underscores. (You can use other characters, but confusion can ensue.)

6. **Pine asks for the folder's nickname.**

   This is the name that Pine will use to refer to the folder. You can type any characters you want — for example, `Fred Smith` if that's who the mail will be from.

That's it. You can create as many incoming folders as you want. If you decide that you don't want one of your folders, just move the cursor to its name and press d.

Saying what to sort

This part is a little trickier. You have to create a pattern file for procmail, a program written by a German character who evidently believed that using any more characters than are absolutely necessary is a terrible waste of time.

The pattern file is called `.procmailrc`. You create or edit it by typing `pico .procmailrc`.

The file consists of *recipes,* each of which identifies a category of mail and what to do with it. Here's a typical recipe:

```
:0
* From:.*fred@flint
mail/fred
```

The `:0` marks the first line of a recipe. (We said he didn't like to waste characters.)

The second line starts with an asterisk to mark it as a *pattern.* Procmail scans the headers of each incoming message to see if the pattern matches. Patterns can be extremely complicated (they're the same as the ones used by the *egrep* program, if you know what that is), but for most purposes, you can get by with only a little knowledge of patternology. The most important thing to know is that `.*` is a wild card that matches anything. So, for example, the pattern above matches any line that contains `From:` and also `fred@flint`.

The third line says in what file to save matching messages. Use the same folder name (not nickname) you gave to Pine.

A realistic `.procmailrc` has several recipes and also some comments to remind you what your sorting criteria are supposed to mean:

```
# identify mail from Fred
:0
* From:.*fred@flint
mail/fred

# this sorts by the subject
:0
* Subject:.*meeting
mail/meeting
```

(continued)

```
(continued)
# this sorts by who the mail is addressed to, usually the
# best way to identify mail to mailing lists
:0
* To:.*bread-bakers
mail/bread
```

Using multiple folders

Once you've created your multiple folders, Pine makes them easy to use. After
you open your Inbox, you can use the Tab key to find the next new message.
When no more new messages are in the current folder, Tab looks through the
rest of your incoming folders for new mail, so you just Tab your way through
until Pine tells you that you have no new mail.

Each time Pine finds a folder with new mail, it asks you whether you want to
look in that folder or continue looking in other folders, so you're in charge of
when you read what.

Incoming folders work the same as any other folders, so you can save messages
from one folder into another the same way we discussed in "Saving messages"
(earlier in the chapter), using the S key.

One minor disadvantage of multiple incoming folders is that UNIX only reports
"You have mail" when you have mail in your main Inbox. You have to use Pine
to look and see if you have mail in any other incoming folder.

Part IV
Using E-Mail at Work

The 5th Wave   By Rich Tennant

"Oh, suure - it's probably a disturbance on the line. You vendors always use that as an excuse!"

In this part . . .

*M*illions of people are using e-mail in the office place. We help you get started with the most popular local-area-network mail systems. In this section, we assume that your mail program is already installed. Using the concepts we cover at the beginning of the book, you can quickly get up to speed in the office environment.

Chapter 17

Microsoft Mail

* * *

* * *

Microsoft Mail is the mail program that comes with Windows for Workgroups, the local area network version of Windows. What does that mean? It means that if your office has Windows computers on a local area network (that is, connected together with a bunch of wires), you may well use Microsoft Mail to exchange e-mail with other folks in your office. If your local area network is attached to the Internet, you can also use it to exchange e-mail with the big, wide world.

Somebody is in charge of your Microsoft Mail system, and with any luck, it's not you. Each Mail network has a person in charge of Mail, and you may need to ask her what your user name and password are before you can sign on. Your Mail manager can create a Mail account for you if you don't already have one. You need to know two facts about your account:

✔ **Your mailbox name:** This is usually your name or something like it. If your name is Zac Young, it might be *zac*, or *zyoung*, or *zacy*.

✔ **Your password:** This can be up to eight characters long. Don't tell it to anyone or write it on a sticky note and stick it to your screen. Be discreet — at least *hide* the sticky note in your files somewhere.

Note: If you use Windows 95, you don't use Microsoft Mail. Instead, you can probably run Microsoft Exchange, which comes with Windows 95. Ask your network administrator about it. If you do use Microsoft Exchange, see Chapter 14 for info on how to read your mail and compose messages.

Getting into Mail

To read your mail or send messages, you run the Microsoft Mail program — easy enough. Here's how:

1. **In Windows Program Manager, find the Network program group.**

   If you can't see it, choose the <u>W</u>indow command from the menu and choose Network from the menu that appears. The Network program group appears, and it contains the Mail icon.

2. **Double-click the Mail icon.**

   Microsoft Mail runs and asks who you are. If you see the Welcome to Mail dialog box instead, your computer hasn't been set up with a mail account. Get your Mail manager to help you create a mailbox for you.

3. **If your mailbox name doesn't appear, type it in the <u>M</u>ailbox box.**

4. **Type your password in the <u>P</u>assword box.**

   If you're completely confident that your PC is in a 100-percent secure location and no one will ever try to read or delete your mail for any reason or try to send mail from your account, you can click the Remember password box so that you don't have to type your password each time you run Mail. If you click this box, Mail doesn't display the Mail Sign In box at all from now on.

   We don't recommend this practice. Once you get used to typing your password, your fingers will remember it and it's not a lot of work. Even if you're not concerned about your own privacy or security, you can compromise other people's when you allow unauthorized access to a system.

5. **Click OK.**

   You see the Mail window.

Getting Out of Mail

After you are finished reading your mail, you can exit from Mail by choosing <u>F</u>ile⇨E<u>x</u>it. You remain connected to your Mail mailbox, which is handy if you use Microsoft Schedule+ or PC Fax, both of which use your mailbox, too. If you want to completely, totally, exit and sever all relations with your mailbox, choose <u>F</u>ile⇨E<u>x</u>it and Sign Out.

You can leave Mail up and running all day if you want. A local area network isn't like an online account — you don't pay by the minute to stay connected! And it's nice to leave Mail running because it checks for new mail periodically (usually every ten minutes). If new mail arrives, it beeps and the cursor appears as a little flying envelope for a few seconds.

Do You Have Mail?

If you have new mail, the messages appear in your inbox. Click the Inbox folder under the Private Folders heading in the Mail window. The messages in your inbox appear on the right side of the window.

A little picture of a closed envelope to the left of a message means that you haven't read the message yet. If the top of the little envelope is open, you've already read the message.

Reading Your Mail

To read a message, double-click on it in your inbox. The message appears in its own window.

When you are looking at a message, you can do the following:

✔ Reply to the message by clicking the Reply button on the toolbar, choosing Mail⇨Reply from the menu, or pressing Ctrl+R. Mail creates a new message addressed to the person who sent the original message and includes the text of the original message in the new message. Type your own text at the top of the message area and click Send to send the message.

✔ Forward the message to someone else by clicking the Forward button on the toolbar, choosing Mail⇨Forward from the menu, or pressing Ctrl+F. Mail creates a new message containing the text of the original message. Type the recipient's mailbox name in the To box and click the Send button.

✔ Delete the message by clicking the Delete button on the toolbar, choosing File⇨Delete from the menu, or pressing Ctrl+D. The message disappears into the wastebasket (we kid you not). To see what's in the wastebasket, double-click Wastebasket under the Private Folders heading on the left side of the Mail window. Your deleted messages are listed on the right side of the Mail window.

✔ Print the message by choosing File⇨Print from the menu or pressing Ctrl+P.

Composing a New Message

Here's how to create a new e-mail message:

1. **Click the Compose button on the toolbar, or choose Mail⇨Compose Note from the menu, or press Ctrl+N.**

You see the Send Note window. As soon as you type something into the Subject box, the name of the window changes from Send Note to the subject of the note.

2. **In the To box, type the mailbox name of the person to whom you want to send the message.**

   You can send it to several people if you want: separate the names with semicolons (;). If your network is connected to the Internet, you may be able to send mail to Internet addresses. Ask your Mail manager how to type an Internet address in the To box.

   You can press the Tab key to move to the next box.

3. **In the Cc box, type the mailbox name of anyone who you'd like to receive a copy of the note.**

4. **In the Subject box, type a short, specific, succinct subject.**

5. **Press Tab to move to the message area, or click in it. Then type the text of the message.**

6. **When your message is ready to send, click the Send button.**

   If you change your mind and decide not to send the message (perhaps you were a little *too* honest about that staff meeting!), double-click the Control-menu box in the upper-left corner of the Send Note window (the little box with a dash in it). Mail asks if you want to save changes to the note; click the No button to cancel the message.

File It, Please!

You can save your messages to refer to later. Just like real paper mail, don't let your e-mail pile up in your inbox. File it instead.

Mail lets you create folders for your mail. You can create private folders, which are for your eyes only and are stored on your own computer. Shared folders are stored in the Microsoft Mail post office on the network.

You start out with just three private folders:

  ✔ **Inbox:** Your incoming messages.

  ✔ **Send mail:** Copies of outgoing messages. These are like carbon copies of the messages you have sent.

  ✔ **Wastebasket:** Messages you have deleted. They are deleted for real when you exit from the Mail program.

Making file folders

Here's how you can create your own folders:

1. **Choose File⇨New Folder from the menu.**

   You see the new Folder dialog.

2. **Click the Options button so that you see the rest of the dialog box.**

   Ah! Now the New Folder dialog box grows.

3. **In the Name box, type a name for the folder, like** Budget **or** Personal.

4. **Choose Private or Shared for the type of folder.**

   For shared folders, click the Read, Write, and Delete boxes in the Other Users Can section of the dialog box to give everyone else in your office permission to read, write, or delete the messages in the folder.

5. **If you want this folder to be a new, separate folder, click the Top Level Folder option. If you want to store it as part of another folder, click the Subfolder option and choose the folder where you want to store it.**

   For example, you might create an *Administrivia* folder as a top-level folder. Then you might create folders named *Budget* and *Staff Meetings* that are stored in the *Administrivia* folder.

6. **Click OK to create the folder.**

   The new folder appears in the folder list on the left side of your Mail window.

The folder list on the left side of the Mail window is entitled Private Folders or Shared Folders. To switch between seeing private and shared folders, click the title — it's actually a button.

Filing messages

Once you have a file folder to put a message into, it's easy to file a message:

1. **Select the message from the list of messages, or view the message.**

2. **Click the Move button on the toolbar (or choose File⇨Move from the menu, or press Ctrl+M).**

   You see the Move Message window.

3. **If you want to move the message to a shared folder, click the Shared Folders button at the bottom to see the list of shared folders.**

4. **Double-click the folder in the Move to list.**

   Mail moves your message.

Looking at the messages in a folder

To see the messages that are stored in a folder, just double-click the folder name on the list of folders. To see a list of the shared folders on your network, click the Private Folders heading. Quick as a wink, it changes to say Shared Folders and lists the shared folders. Click the heading again and you see your private folders again.

Files in Your Mail

When you compose an e-mail message, you can attach a message to it. If you are sending the file to another Mail user on your local area network, it arrives safe and sound. If, however, you try to send a file to someone on the Internet, you may not be so lucky.

Attaching a file to a message

To attach a file to a message:

1. **While you're composing a note, put your cursor where you want the icon for the file to appear.**

2. **Click the Attach button in the Send Note window.**

3. **Choose the file you want to send and click the Attach button again.**

   You can attach more than one file to a message.

4. **Click Close after you are finished attaching files.**

   An icon for each attached file appears in the e-mail message, as shown in Figure 17-1.

5. **Send the message as usual by clicking the Send button.**

For you drag-and-drop fans, there's another way to attach a file to a message. In Windows File Manager, select the filename you want to attach. Then drag the file from File Manager into the Send Note window.

Receiving an attached file

When you receive a message that has a file attached to it, a little paper clip appears on the envelope icon in your list of messages. When you display the message, an icon represents this file (it looks the same as when you send an attached file; see Figure 17-1).

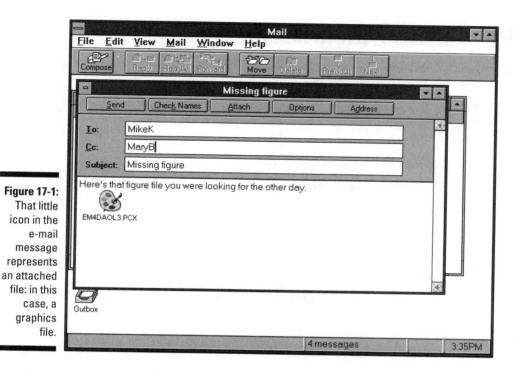

Figure 17-1:
That little
icon in the
e-mail
message
represents
an attached
file: in this
case, a
graphics
file.

To see the attached file, double-click its icon. Windows runs the program that deals with that type of file. For example, if it's a graphic, Windows might run Windows Paintbrush. If it's a WordPerfect document, Windows runs WordPerfect. You see the program with the attached file loaded.

You usually want to save the attached file on your disk. To save it in a separate file, follow these steps:

1. **Choose File⇨Save Attachment from the menu.**

   You see the Save Attachment dialog box.

2. **If more than one file is attached to the current message, choose the attachment you want to save from the Attached Files list.**

3. **Use the Directories and File Name settings to tell Mail where to store the attached file and what to call it.**

4. **Click Save to save the attachment in a file.**

   You can save all the attached files in the same directory, each using its original filename, by clicking the Save All button.

5. **Click Close.**

Your Little Black Books

Mail keeps two address books you can use. The Postoffice List is like the phone book you get from the phone company: It lists everyone, and you can't change it. (Well, we like to write in our phone book, but that's a different story.) The Personal Address Book is like your own little black book: It lists only the people you know.

Let's see that book

To see either address book, start composing a message by clicking the Compose button on the toolbar. On the Send Note window, click the Address button. You see the Address window.

The list in the top half of the window lists one of the address books. You can choose which of the two address books you see first (the Postoffice List or your Personal Address Book). To switch to the other address book, click the Open Directory button (the topmost button, the one that looks like an open book). You see a list of address books. Choose the address book you want and click OK.

Addressing the mail

To address an e-mail message to someone listed in the top half of the address window, double-click on the person's name. The person's name appears in the To list in the bottom half of the Address window. To include a name in the Cc box, select the name and click the Cc button. After you are finished addressing your e-mail message, click the OK button.

Join the group

Your address book is good for something else, too — you can create a small mailing list, which is a group of names that you can send a message using a single address. A small mailing list is called a *personal group*. To create a personal group, choose Mail⇨Personal Groups from the menu.

To create a new group, click the New button. Type the name of the group (say, *Pizza Group* or *Football Pool* or *Accounting Staff*) and click the Create button. You see the Address window with your address books displayed in the top half and the members of the group in the bottom half. Double-click each name you'd like to add to the group and click OK after you have the complete list of people in the group.

When you want to send a message to all of the people in one of your personal groups, use your address book as you do for one person. The groups you have defined appear in your Personal Address Book.

Chapter 18

Lotus Notes Mail

• •

In This Chapter

▶ Sending and receiving mail

▶ Replying to and forwarding messages

▶ Attaching files to your messages

▶ Keeping important messages in folders

▶ Using Lotus Notes 4

• •

*W*hat is Lotus Notes? It's not exactly an e-mail program, but it does send e-mail and *secure* e-mail — most e-mail packages cannot make such a claim. Notes is the first (and arguably the best) *groupware* program — software that allows groups of people to work together. In addition to handling e-mail among people in the group, Notes lets people have ongoing conversations as a group and share databases. Organizations use Lotus Notes for sharing customer databases, managing large projects — you name it. E-mail is just one part of it.

In fact, your group may use Lotus Notes for sharing databases and use some other program for e-mail. Check with your network administrator to find out what to use.

This chapter describes Lotus Notes 3 for Windows (both the 3.1 and 95 varieties). Lotus Notes is also available for OS/2, the Macintosh, and even UNIX. (By the way, would you mind if we just called the program *Notes* instead of *Lotus Notes*? It would save us a ton of typing.) Lotus Notes 4 and Notes Mail 4 are radically different. Even if you have Notes 3, you may want to look at the last section of this chapter on Notes 4 so that you can band together with your colleagues and demand the upgrade. It's way cool.

Up and Running with Notes

Before you can use Notes, your network administrator must set it up on your computer. If you use Windows 95, the Lotus Notes icon appears on your Windows 95 desktop or in one of the menus you see when you click the Start button on the taskbar. In Windows 3.1, the Lotus Notes icon appears in a Program Manager group. Either way, the icon shows a little group of people — groupware strikes again!

Taking Notes

To run Notes, double-click the Lotus Notes icon. (In Windows 95, you instead click the Start button on the taskbar and then choose Lotus Notes from a menu.) You see the Notes window shown in Figure 18-1.

To exit, do the usual — choose File⇨Exit from the menu bar. Windows 95 users can also click the Close button (the X button in the upper-right corner of every Windows 95 window).

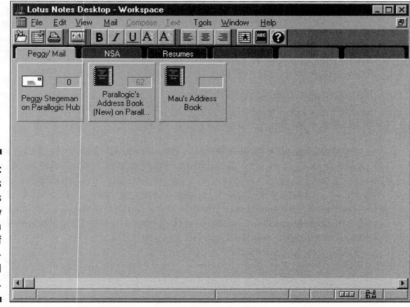

Figure 18-1: The Lotus Notes window looks like a pile of neatly-stacked folders.

Look at all those databases

If someone (maybe you) has already been using Notes on your computer, you may see the icons for databases on the folders. Each icon represents a database that you can look at, and the database might be a personal database stored on your own computer or a shared database stored on the Lotus Notes file server.

We're not going to talk about Notes databases because this book is about e-mail, after all. For information about using Notes databases, you might want to get *Lotus Notes For Dummies* (IDG Books Worldwide, Inc.).

Windows galore

Notes likes to display everything in a window, and you can have a bunch of windows open at once. Use the <u>W</u>indow command on the menu bar to switch between open windows. You can also choose to *maximize* a window (that is, expand one window to take up all the available space in the Notes window), *minimize* a window (that is, shrink it to an icon), or *restore* a window (that is, display it in part of the Notes window) by using the commands on the <u>W</u>indows menu.

Notes has a good-looking row of *SmartIcons* (what any other company would call a *toolbar*) just below the menu bar. To find out what any of the buttons do, move the mouse pointer over any button and click and hold the *right* mouse button. The name of the button appears in the title bar of the Notes window. Changing the buttons that appear on the toolbar is possible, so yours may not match those in Figure 18-1.

Opening Your Mail Database

Your what? Notes considers everything to be a database, and e-mail is no exception. Your e-mail messages are stored in a Notes database. To open it, you click the icon for your mail database in the Notes workspace (the stack of folders in the Notes window). The mail icon looks like a little envelope, and it has a number to its right showing the number of new e-mail messages that are waiting for you.

If you see the mail icon on a folder, double-click it. If you don't see the mail icon, click each folder tab (the tabs are just below the toolbar in the Notes window). As you click each folder tab, that folder comes to the "top of the stack" so that you can see the whole folder and any icons it contains.

If you still don't see a mail icon on any of the folders, you need to add the icon to a folder. Get help from your network administrator to set up your mail icon.

Once you add the mail icon to your workspace, the mail icon will be there in the future when you run Notes. All you'll have to do is double-click it.

If you are not into clicking icons, you can also open the mail database by choosing Mail⟹Open from the menu bar.

When you open the mail database, Notes asks for the password for your mailbox. (If you don't know it, check with your network administrator.) As you type the password, Xs appear in the box — not even the same number of Xs as letters you typed, so that someone looking over your shoulder can't even tell how many characters your password is. (Is someone paranoid or what?) When you click OK, you see your Mail database.

The Mail database window has a title with your name in it, followed by *All by Category*, which means that all your e-mail messages are listed and sorted by category. (We'll talk about sorting e-mail messages in section "Don't Let Your Notes Pile Up" later in this chapter.) Messages you haven't read yet are in the *Not Categorized* category. (Makes sense!) You can see the date, sender, and subject of each message. Messages that you haven't read yet appear in red, and a star appears in the left margin.

Mail's Coming Your Way

Notes automagically gets your mail and displays new messages in your mail window. To read a message, double-click it.

Sending your response

To reply to a message, click the Reply button at the top of the message or choose Compose⟹Reply from the menu bar. If you want everyone who received a copy of the original message to get a copy of your reply, click the Reply to All button or choose Compose⟹Reply to All from the menu bar. Notes creates a new message — see the section "Sending a Note" later in this chapter.

Sharing a note with friends

To forward a message to someone else, click the Forward button or choose Mail⟹Forward from the menu bar. Notes creates a new message containing the text of the original message — see the section "Sending a Note" later in this chapter for how to address and send it.

Deleting messages

To delete a message, open it or select it from the list of messages in your mail window and press the Del key. The message doesn't actually disappear from the mail database, but a little trash can appears in the margin to its left. When you exit from Notes, the program asks if it should throw out all the messages that have been marked for deletion. When you click Yes, the messages actually get tossed.

Keep your mail database from getting bloated with unnecessary messages so that your network administrator won't complain about wasted disk space. Delete messages you don't need, especially large ones or messages with large files attached. (See the section "Dealing with attached files" later in this chapter.)

Printing a message

To print a message, click the File Print button on the toolbar (the little picture of a printer), or choose File⇨Print from the menu bar, or press Ctrl+P. You see the usual Windows Print dialog box asking how many copies you want and asking other info. Click OK to print one copy on your regular printer.

Getting back to your mail window

If the message you are reading takes up the whole Notes window (that is, it is *maximized*) and you want to see your list of mail messages again, choose Window from the menu bar and choose your mail window from the menu bar that appears.

Checking mail

You can tell Notes to check for any new messages by choosing View⇨Refresh from the menu bar or by pressing F9. Notes asks if you want to delete any messages you've marked for deletion, and Notes displays any new mail for you in your mail window.

Sending a Note

Once your Mail database is open, you can send a message. If you are replying to or forwarding a message, some of the information already appears in your new message because Notes has filled it in for you. When you reply to a message, your new message is already addressed to the person you are replying to. If you are replying to or forwarding a message, the new message has the same subject as the original message, but preceded by *Re*, and the text of the original message appears in the body of the message, with each line preceded by a >.

Making note of it

Here's how to create and send a message from Notes:

1. **Choose Compose⇨Memo from the menu bar.**

   Notes opens a New Memo window.

   You can use the Tab key to move from line to line in this window. Press Shift+Tab to move up a line. The little red corner brackets show where you can type.

2. **On the To line, type the address of the person you want to send the message to.**

   If you don't know the person's exact name in Notes (is it *John Smith? Jack Smith?*), you can use the Address button described in the "Notes Has Address Books, Too" section later in this chapter. To check the names that you've typed so far to make sure that Notes understands them, click the Check Names button at the top of the message. In fact, you can type just the first part of the person's name and click Check Names to ask Notes to complete the address. (This works if you have typed enough of the name for Notes to guess who you mean.)

   You can send the message to a bunch of people at once. Just type their names separated by commas, or press Enter between the names.

   To send copies of the message to other people, type their names on the cc or bcc lines. (The bcc line is for *blind copies*, where the person gets a copy but that person's name doesn't appear on the copies that everyone else gets.)

   If you are replying to a message, the sender's address already appears in the To line — you don't have to do a thing!

3. **Type a one-line summary of the message in the Subject line.**

   Make the summary as specific as possible.

4. **Type the text of your message in the space below the Subject line.**

   The little red corners indicate the space you can type in. Don't worry — the space expands to fit what you type. Don't press Enter at the end of each line. Notes can do word wrap, and it looks nicer if you let Notes take care of the margins.

5. **Unless your message is really short, check your spelling.**

   Notes is so thoughtful to provide a spell checker — most e-mail programs don't have one. To check the spelling of a message, click the Tool Spell

Check button on the toolbar (the picture of a book entitled *ABC*). Or choose T̲ools⇨Spell Chec̲k from the menu bar. If any words don't appear in Notes' dictionary, Notes asks you about them.

6. **When you are done typing your message, click the Send button at the top of the message window.**

   You see the Mail Send dialog box.

7. **Click the S̲end button.**

   If your Notes program is set up to save a copy of the message you send (see the section "Customizing Notes" later in this chapter), Notes asks if you want to save the message. Click Y̲es if you want to save a copy of your outgoing message for your own reference. If you choose Y̲es, the message appears in your mail database, in the *Not Categorized* category.

You can send mail from Notes even if your mail database isn't open. Choose C̲ompose⇨M̲emo from the menu bar any time.

If you compose a message and you decide not to send it after all (perhaps you were responding in anger to a particularly brainless message), press Ctrl+W or choose F̲ile⇨C̲lose Window from the menu bar. Notes asks if you actually want to mail or save the message. Click N̲o.

To send a message to someone on the Internet or someone using a mail program other than Notes, you must add the person to your personal address book first. See the section "Notes Has Address Books, Too" for details.

Spiffing up your note

The text in your memo doesn't have to look dull and uninteresting (we're sure that what you're *saying* isn't). You can use Notes' formatting commands to jazz it up. Here are ways to spruce up the formatting of a message:

- ✔ **Make text bold, italics, or underlined:** Select some text and click the Text Bold, Text Italic, or Text Underlined buttons on the toolbar (the ones with the big B, I, and U on them), or press Ctrl+B, Ctrl+I, or Ctrl+U.

- ✔ **Make text bigger or smaller:** Select some text and click the Text Reduce Font or Text Enlarge Font buttons on the toolbar. Or press F2 to enlarge the text or Shift+F2 to make it smaller. You can click the same button or press the same keys again to make the selected text even smaller (or bigger).

- ✔ **Center a line:** Put your cursor on a line and click the Text Align Center button on the toolbar.

- ✔ **Use another color or font:** Choose the T̲ext command from the menu bar and take a look at the available commands.

Formatting doesn't work when sending messages to people who don't use Notes, like people out on the Internet. The formatting looks cool on your screen, but the message won't arrive with the formatting. Bummer.

Take Note of This File

Notes has two ways to send a file along with an e-mail message: importing and attaching. If you import a file, the contents of the file becomes part of the message. If you attach a file, the file stays separate — as if you paper-clipped the file to the message.

Importing files right into your message

To include a picture or text in your message, put your cursor where you want the picture to appear and choose File⇨Import from the menu bar to see the Import dialog box. Choose the graphics file that contains the picture. Click Import to import the file and display it in your message.

Here's what happens when you import various types of files:

- ✔ If you import a text file, the text from the file appears as text in your e-mail message.

- ✔ If you import a picture, like a BMP file, the picture appears in your message. Cool!

- ✔ If you import an RTF file, the text of the file, complete with formatting, appears in your message. An RTF file, if you were wondering, is a *Rich Text Format* file, a standard file format invented by Microsoft that most word processors can read and write. (Try using the File⇨Save As command in your favorite word processor.)

- ✔ If you import a type of file that Notes doesn't know what to do with, the file looks like a bunch of random characters. For example, Notes can't import a COM or EXE file (program files) into a message.

If you are sending a message to someone who doesn't use Notes, don't expect the pictures and other files to arrive intact.

Sending a file with this note

To send other types of files or to send files to people who don't use Notes, attach the file to your message. Choose File⇨Attach from the menu bar, choose the file to attach, and click the Insert button. An icon for the document appears in the message, as shown in Figure 18-2.

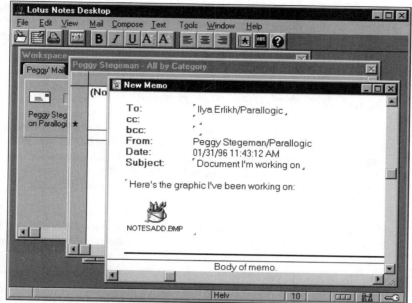

Figure 18-2:
A picture
is attached
to this
message.

Dealing with attached files

If you receive a message with a file attached to it, a paper clip appears next to the message in the list of messages in your mail window. An icon appears in the message, too, as shown in Figure 18-2. What can you do with the file? Detach the file, that's what.

To detach the file, double-click the icon in the message. You see the File Attachment Information dialog box, telling you the filename, date, and size of the file. Click the Detach button in the dialog box to save the attached file on your disk. Click the Launch button to run the program that is associated with that type of file — for example, Notes runs Word to see a Word document or Paint (or Paintbrush) to see a picture. You can use the program that Notes opens to view, edit, or save the file.

Notes Has Address Books, Too

When you are composing a message, you can click the Address button to see the Notes address book. Actually, Notes has a bunch of address books: its own address book (also known as the *Public Name & Address Book*), which contains everyone who has a Notes account on your organization's network, and each person's own address book (called a *Personal Name & Address Book*).

To address a message to someone in an address book, double-click the person's name. Notes adds the name to the message you are working on. Normally, Notes adds the person's name to the To line in your message, although you can change this to the cc or bcc line by clicking the To: box.

Sending a note to a group

The Public Name & Address Book for your system probably contains a few groups, that is, mailing lists of people's names. For example, your system might have a group named *Marketing* that contains the names of everyone in the Marketing department. You can tell that an entry in an address book is a group because the little icon to the left of the name has three little heads rather than one.

To send a note to a group, just double-click the group name in the address book. The name of the group appears in your e-mail message, and your message is sent to each person in the group.

Making notes in your own address book

You can put just the names of the folks you like to write to in your own address book. Your own address book should already exist — if you don't see an icon for it in Notes, select the folder in the Notes workspace where you want the icon to appear, choose File⇨Open Database from the menu bar, double-click the Local option listed in the server box (because your address book is usually stored locally on your own computer), choose your address book from the list that appears in the bottom part of the window, and click the Add Icon button. If that doesn't work, chat with your network administrator.

To open your personal address book, double-click the button for it in your Notes workspace. The icon looks like a blue wire-bound book and is labeled something like *Elvis's Address Book*. (The exact label depends on your own name.)

You don't need to add people who are in the Public Name & Address Book to your own address book. Use your address book to make your own mailing lists (see the section "Making your own groups" later in this chapter) and to put names of people who don't use Notes, like folks with cc:Mail or other types of e-mail accounts.

To add someone to your address book, choose Compose⇨Person from the menu bar. You see the New Person window. This form has dozens of entries, and you don't need to fill them all in. (For example, you may not care what the person's fax number is.)

Ask your network administrator what to type in entries for folks who aren't on your Notes system, like people with other types of e-mail accounts or people out on the Internet. When you have filled in the blanks, click the Close button (in Windows 95) or double-click the Control-menu box in the upper-left corner of the window (in Windows 3.1). Notes asks if you want to save the new entry — click Yes.

Making your own groups

You can create mailing lists (that is, groups) in your own address book. With your address book open, choose Compose⇨Group from the menu bar. You see the New Group window, as shown in Figure 18-3. Type a name for the group (mailing list) in the Group name box and the names of the people in the group in the Members box. When you close the New Group window, Notes asks whether you want to save the group — click Yes.

Figure 18-3:
Here's a
mailing list
that only you
can use
because it's
in your
personal
address
book.

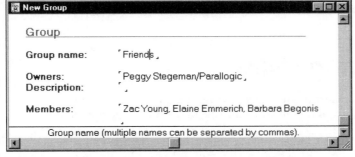

To see a list of the groups in your address book, choose View⇨Groups from the menu bar. To see people again, choose View⇨People.

Don't Let Your Notes Pile Up

What's with these *categories,* anyway? All your mail appears under the heading *Not Categorized* in your mail window. And what are categories good for?

Many of us like to save mail messages, and they can really pile up after a while. To keep your mail window from getting unmanageable, you can move messages you have already read or outgoing messages you have saved into categories.

To categorize a message, select the message in your mail window and choose Tools⇨Categorize from the menu bar. Or open the message by double-clicking it; then click the Categorize button at the top of the message window. Either way, you see the Categorize window.

Choose a category from the list of Categories or type a new category in the New categories box at the bottom of the window. Then click OK.

A message can be in more than one category. If it is, it appears under each category in the listing in your mail window. To fix this situation, categorize the message again and click the unwanted categories so that they aren't highlighted.

A message with a subject line that doesn't properly identify the contents of the message can be annoying. You can change the subject line of messages you keep in your mail database. Select the message and choose Edit⇨Edit Document from the menu bar or press Ctrl+E. The message appears and you can change the subject line. When you close the message window, Notes asks if you want to save or mail the message. Since you only want to save it — and not mail it — click the Mail box to clear the little × and click Yes to save it.

Customizing Notes

You can sort the messages in your mail window by choosing View from the menu bar and then choosing one of the following commands:

- **All by Category:** Lists your messages by the category you've assigned them, with a heading for each category. Incoming messages are in the *Not Categorized* category. See the section "Don't Let Your Notes Pile Up" earlier in this chapter for information on how to put your messages into categories.

- **All by Date:** Lists your messages in chronological order.

- **All by Person:** Lists your messages by the person they are from, with a heading for each correspondent.

- **All by Size:** Lists your messages with the largest messages first. (Strange, but it might be useful, we suppose, once in a blue moon.)

- **Show Only Unread:** If a lot of messages you've already read are lying around in your mail window, this command lists only the new ones that you haven't read. A check appears by this command on the View menu, and you see only unread messages until you choose this command again.

You can change other things about the way Notes' e-mail works, too. Choose Tools⇨Setup⇨Mail from the menu bar. You see the Mail Setup dialog box.

In the Mail Setup dialog box, don't fool with the top two settings, which determine where your mail is stored. Your network administrator knows about this stuff, and you probably don't want to know. However, here are the settings you might want to change:

- ✔ **Save Sent Mail:** When you send a message, Notes asks if you want to save it.

- ✔ **Sign Sent Mail:** This doesn't have anything to do the traditional signature that can be added to the end of e-mail messages. Notes signatures are a security feature that lets others people know that this e-mail really came from you.

- ✔ **Check for New Mail Every ___ Minutes:** This setting tells Notes how often to check for new messages on the mail server. If you want Notes to check your mail periodically, click this box so that an × appears in the box and then type a number (how about 15 or 30) in the box to the left of the word *Minutes*.

When you have changed the setting to your liking, click OK.

Taking Notes Out for a Spin

If you take your computer on the road, you may be able to use Notes even when your computer is not connected to your organization's local area network. Your computer may be able to call the company's Notes system and get your mail no matter where you are, as long as you can find a phone to connect your computer to and as long as your computer has a modem.

When you are on the road, you take a copy (or *replica*) of your mail database with you on your computer. You can compose messages any time without having to call the main Notes system. To mail your message and pick up your new mail, you call your company's Notes system, log in, and exchange information between the replica of your mail database on your own computer and your original mail database at home base.

To find out if your Notes system can handle *Dial-In Notes* (as they call it), ask your network administrator. She may have to install software on your computer to set up Dial-In Notes. In the process, you'll get a *Remote Connection document* in your personal address book containing all the information about how to call your Notes server.

Once your computer is set up for Dial-In Notes and you have a replica of your mail database on your computer, you use the Tools⇨Replicate command to call your Notes server back at the office and bring your copy of your mail database up to date. Notes sends any messages you've composed and receives any new mail that has come in for you.

Notes Mail 4

Lotus has just started shipping Notes 4 and, with it, the all new Notes Mail. Not just for Notes users anymore, Notes Mail is also being sold as a stand-alone mail package. Because Lotus just happens to own cc:Mail, it used the crowd-pleasing, award-winning, cc:Mail user interface for its spiffy, all-new mail product.

We don't have room here for a blow by blow description of how to use Notes Mail. Instead, we tell you all the cool things Notes Mail purports to do and why we think it's worth checking out.

If you're coming from the Notes world, Notes Mail 4 is a major leap forward into serious e-mail. If you're coming from any other e-mail environment, Notes Mail 4 is a serious step into high-end, bells and whistles, toe-tapping e-mail that will make your neighbors drool.

We're rich!

Notes Mail supports rich text. No, this isn't some sort of classist comment. *Rich text* means that messages can use different fonts and formatting features, like bold and italics. You can include graphics and documents created by other programs, and your readers will be able to read these foreign documents without having to run the actual programs that created them.

Your mail can start to look pretty fancy when you use different letterhead and mood stamps. You can even structure your mail so that sections collapse and your reader sees an outline of your mail; when the reader is ready to read a particular section, she can expand it.

Web Notes

Notes Mail has a powerful World Wide Web browser built in so that you bring the Web to your e-mail and e-mail to the Web. Here are some examples:

✔ Notes mail understands *URLs,* those cryptic addresses of pages on the World Wide Web. You can make *hot links* in your e-mail so that your reader clicks on a link and — POOF — she's at the Web site. Hot links usually appear in color and underlined.

✔ With some amount of work on your part, you can send a *mail agent* (more about them in a minute) to do your Web searching for you.

✔ The Notes Mail browser is a full-fledged Web browser in its own right, so it's all you need to access the Web.

"Agent 99? Smart here . . ."

Notes Mail is smarter than your average bear and comes with a tool to help you automate certain things that you do on regular basis. Once created, these automated tasks are known as *mail agents*. Notes Mail comes with a handful of useful agents for you to put to work right away.

If you can think of other things you'd like a mail agent to do, you can create new mail agents using LotusScript or Notes Simple Actions. For the average user, this might look a lot like programming and may not be the part of the system that you gravitate toward first. However, if you have any latent computer-geek tendencies, here's a place to let your fancy fly. You can create *mail agents* to filter your incoming mail, search the Web, or send messages telling people you're out of the office. Even if you in particular aren't inclined to try this on your own, chances are someone in your organization, perhaps your network administrator, has the requisite genes for the task and can help you set up your mail to do exactly what you want.

Filter, folder, and thread

Notes Mail allows you to group your mail (both incoming and outgoing) by *thread* (that is, what the messages pertain to) and by other criteria using those ambitious mail agents. When we use "other criteria" to group our messages, we call it *filtering*.

When searching through mail for the criteria you've specified, Notes Mail is capable of sorting through attachments as well.

Not exactly leading-edge technology, but new to Notes Mail, you can file your mail into hierarchical folders, just like Eudora and a lot of other fine mailers. What *is* leading-edge is that you can keep multiple *views* of a message in various folders. This means that if you'd like to file mail under more than one category, you can, *and* Notes Mail cleverly stores only *one* copy while maintaining pointers for additional "views." Essentially, you get the flexibility of multiple copies while only chewing up enough disk space for one copy.

But wait, there's more. This capability to store only one copy can be expanded to include a group of users so that when you send a giant file to ten different people on the same server, only one copy is stored and everyone's mail points to that one copy.

Feeling secure

Notes Mail encrypts your mail so that only the people you intend to see it can. Electronic signatures let you know that the person who sent the mail is really who she says she is. Return receipts let you know your mail got where it was going. And for those extra sensitive messages, you can send them "For Your Eyes Only" — a great feature that allows only your intended reader to read the message; she can't forward it, copy it, or even cut and paste from the window that displays it. This feature doesn't prevent someone from leaning over her shoulder, but it does limit the message's circulation.

Remote control

Notes Mail lets you set up various location profiles so that picking up your messages remotely is easy and doesn't require perpetual reconfiguration. When you're connected from a remote site, you have full Notes Mail capability including access to the Web. You don't have to worry about doing things over when you get back to the office — you have your own virtual office at your fingertips.

Usenet newgroups in your mail

You can use Notes Mail to read your favorite Usenet newsgroups and file articles into folders, just like mail messages.

On the down side, the rest of the e-mail industry hasn't caught up yet, and most of the features that make Notes Mail so spiffy don't work when you try to send mail to a no-Notes kind of person. When your addressee doesn't have Notes, Notes Mail tries its best to convert the Notes-specific features into something your reader's mailer can handle. A lot of people using older mailers won't be able to see graphics without a lot of extra work, so for them, you might want to stick to plain text. But the world is moving in the rich text direction, and we hope it is just a matter of time until smarter mailers will know how to do the right thing with rich text — display it in all its glory.

Chapter 19
Lotus cc:Mail

●●

●●

C c:Mail is the most popular e-mail package for local area networks, with some thirteen million users.

cc:Mail is available for Windows, Macintosh, DOS, OS/2, and UNIX. This chapter describes cc:Mail version 2.2 for Windows, but Mac users should be able to follow along easily. If your organization uses cc:Mail but the software is not installed on your computer, ask your supervisor or your network administrator to help you.

Starting cc:Mail

To start cc:Mail, double-click its icon, which looks like small stack of stamped envelopes. You see the cc:Mail window, as shown in Figure 19-1.

Along the very top of your cc:Mail window is a thin header that tells you what mailbox or folder you are looking at. Below that header are your menu and toolbar.

Down the left side of the cc:Mail window is a column of small icons named Inbox, Drafts, Message Log, Trash, and so on. These are the folders in which you can store your messages. The exact list depends on how you set up your mail folders (see the section "Saving Your Messages" for more about folders). One of the folders is selected (it appears highlighted in gray). Down the right side of the cc:Mail window is a list of the messages in the selected folder.

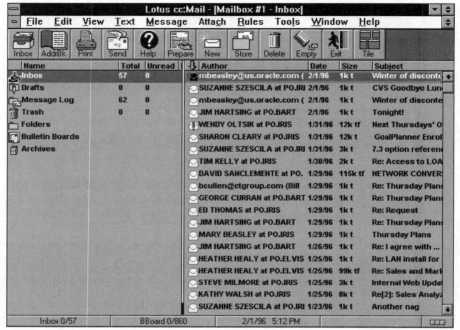

Figure 19-1:
cc:Mail
says hello.

Reading Your Mail

To see what mail you have, double-click the Inbox icon, which looks like a tray piled high with envelopes. You see a list of your messages, one per line (see Figure 19-1). The list shows who sent the message, the date the message was sent, its size, and the subject.

Double-click a message to open it. The message looks like Figure 19-2. Below the toolbar you see boxes that tell you who the message is from, who it's to, the subject, and (finally!) the text of the message.

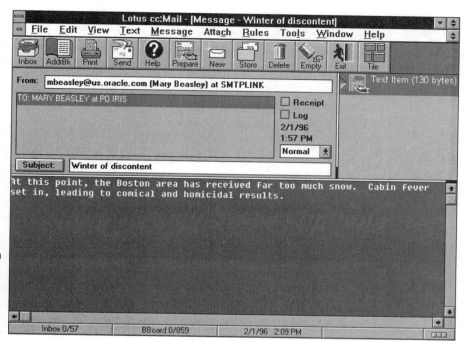

Figure 19-2:
cc:Mail
shows you a
message.

Where's my message?

So you dutifully double-click your message, the message window opens and . . . nothing — zip, zilch, nada! Is some practical joker sending blank messages? Well, maybe. But odds are that your incoming message is just a tad verbose, or that something more than simple ASCII text is being sent to you.

Take a look in the upper-right corner of your cc:Mail window, just below the toolbar, an area called your *attachments pane.* If you see an icon of a diskette followed by a number in parentheses, then your message is longer than 20 Kilobytes. cc:Mail gives you a chance to decide if you really want to open that message right now. If you do, double-click the diskette icon and, voilà, your message appears. If double-clicking doesn't open the message, then try holding down the Shift key while you double-click.

cc:Mail has several *view filters* that allow you to read documents prepared by applications that you may not have on your computer. If you get mail with an Excel spreadsheet attached, for example, a different icon appears in the upper-right corner of your cc:Mail window with the name of the attached file next to it. (The kind of icon you see depends on what kind or file is being sent.) To open the attachment, click its icon. Though a variety of common file formats are supported, we can't guarantee that every file will be readable.

If you know the kind of application (for example, spreadsheet, database, graphic, and so on) that the attachment was created in, but you don't have that particular application, save the attachment to disk and try opening the attachment with a different brand of the same type of application. For example, if you receive a spreadsheet created in Lotus 1-2-3 and you only have Excel, try opening the attachment with Excel. Many applications come with translators that allow you to open documents created in other, similar applications.

Replying to a Message

To reply to a message, click the Reply icon — that's the one that looks like an envelope with an arrow curving back to the left. A dialog box appears asking you if you want to reply to Sender or to All Addresses. Think before you click! If the original message was sent to others besides yourself, do you want them to receive your comments as well? If so, check All Addresses. Otherwise just check Sender. The appropriate addresses appear on the To: line. cc:Mail also asks you if you want to Retain Original Item. Click here if you want to include the original message in your reply. (This option is useful if you want to respond to specific points without reminding the sender of what was said originally.)

If you did not check Retain Original Items in the dialog box, you have a clean slate on which to prepare your message. However, if you did check Retain Original Items, cc:Mail includes a copy of the original message in your reply. The copy appears under a line labeled

```
_____Reply Separator_____
```

Your *insertion point* (the place where letters appear on the screen when you type) is automatically above this line so that your message comes first. If needed, your recipient can scroll down to see the original message. However, you can insert your text any place you want. So if, for example, you were sent a list of questions, you can just point-and-click under each question and type your answer right there.

Forwarding a Message

To forward a message, click the Forward icon — the one that looks like an envelope being passed from hand to hand. A dialog box asks if you want to Retain Forwarding History? If you check this box, your recipient can track how the message went from A to B, who forwarded it to C, and who felt the need to pass it on to D. We generally check this box. Doing so may save your recipient the effort of forwarding a message to someone who has already seen it. Besides, seeing how far and wide a message has traveled is always interesting!

Deleting Messages

To delete a message that's open or highlighted in your Inbox, click the Trash can icon on the left side of your cc:Mail window. If you have second thoughts after you hit the delete key, double-click the Trash can icon inside the cc:Mail window and then reopen the message. (This feature works until you empty your trash. After that, your message is history.)

Not all trash cans are created equal. Just because both trash cans look the same, don't believe for a moment that they work the same way. If you click the Trash can icon from the toolbar, your message is gone forever. If you drag your message over to the Trash can icon on the left side of your cc:Mail window, you place the message in a *folder* called *Trash,* and you can dumpster-dive to pull it back out. This Trash icon lets you recycle. The toolbar Trash can just hauls the trash away, never to be seen again!

Saving Your Messages

cc:Mail lets you save your messages two different ways. Save messages you want to continue to use in folders. Save messages you want to keep for histori-cal reasons in *archives* (a sort of cold storage for messages). You can move messages from folder to folder and delete them at any time. Once a message is in an archive, you can't delete the message unless you delete the entire archive. You can create as many folders and archives as you like.

To create a folder or archive, click the Folder icon on the left and then choose File⇨New from the menu. A dialog box asks if you want to create a new folder or a new archive. Take your pick and give it a name.

To save a message, drag the closed message to the folder or archive and drop the message there. To reread the message, double-click the folder or archive and then click the message.

When cc:Mail shuts down, it hides your folders to tidy up the cc:Mail window. To see them, double-click the original folder icon. To hide them again, double-click the folder icon once more.

Writing and Sending Mail

To create a new message, click the Prepare icon — the one that looks like a hand writing on a piece of paper. A new message window appears, as shown in Figure 19-3. Enter the e-mail address of the person you want to send a message to in the To: field. To send copies to other people, click the little downward pointing arrow right next to the field and enter addresses in the cc: field. The bcc: field is for *blind copies* — copies you don't want other people to know about.

Ask your cc:Mail administrator about any special instructions for addressing e-mail. Some companies have internal directories that let you simply click a person's name to put her e-mail address in a field. Some companies require you to first type **SMTP** (which stands for *Simple Mail Transfer Protocol*, the Internet's method of sending mail) when you send mail outside the company. Find out. Addressing e-mail messages outside of your cc:Mail system is not well standardized. Sorry.

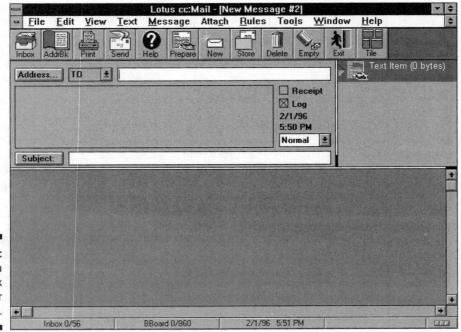

Figure 19-3:
Here's a nice, blank message for you to write.

Public and private mailing lists

To create a private mailing list of e-mail addresses, click the Address Book icon — the one that looks like an open book. When the Address Book window appears, click the Add New button. Select Private Mailing Lists and type in a name for your list; click OK.

To add names to this private mailing list, open the Address Book window. Double-click the Private Mailing Lists folder in the left column on your cc:Mail window. Below this folder appears a list of all the private mailing lists you have created. Click the Add New icon (an envelope with a star behind it). When the dialog box appears, select Mailing List Participants. A Participants List dialog box appears. You can now add e-mail addresses to your list.

You can add e-mail addresses in a few ways:

- ✔ Carefully type in the address. When you finish, click Add.
- ✔ Select the desired address in the list of messages and click Add (or drag and drop the address into the address list).
- ✔ Start typing in the address until cc:Mail recognizes it and fills in the rest for you. (cc:Mail recognizes the people on the cc:Mail system.) Then click Add.
- ✔ If the address is in an e-mail message, you can open the message. With the Address Book open, select the Private Mailing List to which you want to add the address. Arrange the two windows on your screen so that you can see both of them. (Windows users can choose Window➪Tile Horizontal from the menu). Now select the desired address from your message and drag and drop the address on top of your Private Mailing list. The address you selected is now part of your list.

While you are in the Address Book window, see if your mail administrator has created any public mailing lists for your use. They work exactly the same way as your private lists, except that only your mail administrator can add or delete names from them.

Your company may have cc:Mail configured so that you can only put other members of your network on a mailing list. So, for example, if you need to type SMTP before addressing e-mail to someone outside of the network, you may not be able to put her in a private mailing list. Try it and see.

The message

To continue creating your message, press Tab or position your cursor and click the Subject: line. Fill in something appropriate, informative, and pithy, and then press Enter.

Enter your message. When you finish, spell check your message by clicking the Spell Check icon, a little blue book with ABC on the cover. Then click the Send button to send the message.

Attaching Files to Messages

You can attach up to 20 files to one message. To attach a file to your message, click the Attach icon — the one that looks like a paper clip. A dialog box appears. Double-click the filename you want to attach. When you finish, click OK or press Enter. The files you selected appear in the Attachments Pane of your message.

If you change your mind, select the attachment you want to delete by clicking it once and pressing Delete. If you want to change the name of an attachment, highlight the attachment and choose Message⇨Rename Item from the menu. When its dialog box opens, type in the new name for your attachment and click OK.

To send your mail, click the Send icon — the envelope with wings.

Part V
Advanced
E-Mail Topics

The 5th Wave   By Rich Tennant

"You know, I liked you a whole lot more on the Internet."

In this part . . .

Sending and receiving e-mail is just *part* of the fun. In this section of the book, we help you find e-mail addresses. Then we tell you all about mailing lists, including how to join them. We tell you all about e-mail security — why it's important and how to use it. And then, as a special treat, we show you how to get to many Internet services using just e-mail.

Chapter 20
How to Find Someone's E-Mail Address

In This Chapter

▶ Looking for an address

▶ Using online directories

Where Is Everybody, Anyway?

You might have figured out one teensy detail keeping you from sending e-mail to all your friends: you don't know their addresses. In this chapter, you learn lots of different ways to look for addresses. But we save you the trouble of reading the rest of the chapter by starting out with the easiest, most reliable way to find out people's e-mail addresses:

> Ask them.

Pretty low-tech, huh? For some reason, this way seems to be absolutely the last thing people want to do. But try it first. If you know or can find out the phone number, calling and asking is much easier than any other method.

They won't mind if you give them the finger

One of the most useful commands, if you generally know where someone receives mail, is *finger*. On most UNIX shell provider systems, you can use finger to find out who is currently logged in and to ask about particular users. Most other service providers support the finger command; check with the help desk to find out if yours is one.

What if you don't know your own address?

For people who've *always* known their e-mail address, not knowing your own address seems impossible. But it happens frequently — usually because someone's using a private e-mail system that has a gateway to the outside world that provides instructions for how to send messages to the outside but no hint about how outsiders send stuff in. Fortunately, the solution is usually easy: tell your friend to send you a message. All messages have return addresses, and all but the absolutely cruddiest of mail gateways put on a usable return address. Don't be surprised if the address has a great deal of strange punctuation.

After a few gateways, you always seem to end up with things like this:

`"blurch::John.C.Calhoun"%farp@slimemail.com`

Usually if you type the strange address back in, it works, so don't worry about it.

You can find out your own address this way by sending a message to our ever-vigilant mail robot at `email@dummies.com`, which will send you back a note telling you what the return address in your message was. The human authors see those messages as well, so feel free to add a few words telling us whether you like the book.

Fingering from UNIX

To run finger from a shell prompt, simply type **finger *username@hostname*** and press Enter. For example, to finger someone whose e-mail address is `elvis@bluesuede.org`, you would type this line: `finger elvis@ bluesuede.org`.

You get back something like the following:

```
Login name: elvis               In real life: Elvis A. Presley
Directory: /usr/elvis           Shell: /bin/sh
On since Jun 30 16:03:13 on vt01         1 day 9 hours Idle Time
Project: Working on "Hound Dog"
Plan:
Write many songs, become famous.
```

The exact format of the response varies a great deal from one system to another because fiddling with the finger program is a bad habit of many UNIX system hackers.

Fingering with Eudora

If you don't have a UNIX shell account but do use SLIP or PPP, have no fear. The Windows and Mac versions of Eudora can finger people for you. In Eudora, choose Window⇨Ph (or press Ctrl+U) to open the Finger window. Type the address you want to finger in the <u>C</u>ommand box and click <u>F</u>inger. The results appear in the big text box. Press Ctrl+F4 to close the Finger window.

If you use Windows, an intrepid programmer out in Netland named Lee Murach has created a WinSock program called WS Finger just for you. You can get WS Finger via FTP from `sparky.umd.edu` in the `/pub/winsock` directory, among other places.

Using finger works only if the fingeree's Internet provider runs a program called (intriguingly enough) a *finger server*. It doesn't hurt to try; the worst that will happen is a "Connection refused" message.

Fingering otherwise

If you use a SLIP/PPP Internet connection and your provider gave you a package of software to use, it may well include a finger program (commercial packages such as Chameleon all do; shareware packages may or may not).

You can download and install a shareware or freeware finger program if you have a SLIP/PPP account. The details of doing so are beyond the scope of this book, but we cover them in our *More Internet For Dummies.* You can also ask your provider for help.

Finally, if you have access to a World Wide Web browser such as Netscape, quite a few Web pages will do finger requests for you. Here are some of them:

```
http://www.middlebury.edu:80/~otisg/cgi/HyperFinger.cgi
http://www.rickman.com:80/finger.html
http://www-bprc.mps.ohio-state.edu:80/cgi-bin/finger.pl
```

The giant finger

Some places, universities in particular, have attached their `finger` programs to organizational directories. If you finger `levine@bu.edu` (Boston University), for example, you get the following response:

```
[bu.edu]
 There were 55 matches to your request.

 E-mail addresses and telephone numbers are only displayed
 when a query matches one individual. To obtain additional
 information on a particular individual, inquire again with
 the index_id.
```

The finger program then lists all the matches. It gives the actual mail address (or occasionally some other ID code) for all of the people who match your request, so you can then finger the address for the person you want.

Other universities with similar directories include Cornell, MIT, and Yale. It's worth a try — the worst that can happen is that it will say `not found`.

SLED Corp.'s Four11 Online User Directory

SLED Corp.'s Four11 Online User Directory is an Internet white pages service you can use to look for someone's e-mail address or home page. Anyone can be listed for free. Four11 will also certify and list your PGP key for a fee. See PGP in Chapter 23.

To try out the service and at least register your address, send e-mail to `info@Four11.com`.

Whois whatzit

Quite a long time ago (at least, a long time ago in the *network* frame of mind — 15 or 20 years), some of the network managers began keeping directories of network people. This time, of course, was when Men were Men and Internet connections were UNIX. The shell command that lets you look up people in these directories is called *whois*. Some systems have a whois command, so in principle you can type the line `whois Smith`, and it should contact the whois database and tell you about all the people named Smith.

In practice, however, whois isn't quite that simple. For one thing, around the end of 1992, the main system that keeps the Internet whois database moved, and some whois commands still haven't yet been updated to reflect that move. The old standard server now holds only the names of people who work for the Department of Defense.

Fortunately, you can tell the whois program to use a particular server, as in `whois -h whois.internic.net Smith` because the civilian Internet service is now at `whois.internic.net`. The `-h` stands for *host,* as in the host where the server is located. But keep in mind that it still lists only network managers and administrative contacts. Here at *Internet For Dummies* Central, for example, `whois` will find John because he's the network manager; and Margy, who manages some name domains; but you won't find Carol, who, instead of being a network manager, has a life.

Please, please Mr. Postman

Sometimes you have a pretty good idea what machine someone uses, but you don't know the name. In that case, you can try writing to the *postmaster*. Every *domain,* the part of the address after @ (the at sign) that can receive Internet mail has the e-mail address postmaster, which contacts someone responsible for that machine. So if you're pretty sure that your friend uses my.bluesuede.org, you might try asking (politely, of course) postmaster@my.bluesuede.org what the address is (we assume that, for some reason, you can't just call your friend and ask what the e-mail address is).

Most postmasters are overworked system administrators who don't mind an occasional polite question, but you shouldn't expect any big favors. Also keep in mind that the larger the mail domain, the less likely that the postmaster knows all the users personally. Don't write to Postmaster@ibm.com to try to find someone's e-mail address at IBM. Fortunately, for people who want to find correspondents in the Blue Zone, IBM has a whois server — see the section, "Whois whatzit" in this chapter.

Postmaster is also the appropriate place to write when you're having trouble with mail to or from a site. If your messages to someone are coming back with a cryptic error message that suggests the mail system is fouled up, or if you're receiving a flood of mechanically generated junk mail from a deranged automatic mail server, the postmaster at the relevant site is the one to contact.

For systems that don't have the whois command but do have other Internet services, you can use telnet instead (see *More Internet For Dummies,* 2nd Edition, for the poop on how to telnet). You can telnet to whois.internic.net; then at the prompt, type whois whoever. For European Net people, try typing whois.ripe.net. A large list of whois servers (lots of organizations run their own whois service for their own employees) is in a file you can FTP from sipb.mit.edu; its filename is /pub/whois/whois-servers.list.

Maybe the knowbot knows

One more address-finding system worth trying is *knowbot.* It's at http://info.cnri.reston.va.us/kis.html on the Web. Just type the person's name, click the Search button, and wait, sometimes for as long as several minutes, as it looks through a bunch of directories and tells you what it finds. Knowbot has access to some directories not otherwise easily accessible, including the one for MCI Mail, so it's worth checking.

Finding people at big companies

Some companies have services that let you look up people's addresses. IBM, for example, has a mail server that lets you look up people's names. Send a message to nic@vnet.ibm.com that contains a line like this: whois Watson, T.

The service lists any users with e-mail addresses whose names match your request. Although nearly all IBM employees have internal e-mail addresses, only a fraction can receive mail from the outside, and you can see only those addresses (makes sense — no point in telling you about mail addresses you can't use).

Many other companies have a straightforward addressing system that gives everyone at the company an alias such as Firstname.Lastname. This works at AT&T, so mailing to the address Theodore .Vail@att.com finds someone pretty reliably. This technique also works at Sun Microsystems (sun.com). It's always worth a try because the worst that can happen is that you get your message back as undeliverable. If several people have the same name, you usually get a mechanical response telling you how to figure out which of them you want and what the correct address is.

Chapter 21
Mailing List Fever

In This Chapter
▶ Mailing lists
▶ Getting on and off
▶ A few interesting mailing lists

Pen Pals Galore

So you've heard that gazillions of people are out there just ready to send you mail. How do you find them and how can they find you? Well, since you probably don't really want to correspond with all of them, we suggest you start by thinking about what interests you. You may have gone your whole life without ever finding someone who shares your interest in shitake mushrooms, tantric yoga, and Alfonso Sastre. Now's your chance.

The Internet is chock-full, and getting chock-fuller every second, of people with shared interests using electronic mail mailing lists to create a running conversation. E-mail mailing lists are a source for both information and entertainment, and with over twelve thousand of them out there, one is bound to appeal to your interests or tickle your fancy.

How a mailing list works is simple. The list has its own special e-mail address, and anything that you send to that address is sent to all the people on the list. Because some of the people on the list, in turn, may respond to your messages, the result is a running conversation.

Different lists have different styles, tones, and senses of focus. Some are relatively formal, hewing closely to the official topic of the list. Others tend to go flying off into outer space, figuratively and literally. You have to read them for a while to be able to tell which list works which way.

Some mailing lists generate hundreds of messages per day or more. Don't get carried away and join ten mailing lists in one sitting. Join them one or two at a time and see how it goes.

Sign Me Up!

The way you get on or off a mailing list is simple: You send a mail message.

The message you send to get on and off a mailing list goes to a special *administrative address*, not the address where you send messages to distribute to the members of the list. Sending a "put me on the list" or "take me off the list" message to the entire group is one of the big no-nos of mailing lists. Figuring out the right way to do these things is a bit complex, but that's what we're here for. Read on.

Two general schools of mailing-list management exist: *manual* and *automatic*. Manual management is the low tech way: Your message is read by a human being who updates an address file to put you on or take you off the list. The advantage of manual management is that you get personal service; the disadvantage is that the list maintainer may not get around to handling your request for quite a while if more pressing business (such as her real job) intervenes.

These days, having lists maintained automatically is more common. Such lists only need human attention when things get fouled up. Automatic lists are managed by computer programs known as list managers. LISTSERV, Majordomo, and Listproc are the most common names you'll see, and they each get their own sections later in this chapter.

A widely observed convention regarding list and maintainer addresses exists for the manual lists. Suppose that you want to join a list for fans of Chester Alan Arthur (the 21st President of the United States), and the list's name is `arthur-lovers@dummies.com`. The manager's address is almost certainly `arthur-lovers-request@dummies.com`. In other words, just add `-request` to the list's address to get the manager's address. Because the list is maintained by hand, your request to be added or dropped doesn't have to take any particular form, as long as it's polite. `Please add me to the arthur-lovers list` does quite well. When you decide that you have had all the Arthur you can stand, another message saying `Please remove me from the arthur-lovers list` does equally well.

Messages to `-request` addresses are read and handled by human beings who sometimes eat, sleep, and work regular jobs as well as maintain mailing lists. Therefore, they don't necessarily read your request the moment it arrives. Being added to or removed from a list can take a day or so, and after you ask to be removed, you usually get a few more messages before they remove you. Be patient. And *don't* send cranky follow-ups — they just cheese off the list maintainer.

Yeah, Now What Do I Do?

Here's a handy tip: After you subscribe to a list, don't send any messages until you read it for a week. Trust us — the list has been getting along without your insights since it began, and it can get along without them for one more week.

This method gives you a chance to learn the sorts of topics that people really discuss, the tone of the list, and other helpful hints about behavior on this particular list. Reading the list for a week also gives you a fair idea about which topics people are tired of. The classic newcomer gaffe is to subscribe to a list and immediately send a message asking a dumb question that isn't really germane to the topic and that was beaten to death three days earlier. Bide your time, and don't let this faux pas happen to you. (As a small exception to this rule, a few lists ask new members to send a message introducing themselves. Check the introductory message you get when you join a list to see if an intro is expected.)

The number-two newcomer gaffe (as mentioned earlier) is to send a message directly to the list asking to subscribe or unsubscribe. This type of message should go to a request or LISTSERV, Majordomo, or Listproc address, where the list maintainer (human or robotic) can handle your request, _not_ to the list itself, where all the other subscribers can see that you screwed up.

Make sure that you read all the information the list has sent you before you start asking questions. Look for the _FAQs_ — the list of frequently asked questions (and their answers) — that people have thoughtfully provided so that when a newcomer like you joins up, they don't have to answer the same question for the fifty-gazillionth time.

When you _are_ ready to post something to the group, read and reread what you've written thoroughly. You are what you type. Make sure that you're saying what you think you're saying, keep the message civil, and observe the conventions of the group. We talk more about sending messages to the list later in this chapter.

Automagic Mailing List Service: LISTSERV

Once upon a time, the _BITNET network_ (a network of large computers, now mostly merged into the Internet) could _only_ ship files and messages from one system to another. As a result, BITNET users quickly developed lots and lots of mailing lists because no other convenient way — such as USENET news — was available to stay in touch.

Because maintaining all those mailing lists was (and still is) a great deal of work, the BITNET crowd came up with a program called _LISTSERV_ to manage the mailing lists. Originally, only users on machines directly connected to BITNET could use LISTSERV, but current versions have been improved so that anyone with an Internet address can use LITSERV. Indeed, LISTSERV has grown to the point where it is an all-singing, all-dancing, mailing-list program with about 15 zillion features and options, almost none of which you care about.

LISTSERV is a little klunky to use but has the great advantage of being able to easily handle enormous mailing lists that contain thousands of members — something that makes the regular Internet mail programs choke.

Enlisting with LISTSERV

You put yourself on and off a LISTSERV mailing list by sending mail to LISTSERV@some.machine.or.other, where some.machine.or.other is the name of the particular machine on which the mailing list lives. Because they're computer programs, LISTSERV list managers are pretty simpleminded, so you have to speak to them clearly and distinctly.

Suppose that you want to join a list called SNUFLE-L (LISTSERV mailing lists usually end with -L) that lives at bluesuede.org. To join, send to LISTSERV@bluesuede.org a message that contains this line:

```
SUB SNUFLE-L Roger Sherman
```

You don't have to add a subject line or anything else to this message. SUB is short for subscribe, SNUFLE-L is the name of the list, and anything after that is supposed to be your real name. (You can put whatever you want there, but keep in mind that the name you use shows up in the return address of anything you send to the list.) Shortly afterward, you should get two messages back:

✔ A chatty, machine-generated welcoming message, telling you that you've joined the list, along with a description of some commands you can use to fiddle with your mailing-list membership. Sometimes this message includes a request to confirm that you got this message. Follow the instructions by replying to this message with the single word *OK* in the body of the message. This helps lists ensure that they aren't mailing into the void. If you don't provide this confirmation, you don't get on the list.

✔ An incredibly boring message, telling you that the IBM mainframe ran a program to handle your request and reporting the exact number of milliseconds of computer time and number of disk operations the request took. (It is sobering to think that somewhere there are people who find these facts interesting.) Whoopee.

Keep the chatty, informative message that tells you about all the commands you can use when dealing with the list. For one thing, this message tells you how to get *off* the mailing list if you choose to. We have a folder called *Mailing Lists* in our mail program in which we store the welcome messages from all the mailing lists we join.

To send a message to this list (after you subscribe), mail to the list name at the same machine — in this case, `SNUFLE-L@bluesuede.org`. Be sure to provide a descriptive `Subject:` for the multitudes who will benefit from your pearls of wisdom. Within a matter of minutes, people from all over the world will read your message.

To get off a list, you again write to `LISTSERV@some.machine.or.other`, this time sending

```
SIGNOFF SNUFLE-L
```

or whatever the list's name is. You don't have to give your name again because after you're off the list, LISTSERV has no more interest in you and completely forgets that you ever existed.

Some lists are more difficult to get on and off than others are. Usually you ask to get on a list, and you're on the list. In some cases, however, the list isn't open to all comers, and the human list owner screens requests to join the list, in which case you may get some messages from the list owner to discuss your request to join.

To contact the actual human being who runs a particular list, the mail address is `OWNER-` followed by the list name (`OWNER-SNUFLE-L`, for example). The owner can do all sorts of things to lists that mere mortals can't do. In particular, the owner can fix screwed-up names on the list or add a name that for some reason the automatic method doesn't handle. You have to appeal for manual intervention if your mail system doesn't put your correct network mail address on the `From:` line of your messages, as sometimes happens when your local mail system isn't set up quite right.

Telling LISTSERV how to behave

The people who maintain the LISTSERV program have added so many bells and whistles to it that it would take an entire book to describe them all, and, frankly, they're not that interesting. But here are some of the things LISTSERV can do. For each of them, you send a message to `LISTSERV@some.machine.or.other` to talk to the LISTSERV program. You can send several commands in the same message if you want to do two or three tricks at one time.

✔ **Temporarily stop mail:** Sometimes you're going to be away for a week or two and you don't want to get a bunch of mailing-list mail in the meantime. But because you're planning to come back, you don't want to take yourself off the list, either. This feature is especially useful for restricted lists where you had to get approved by the list owner to join.

To stop mail temporarily from the SNUFLE-L mailing list, send SET SNUFLE-L NOMAIL and the list stops sending you messages. To turn the mail back on, send this message: SET SNUFLE-L MAIL

Turning off your mailing lists temporarily when you go on vacation or won't be reading your mail for some other reason is a good idea. Be aware that some mailing list programs send a confirmation message, asking if you really want to do stop mail. So if you send out your NOMAIL messages, turn out the lights, and hop in the car, you may be unpleasantly surprised when you get back to find your mailbox has overflowed and you did not get important mail. Moral: don't wait until the last minute to NOMAIL.

✔ **Get messages as a digest:** If you're getting a large number of messages from a list and would rather get them all at one time as a daily digest, send this message: SET SNUFLE-L DIGEST

Not all lists can be digested, but the indigestible ones let you know and don't take offense.

✔ **Find out who's on a list:** To find out who subscribes to a list, send this message: REVIEW SNUFLE-L

Some lists can be reviewed only by people on the list, and others not at all. Some lists are enormous, so be prepared to get back an enormous message listing thousands of subscribers.

✔ **Get or not get your own mail:** Sending a message off into cyberspace leaves many folks wondering if it really went anywhere, or if the computer just burped when you clicked send. So most mailing lists are set up so that you automatically receive a copy of any message you send to the list, just like anyone else. Just to be perverse, some list owners set things up the other way: so you *don't* automatically receive a copy of your own message. If you want to be sure that you receive a copy of your own messages, send the following command to the LISTSERV address: SET SNUFLE-L REPRO

To stop getting copies of your own messages, send this one: SET SNUFLE-L NOREPRO

If you are only interested in knowing that your message made it to the list but don't want a copy of the message itself, send the command: SET SNUFLE-L ACK

To stop getting acknowledgments, send this one: SET SNUFLE-L NOACK

✔ **Get files:** Most LISTSERV servers have a library of files available, usually documents contributed by the mailing-list members. To find out which files are available, send: INDEX

To have LISTSERV send you a particular file by e-mail, send the message GET*fname* where *fname* is the name of a file from the INDEX command. On IBM systems, files have two-part names separated by a space (for example, GET SNUFLE-L MEMO).

✔ **Find out which lists are available:** To find out which LISTSERV mailing lists are available on a particular host, send this message: LIST

The LIST command gives you the local lists, one per line. If you want more information on each list, send the command: LIST DETAILED

> *Note:* Keep in mind that just because a list exists doesn't necessarily mean that you can subscribe to it. But trying never hurts.

✔ **Get LISTSERV to do other things:** Lots of other commands lurk in LISTSERV, most of which apply only to people on IBM mainframes. If you are one of these people or if you're just nosy, send a message containing the line `HELP` and you'll receive a helpful response that lists other commands.

Major Major Domo Domo

The other widely used mailing-list manager is Brent Chapman's *Majordomo.* Majordomo started out as a LISTSERV wannabe for workstations but has evolved into a system that works quite well. Because of its wannabe origins, Majordomo commands are almost, but (pretend to be surprised now) not quite, the same as their LISTSERV equivalents.

The mailing address for Majordomo commands, as you might expect, is `majordomo@some.machine.or.other`. Majordomo lists tend to have long and expressive names. One of our favorites is called `explosive-cargo`, a very funny weekly column written by a guy in Boston who also writes for a computer magazine. To subscribe, because the list is maintained on host `world.std.com`, send this message to `Majordomo@world.std.com`:

```
subscribe explosive-cargo
```

Unlike with LISTSERV, you *don't* put your real name in the subscribe command.

To unsubscribe

```
unsubscribe explosive-cargo
```

Once you subscribe, you can send a message to everyone on the mailing list by addressing it to `listname@some.machine.or.other`. (You can't post messages to `explosive-cargo` because it's an *announcements-only list*, that is, only the guy in Boston who runs the list is allowed to post messages.)

Not to be outdone by LISTSERV, Majordomo has its own set of not particularly useful commands (as with LISTSERV, you can send in a single message as many of these as you want):

✔ To find out which lists at a Majordomo system you are subscribed to, enter **which**.

✔ To find all the lists managed by a Majordomo system, enter **lists**.

✔ Majordomo also can keep files related to its lists. To find the names of the files for a particular list, enter **index name-of-list**.

✔ To tell Majordomo to send you one of the files by e-mail, enter **get name-of-list name-of-file**.

✔ To find out the rest of the goofy things Majordomo can do, enter **help**.

✔ If you need to contact the human manager of a Majordomo system because you can't get off a list you want to leave or otherwise have an insoluble problem, send a polite message to `owner-majordomo@hostname`. Remember that humans eat, sleep, and have real jobs, so getting an answer may take a day or two.

It's Not a Crock, It's Listproc

Listproc is not as widely used as LISTSERV or Majordomo, but Listproc is increasing in popularity because it is easier to install than LISTSERV, cheaper, and almost as powerful.

To subscribe to a Listproc mailing list, you send the message `subscribe listname yourname` to `listproc@some-computer`. For example, to subscribe to the `chickens` mailing list on `dummies.com`, you send the message `subscribe chickens George Washington` to `listproc@dummies.com` (assuming that you were named after the same person that the first President of the U.S. was named after).

To get off the mailing list, send the message `signoff` listname to the same address. You don't have to provide your name — the Listproc program should already know it!

Once you subscribe to the list, you can send messages to everyone on the list by addressing e-mail to `listname@some-computer` (for example, `chickens@dummies.com`).

To find out other things that Listproc can do, send the message *help* to `listproc@whatever`, where *whatever* is the name of the computer on the Listproc mailing list lives.

Sending Messages to Mailing Lists

Some lists encourage new subscribers to send in a message introducing themselves and saying briefly what their interests are. Others don't. So don't send anything until you have something to say.

After you watch the flow of messages on a list for a while, what we're talking about will become obvious.

Mailing list protocol

Some mailing lists have rules about who is allowed to send messages, meaning that just because you're on the list doesn't automatically mean that any messages you send will appear on the list. Some lists are *moderated:* Any message you send in gets sent to a human moderator, who decides what goes to the list and what doesn't. This policy may sound sort of fascist, but in practice, the arrangement makes a list about 50 times more interesting than it would be otherwise because a good moderator can filter out the boring and irrelevant messages and keep the list on track. Indeed, the people who complain the loudest about moderator censorship are usually the ones whose messages most deserve to be filtered out.

If your message to a moderated list doesn't appear, and you really don't know why, post a polite inquiry to the same list.

Another rule that sometimes causes trouble is that many lists allow messages to be sent only from people whose addresses appear on the list. This rule becomes a pain if your mailing address changes. Suppose that you get a well-organized, new mail administrator and that your official e-mail address changes from `jj@shamu.pol.bluesuede.org` to `John.Jay@bluesuede.org`, although your old address still works. You may find that some lists begin *bouncing* your messages (sending them back to you rather than to the list) because they don't understand that `John.Jay@bluesuede.org`, the name under which you now send messages, is the same as `jj@shamu.pol.bluesuede.org`, the name under which you originally subscribed to the list. Worse, LISTSERV doesn't let you take yourself off the list for the same reason. To resolve this mess, you have to write to the human list owners of any lists in which this problem arises and ask them to fix the problem by hand.

Mailing-list etiquette

The list of e-mail etiquette rules listed in Chapter 4 applies even more to messages sent to mailing lists because *far* more people will read the message you send. Here are some other rules you should follow:

✔ Be sure that your message is appropriate for the list.

✔ Don't send a message saying another message. A *spam* (a message sent to many lists without regard to their content), for example, is inappropriate. The sender probably knows and doesn't care. Even worse, the responses to the ad, the responses to the responses, and so on only create a flood of messages that wastes everyone's time and gives the sender even more publicity. Silence is the best answer.

✔ If you have to complain about an message, send e-mail to the postmaster at the sender's host.

✔ Make your subject line as meaningful as possible.

✔ Don't post a two-line follow-up that quotes an entire 100-line message. Edit down any quoted material in your message to the bare minimum needed to establish the context of your reply.

✔ Don't crosspost to multiple lists.

✔ Watch out for *trolls*. These are messages calculated to provoke a storm of replies. Not every stupid comment needs a response.

✔ Many lists periodically post a list of Frequently Asked Questions (or *FAQ*). Read the FAQ before asking a question.

The Gentle Art of Replying to Mailing-List Messages

Often you receive an interesting message from a list and want to send a response. But does your reply go *just* to the person who sent the original message, or does your reply go to the *entire list?* The answer depends mainly on how the list owner set up the software that handles the list. About half the list owners set the list up so that replies automatically go just to the person who sent the original message, on the theory that your response is likely to be of interest only to the original author. The other half set the list up so that replies go to the entire list, on the theory that the list is a running public discussion. In messages coming from the list, the mailing-list software automatically sets the `Reply-To:` header line to the address where replies should be sent.

Fortunately, you're in charge. When you start to create a reply, your mail program shows you the address to which you're replying. Look to see if your mail is going to the group or to an individual. If you don't like the address being used, change it. Check the `To:` and `Cc:` fields to make sure that you're sending your message where you want it to go.

While you're fixing the recipient's address, you may also want to change the `Subject:` line. After a few rounds of replies to replies to replies, the topic of discussion often wanders away from the original topic, and changing the subject to better describe what is really under discussion is a nice gesture.

Special Requests to Mailing Lists

You can ask list servers to do other cool things. Following are a few of them:

Finding old messages

Many mailing lists store their messages for future reference. To find out where these archives are kept, send the following message to the administrative address: `INDEX listname`

Who else is out there?

To get a list of (almost) all the people who subscribe to a list, send the following message to the administrative address:

Listproc servers	RECIPIENTS _listname_
LISTSERV servers	REVIEW _listname_ BY NAME F=MAIL
Majordomo servers	WHO _listname_

An increasing number of systems no longer reveal subcriber lists to deter people who steal the lists and send junk e-mail.

Keep me out of this

Listproc and LISTSERV mail servers won't give your name out by the preceding process if you send the following message to the administrative address:

Listproc servers	SET _listname_CONCEAL YES
LISTSERV servers	SET _listname_CONCEAL

To unconceal yourself, send the following message:

Listproc servers	SET _listname_CONCEAL NO
LISTSERV servers	SET _listname_NOCONCEAL

Listservers can do many more tricks. For a list of those tricks, send an e-mail message to `LISTSERV@UBVM.cc.buffalo.edu` with the following test as its body:

```
GET MAILSER CMD NETTRAIN F=MAIL
```

Starting Your Own Mailing List

You can start a simple manual list with nothing more than an e-mail program that supports distribution lists. When a message comes in, you just forward the message to the distribution list. That's all there is to it; you have a mailing list!

Before you start a new list, check to see if a list that meets your needs already exists.

You will soon tire of administering your list manually. Many local Internet providers offer mailing list support, sometimes for a small fee. Many universities also maintain mailing lists. If someone in your group has a university affiliation, she may be able to have a list maintained there.

Some Neat Mailing Lists

A large number of lists reside on the Internet — so many, in fact, that entire *books* have been written that just enumerate all the *lists*. To get you started, here are a bunch of lists we find interesting in addition to short descriptions of what they are.

Ghostletters

Join lively two-, three- or even all-way conversations between a host of historical and fictional characters! You choose a persona from fiction, history, or of your own making, and you may soon find yourself discussing any number of topics with personalities from literature, figures from your nation's past, animals, Hollywood celebrities, mythical creatures, or unique and unusual members of your own community. Only one person is permitted to take on any individual persona, so confirmation is required.

To subscribe, send the following message: `subscribe GHOSTLETTERS yourcharactersname` to `listserv@listserv.aol.com`.

For example, `subscribe GHOSTLETTERS King David`

Internet TourBus

A virtual tour of cyberspace that comes out every week or so. Entertaining even if you do not have full Internet access. Their motto is "Why Surf When You Can Ride The Bus?"

To subscribe, send the message `Send SUBSCRIBE TOURBUS Firstname Lastname` to `LISTSERV@LISTSERV.AOL.COM`.

PBS Previews

The weekly online newsletter of the U.S. Public Broadcasting Service.

To subscribe, send the message `sub web-update` to `www@pbs.org`.

E-Zines

This Internet Web site has a long list of electronic magazines or *e-zines* that are delivered via e-mail. You can subscribe to most of them using only e-mail as well.

`http://www.merak.com/~tkuipers/elists/elists.htm`

Kid's Time Magazine

The Kid's Time Magazine is run by two grade school students in Hawaii. You can go to their Web page and select what parts you want to read, or you can get the whole magazine by e-mail. Check them out at: `http://www.primenet.com/ ~hawaii/` or send e-mail to `hawaii@primenet.com` and tell them you want to subscribe.

Dilbert Newsletter

A sporadic newsletter written by Scott Adams, author of the most authorative source of information on the computer industry, the comic strip `Dilbert`. `listproc@internex.net`.

To subscribe, send the message `subscribe Dilbert_list yourfirstname yourlastname` to `listproc@internex.net`.

Internet-vet Newsletter

Internet-vet Newsletter seeks to guide you in making good health care decisions for your pets. People send in questions and a handful of vets take turns answering about three or four of them each time. Because they can't see the animal, and what they get from folks in e-mail isn't always the whole story, they cannot provide diagnoses or tell you how to treat a given problem. Comes out about once a week.

To subscribe, send a message with `subscribe internet-vet` in the subject line to `internet-vet-request@netcom.com`.

E-mail your questions to `internet-vet@netcom.com`.

Archives are available at `http://www.zmall.com/pet_talk/pet-faqs/ivc/`.

net-happenings-digest mailing list

A great way to keep up with what is happening on the Internet between editions of *The Internet For Dummies*. To subscribe, send the message

```
subscribe net-happenings firstname lastname
subscribe net-happenings-digest yourfirstname yourlastname
```

to `majordomo@lists.internic.net`.

This Just In

This Just In is a free, weekly e-mail newsletter by Randy Cassingham that summarizes recent bizarre-but-true news stories from the nation's press, punctuated by Cassingham's ironic comments.

To subscribe, send the message `subscribe this-just-in` to `listserv@netcom.com`.

U.S. Government Sales

GovSales is a free, public list for government sales and auction announcements from FinanceNet. FinanceNet, established at V.P. Al Gore's National Performance Review, is a "one-stop-shop" for information on the sale of all manner of public assets from real property and loans to planes, boats, cars, jewelry, and just about anything that any government (federal, state, local, or international) will be offering for sale to the general public electronically.

You can subscribe to their free public list for GovSales and begin to automatically receive many of these sales and auction announcements and notices by direct e-mail.

To subscribe, send the message `subscribe govsales firstname lastname` to: `listproc@financenet.gov`.

Pen Pals

Finally, we did promise you pen pals at the beginning of this chapter. Here is a Web site where you can register and be matched up with a pen pal somewhere else in the world. Just for general chatting and whatnot.

Unfortunately, you need Internet access and a Web browser to use this site. But once you have your e-pal's address, you can correspond using only e-mail.

```
http://www.comenius.com/keypal/index.html
```

More, More, More Mailing Lists

Thousands of mailing lists exist. Keeping score is difficult. In the "Part of Tens" later in this book, we give you some more to try. We included a disk full of mailing lists in our book, *Internet Secrets* (IDG Books Worldwide, 1995). The disk can be read by DOS, Windows, and any Macintosh that can read a PC disk — most can these days.

You can find out if a LISTSERV list has "XYZ" in its name or title by sending the following message to any LISTSERV server: LIST GLOBAL/XYZ

The LISTSERV server sends you e-mail with all the matches. If you leave out the /XYZ, you will get back a message containing all known LISTSERV mailing lists. That's one loooooong list.

The USENET group news.lists also has an extensive monthly list of mailing lists. If you get USENET news, you can probably find this list there. Or you can get the list via mail by sending the following cryptic message to mail-server@rtfm.mit.edu:

```
send USENET/news.lists/P_A_M_L,_P_1_21
send USENET/news.lists/P_A_M_L,_P_2_21
```

(That last weird part stands for *p*ublicly *a*ccessible *m*ailing *l*ists, Part 1 of 21, and so on. If you like what you see, you can get the rest of the parts in the same way.) FTP users can FTP the list from rtfm.mit.edu, where it's in the directory pub/USENET/news.lists under the same names, or read it in USENET, where it's posted monthly to the newsgroup news.lists. The lists are growing fast, so by the time you read this book, you may find more than 21 parts.

Stephanie da Silva maintains and updates monthly a large directory of publicly available mailing lists. This directory is the most complete list of lists we know. She posts her lists to the USENET group `news.lists`. The list is also available at `http://www.neosoft.com/internet/paml`.

Another good place to look if you have Web access is `http://www.tile.net`, where you can search a complete listing of all LISTSERV discussion groups.

Chapter 22

E-Mail Security

*W*e are nice people. We're sure that you, having the discernment to buy this book, are a nice person. We bet that most of your friends are nice people, too. Nice people just don't read mail that is not intended for them.

But not everyone has such scruples. Some people are just nosy busybodies. Others believe what they are doing is *sooo* important that they *need* to read your e-mail — as, for example, in the following situations:

✔ Your boss may believe that she has a right to know what the company's computers are being used for, so she monitors everyone's e-mail. Depending on where you work, she may actually have a legal right to do this.

✔ The United States government, which just wants to protect you from terrorists, drug dealers, and child pornographers, believes so strongly that its agents must read your mail that it has pressured e-mail software suppliers not to provide security features.

✔ Other governments, which just want to help their local corporations keep up on the competition, are using their intelligence agencies, built up during the Cold War, to monitor commercial communications.

Many people, ourselves included, find that the general lack of security for e-mail is a real threat to personal privacy. We would like all mail users to have the option of sending their e-mail messages in a coded form that no one but the intended recipient can read — a process called *encryption*.

Phil Zimmermann, an Internet folk hero who invented a popular encryption program called *PGP* — which we discuss in the next chapter — offers the following neat analogy to emphasize the e-mail users' need for encryption:

Perhaps you think your e-mail is legitimate enough that encryption is unwarranted. If you really are a law-abiding citizen with nothing to hide, why don't you always send your paper mail on postcards? . . . Are you trying to hide something? You must be a subversive or a drug dealer if you hide your mail inside envelopes. Or maybe a paranoid nut. Do law-abiding citizens have any need to encrypt their e-mail?

A major reason for the lack of Internet and e-mail security has been the United States government's strong opposition to the widespread commercial availability of secure computer systems. For much of this century, the U.S. intelligence community has used intercepted communications as a major source of intelligence on foreign and domestic activities considered hostile and does not want to give up that strategic advantage.

Other governments like to eavesdrop, too, of course, but the United States is the world's largest source of computer systems, and our government uses its laws to limit the export of secure computer systems. U.S. computer manufacturers avoid export hassles by keeping their products cryptographically inoffensive. As a result, the components on which the Internet is built are full of security holes.

When e-mail was a toy for computer geeks, its lack of privacy may not have mattered. With e-mail poised to become a nearly universal means of communication in the 21st century, privacy matters now. No perfect solutions to this problem are out there yet, but the following sections described some of the best options you have for now.

How Can Anyone Even See My Mail?

You may wonder how all those supposed snoops out there can get their dirty hands on your e-mail. Unfortunately, accessing e-mail messages is not that hard to do. As your e-mail message makes its way to its destination, that message passes through many different computers. In most of these computers, your message is stored for only the briefest moment while the computer decides what to do with it. Someone who knows what she's doing and has access to the inner software sanctum of these wayside computers, however, can install a special program called a *packet sniffer*. This program can intercept all the messages that pass through that computer or, if so instructed, can nose out only those messages with *your* name in the address.

In fact, e-mail is especially vulnerable to snooping. Electronic eavesdroppers can program computers to filter, sort, and file away intercepted messages. Wiretapping a phone call is a much more labor intensive task — a human ultimately must listen to each conversation.

Unless you encrypt your e-mail, anyone who intercepts your message can read it as easily as you can. These days, nothing is safe without precautions.

Should I give out my credit card number over e-mail?

Two different views on this practice prevail.

One camp says that many other ways are available for crooks to steal credit card numbers, so why worry about sending yours over the Net? Crooks can fish discarded paper receipts out of dumpsters much more easily than they can intercept e-mail messages.

The other camp counters that computer use enables fraud to occur on a much more massive scale than we have seen in the past. The best technology available, therefore, should be used to make cyberspace as safe as it can be, and everyone should insist on secure links before using e-mail or the Internet for credit card and other financial transactions.

Encryption

Well, that's life in the '90s. So what is this encryption stuff, anyway? If you ever found a secret decoder ring as a prize in a candy box or worked a cryptoquote puzzle in the newspaper, you have an idea of how encryption works.

Roughly speaking, each letter in your message is replaced by a different letter based on some predetermined rule. The secret decoder ring, for example, may replace all A's with C's, all B's with D's, and so on. The person on the other end reverses the process to read the message.

Encryptors used for e-mail, however, employ much more complicated rules. Exactly how these rules work is determined by a string of *bits* — ones and zeros — in the computer. This string is called a *key*. If you and the person with whom you're corresponding both have the same key, you can communicate with one another. If you keep your shared key secret from everyone else, no one but the two of you can read your mail. Those nasty folks using the sniffer to try to read your e-mail see only nonsense, such as the following lines of code:

```
I9UOKi724BTVqbTlcc+VfolfWv/szrYO+KrUNEnq1hyAVkJRpbhY46v
yU1aCMKL4C/QCXA3OTZRhYM1yJi24csvEZwaMkAKRcRk5QwcPRAAR
```

People who work with codes call these scrambled nonsense letters *ciphertext*. The original message is called *plaintext*. The rules used for scrambling the letters is called the *encryption algorithm* or just the *cipher*.

My key is bigger than your key

For the most part, you don't need to know how encryptors work. One fact about an encryptor, however, does affect you: how many bits are in the keys it uses. If an encryptor is well-designed, the only way you can crack a message encrypted by it is to try all the possible keys until you find the right one. If the encryptor's key length is long enough — 128 bits is sufficient — trying all the keys that may exist is physically impossible. If the key length is shorter, security depends on how big the cracker's computer is and how short your key is. Key length is a major factor that the U.S. government considers in deciding whether you may export software that uses encryption.

Table 22-1 lists key length, products that use keys of that size, and how strong each key is in terms of its security.

Table 22-1	Key Lengths	
Size	*Where Used*	*How Strong*
128 bits	PGP, Netscape Navigator 2.0 (U.S. version)	Secure for the foreseeable future.
80 Bits	Clipper, Tessara	Secure for the next twenty years at least.
64 bit	Lotus Notes, Domestic version	Secure against all but the most powerful opponent.
56 bits	DES	Can be broken with moderate resources.
40 bits	Export versions of Netscape Navigator	Can be broken with a few high-end PCs.

The keys to the kingdom — public key cryptography

You may be thinking, "I keep losing the keys to my car. How am I going to keep track of all the e-mail keys I need to talk to my friends? I need a key for each person I want to talk to. That can be a *lot* of keys. And how do I have a private conversation with someone I have never met? Keeping all those keys secret isn't easy either."

Some people think they have a solution to this messy key management problem — one called *public key cryptography*.

Invented in the mid-1970s, public key cryptography simplifies encrypted communication. Public key cryptography gives you *two* keys, one that you keep secret (your *private* or secret key) and another that you can give to everyone (your *public* key). Here's how the system works:

1. **For two people (say, John and Tonia) to communicate by using encrypted e-mail, each must first have the other's public key in the computer.**

2. **John encodes messages to Tonia by using Tonia's public key.**

3. **Tonia decodes John's messages by using her secret key.**

4. **Tonia encodes her reply to John by using John's public key.**

5. **John decodes Tonia's reply by using his secret key.**

You use public keys to encode messages; you use secret keys to decode them. The only secret key you ever need is your own. You never need to and never should give anyone else your secret key.

The following is Arnold's public key: set of code represents what one public key may look like:

```
—BEGIN PGP PUBLIC KEY BLOCK—
Version: 2.6.2

mQCPAy9MyROAAAEEANejhFb64tLhD1xa/kOmLHRPuXNW2vVvja0luCX1Ntcu7EWA
K8PnmWqruEOWflkBA42g6iwta9B/Bm8J0Yfkk6T7CrnAeBN/IuepQa4uJXXk7AqO
whO3vF8TzPk6STIJAPTQ9CWQ+6MHnwmDk9RzDwxtnS8dMKGXiWtruC2sMYShABEB
AAG0KOFybm9sZCBHLiBSZWluaG9sZCA8cmVpbmhvbGRAd29ybGQuc3RkLmNvbVT6J
AJUDBRAwwLyzkGCWpQlZ7KkBARKaBADCggEzWe2tLvHn9/QkSfPnTMJhXiSDzz6V
K2Xwzyo/TE1V632ZNQ6yQ9IMRObQAs95LNwwd4iGPoeZ3OCqNvqaGkU4fJjz6gW9
v/szgwOfINa91sRtfOJWvKyBiq9J9JC/q9mA6T7mmhDsoWXJZ6/h49AeNF2KCszE
LyybOtAgAokA1QMFEC925FzVMiHPX2O1uQEBxCMD/33cCtdo6yGPWdCddZlx+aBh
tTrat81WwYc2QfIdSphryVeP5nK95YOmsR+94ESgKEzpJQGIYJsK8ZLsu7AaQrYE
CNHkQhe6EkW/Oy4t4X36Yx3qufwKmP4jc5WCliT6o4T+RpCidbrGm3mw91oWJexV
UBp4apxK/rRPaZX7AgoriQCVAwUQLOzKK2truC2sMYShAQELTAQAyOAbV87SYPAJ
tzm3iJwBkcxDoBE/VOdY29H9ZgKSGnebVSySqKpeo5rJq+XFr1sDZ7cZyYacOpaR
FcCFE7sAZoy7bLTMBu6KbhX5YndWqRL+uT8xkNscugPi6O9RTo71roMeA847TuQ7
fl9tYFB25HpDWeKh+CR2Gh3mf4LnvCc=
=M7fR
—END PGP PUBLIC KEY BLOCK—
```

Ugly, huh? Fortunately programs such as PGP enable you to keep all your friends' public keys in a special file called a _key ring_ so that you never need to look at this stuff. In addition, a number of key servers exist around the world — many accessible by using only e-mail — where you can look for a friend's public key and list your own.

Three popular programs use public key cryptography to protect e-mail: PGP, Netscape Navigator 2.0, and Lotus Notes. The cryptography features of Netscape Navigator 2.0 and Lotus Notes are described later in this chapter. PGP is described in Chapter 23.

Sign on the Dotted Line

Public key cryptography can be used for more than just keeping information secret; it can also be used to add to your e-mail messages an electronic signature that cannot be forged — at least in theory. The same technique that creates the electronic signature can tell you whether a signed document that you receive is complete and unaltered. This signature and message verification process is called *authentication*.

Authentication is really neat and may well be the first mass-market application of modern cryptography. You may not want to be the first person on your block to use it, however. See the sidebar "Are you sure you want an electronic signature?"

How do they do that?

Here's how authentication works: The electronic version of your document is passed through something called a *hashing function*, a little computer program that produces a string of bits that depend on all the information in the documents. A simple way to perform this hashing is to break your document's binary representation into pieces and then add up all those pieces as though they were numbers. Actual *hash algorithms* used for signing documents throw in some cryptographic magic that makes difficult predicting how a given change in the document may affect the hash. (This technique keeps bad guys from altering a document in such a way that its hash value remains unchanged — for example, in an attempt to change the sale price in a contract.)

The hash bits are then encrypted with the signer's secret key, and the resulting signature field is transmitted along with the document. The recipient can then hash the received document, decrypt the signature field, and compare the two; if both hashes match, the recipient can be sure that the sender whose name appears on the document actually sent it. The recipient can also be sure that the document she received is exactly what was sent.

Gimme that key

This theory, however, has two holes. First, it assumes that the sender's private key has not been stolen. The sender must protect her private key at all times. Suppose that she was a bit sloppy one time. How do you prove that her key was not compromised? Fortunately, U.S. law, as we understand it (lawyers we ain't), takes a broad view as to what constitutes a valid signature, so electronic signatures are likely to remain widely accepted in commercial practice.

The second hole is that this concept assumes that the recipient has a valid copy of the sender's public key. If a criminal learns someone's private key or sneaks in an ersatz public key, she can forge an apparently valid signature. This problem is not unique to digital signatures; managing keys is the biggest problem in all forms of practical cryptography.

One solution is to use *central key-distribution agents* who issue keys to the general public that were signed by the agent, as proposed as part of an international standard called X.509. Some observers have criticized these agents as being unwieldy and potentially dangerous. The PGP people use a different method, known as *a web of trust*. In the latter method, you sign your friends' signatures; they sign yours; their friends sign *their* signatures; and so on. Eventually, enough of these signature chains exist that you can find someone you know who has signed the signature of someone else who has signed the signature of the stranger with whom you need to establish signature trust. This concept somewhat resembles the letters of introduction of olden days.

How secure is public key cryptography?

Subject to the following several big *ifs,* public key cryptography is quite secure:

- ✔ If the program you use is carefully written. Only careful scrutiny by cryptographic experts over an extended time, however, can determine just how carefully such a program is written. In the fall of 1995, for example, errors in the encryption code then used by Netscape enabled two graduate students, Ian Goldberg and David Wagner, to discover ways to break Netscape's code. Fortunately, those errors have now been fixed, and we hope this kind of public review catches other errors quickly.

- ✔ If your key is long enough. (See the following section.)

- ✔ If no breakthroughs occur in the mathematical knowledge needed to crack public keys. (Progress to date has been slow but steady.)

- ✔ If you use it correctly and can ensure security for the computers that encrypt and decrypt your messages.

Although public key technology is strong now, you cannot rely on the current technology to keep your messages secret forever.

Are you sure you want an electronic signature?

Years ago, while we were visiting Japan, our hosts gave us a *chop*: a carved wooden stamp with our name translated into Japanese kanji characters (see the following figure). They offered to take us to an office in Tokyo where we could register our chop. For a few yen, we could get a nicely calligraphed certificate that we could frame. The only problem was that the chop would then become "official," and anyone who stole it could sign our name in a legally binding way. We declined.

An electronic signature is much like a chop, with one big difference: You are likely to notice if your chop is stolen; on the other hand, your private key and its enabling pass phrase can be copied off your computer in several ways, and you may never learn about the theft until it is too late.

Try a simple experiment. With a pen, write "*Internet E-mail For Dummies* Private-Key Awareness Test" on a blank 3½-inch floppy disk. Now try for a week to keep the disk under your total personal control. Keep it in your pocket during the day; put it under your pillow at night; don't forget to take it into the shower with you. If you do need to put it down, make sure that you hide it well or lock it up. At the end of the week, think about who could possibly have had access to it while you weren't watching. Then ask yourself, "Do I want to add to my life a physical object that requires this kind of attention as long as I live?"

Some public-key schemes encrypt the private key by using a *pass phrase*. This pass phrase makes theft more difficult but not difficult enough that you can be careless with your key disk. So think carefully before issuing a public electronic signature. Unless you really need one, you may want to wait until better technology is available — for example, secure PCMCIA key cards. If you can't resist or if your work requires you to have an electronic signature, be prepared to protect it as one of your most important possessions.

How big should my public key be?

If you use PGP for your public key encryption, you are asked in the beginning how big you want your public key to be. We recommend that you select the 1,024-bit option.

Netscape 2.0 and Lotus notes, however, currently limit you to 512 bits because of United States export restrictions. Is this big enough? Not if you are worried about someone with the resources of a large government or major corporation behind them reading your mail.

Your public key is formed by multiplying together two *prime numbers* — numbers that cannot be divided evenly by any other number. The numbers 3, 5,

13, and 127, for example, are prime numbers, but 4, 15, and 49 are not. Your secret key is the *pair of prime numbers*, each typically 75 to 150 digits long, that your program uses in making up the public key.

Public key cryptography works because mathematicians have a difficult time determining the two primes that produce the public key if the key is big enough. If, for example, we ask you for the product of 1,823 times 2,617, you can probably figure out the answer, 4,770,791, even without a calculator. If, on the other hand, we ask you to find the two numbers that you need to multiply together to get 51,978,374,799,051, you are almost certain to have a hard time calculating the answer without a computer. And the bigger products used in public key cryptography are *very* hard to crack even *with* a computer.

As for what's big enough . . .

- ✔ RSA Data Security, Inc., the company that owns the patents on this type of public key cryptography recommends that your public key be at least this long for varying lengths of security:
  - For short-term security, 768 bits.
  - For medium-term security, 1,024 bits.
  - For long-term security, 2,048 bits.
- ✔ Any 512-bit keys, the largest the United States currently allows in software for export, can be broken, albeit with considerable effort.
- ✔ Most PGP users choose at least 1,024-bit keys.

Public Key Encryption Programs

Three major public key encryption programs are available today. *PGP*, which stands for *Pretty Good Privacy*, is the strongest, most widely available worldwide, and the most notorious. We devote the following chapter to a discussion of PGP. The two others currently in use, Netscape Navigator 2.0 and Lotus Notes, come in two versions, one for use only in the United States and Canada and one for use in the rest of the world.

Why are there domestic and international versions of software?

Using encryption within the United States is not illegal — at least not yet. What *is* illegal is exporting encryption software from the United States without a license. The U.S. State Department grants export licenses only to encryption software that is relatively weak. Usually, this means that the maximum key sizes allowed are 40 bits for conventional encryption and 512 bits for RSA encryption.

This also means that software vendors who want to sell in the United States any product with credible strength must make two versions, one for sale and use in the North America and one for overseas sales.

Both 40-bit session keys and 512-bit RSA keys can be broken by an organization with enough computers. A recently reported crack of the type of 40-bit code that Lotus Release 3 and Netscape use took just eight days on a single Integrated Computing Engines graphics computer, at an estimated cost of less than $600.

In Netscape Navigator, which uses 128-bit session keys, the export version reveals all but 40 bits of the session key in the message header. The most recent version of Lotus Notes, Release 4, which uses 64-bit session keys, also transmits all but 40 bits of each session key in its export version, but with a twist. The transmitted key bits are first encoded in a special way known only to the U.S. government. Thus the export version of Lotus Notes Release 4 is as secure as the North American version — except against the U.S. government.

Both Netscape Navigator and Lotus Notes use 512-bit RSA keys in all versions (as far as we know). In 1994, a large group of computer users working over the Internet for the better part of a year succeeded in breaking a 429-bit RSA public key presented as a challenge in a 1977 *Scientific American* article. (The secret message turned out to be "squeamish ossifrage.") The same group seems about ready to try breaking a 512-bit key. This accomplishment strongly suggests that a very large organization willing to devote a sufficient resources could almost certainly break a 512-bit key.

PGP also comes in domestic and international versions, but in its case, the two versions are necessary because of patent problems, not allowable key sizes. Both versions use 128-bit session keys and allow RSA keys up to 2,048 bits in length. Both are equally strong. The United States government does not approve of the export of PGP, and, for a while, was considering prosecuting Phil Zimmermann when someone (not Phil) did export it.

Netscape Navigator 2.0

Netscape Navigator 2.0, described in Chapter 10, supports encrypted e-mail through a version of public key technology called *SSL*.

Netscape Navigator shows a key icon on the bottom left of the screen. If the key is depicted as broken, the connection is not secure.

Only the version of Netscape Navigator sold in North America offers full security. The export and free versions have been deliberately weakened to comply with U.S. export regulations. Even the fully secure version is believed less secure than PGP.

To use Netscape Navigator 2.0 for encrypted e-mail, you first must obtain your public and secret key certificate from a central key vendor. The only company authorized so far to sell key certificates is VeriSign, Inc., 2593 Coast Avenue, Mountain View, CA 94043. You can get more information about VeriSign by sending e-mail to info@verisign.com or by visiting the company's Web site at http://www.verisign.com.

VeriSign calls the key certificates "Internet Driver Licenses." They offer these licenses at the following four levels:

- *CLASS 1.* Low level of assurance used for secure e-mail and casual browsing. Noncommercial and evaluation versions are offered for free, with a VeriSign-supported commercial version for $6 per year.

- *CLASS 2.* Next level of assurance for a higher degree of trust and security. Used for access to advanced Web sites. Cost is $12 for one year.

- *CLASS 3.* A higher level of assurance used for big ticket purchases and inter-company communications. Cost is $24 for one year.

- *CLASS 4.* A maximum level of identity assurance for high-end financial transactions and trades. Pricing is application-specific.

The encrypted e-mail technology in Netscape Navigator 2.0 is still very new and still being studied by cryptographic experts, but the full-strength version may well offer easy-to-use encrypted e-mail with enough security for most users.

Lotus Notes

Lotus Notes is a powerful distributed database system designed to support company-wide communication and collaboration. Notes included secure e-mail from the beginning. At the time it was first introduced, in late 1989, Notes was among the major first software products to use public key technology.

For export, the latest version of Lotus Notes, Release 4, uses a technique Lotus calls *differential workfactor cryptography*. This new method allows the international edition of Notes to use an encryption key equal in strength to the 64-bit key in the North American Edition, except against the U.S. government.

Here is how differential workfactor cryptography works: Whenever the international edition of Release 4 generates an RSA encrypted 64-bit session key, Notes creates from the key a *workfactor reduction field*. This workfactor reduction field is then separately encrypted using a key known only to the U.S. government. This process gives the U.S. government exclusive access to 24 of the 64 key bits. Thus the U.S. government considers Release 4 to have only a 40-bit key length, and Notes Release 4 is therefore exportable under current U.S. policy.

For anyone other than the U.S. government to access a Notes-encrypted message, that person or organization would need to crack the full 64-bit key, which is 24 million times harder than cracking a 40-bit key. Such a task is just at the edge of feasibility, even for a large country's signal intelligence agency.

The North American edition of Release 4, when used in the United States and Canada, makes a full 64-bit encryption without providing the workfactor reduction field. The two editions of Notes can exchange encrypted data and e-mail with each other.

In some ways, Lotus' differential workfactor cryptography solution to the export problem is worse than *key escrow* (see the section "What Is Key Escrow?" later in this chapter) because no external mechanism exists to make sure that U.S. intelligence agencies have to actually obtain a court order before reading your mail. Lotus seems to recognize that its approach is only a temporary compromise. Ray Ozzie, president of Iris Associates, the developer of Lotus Notes said:

> We are very pleased to have arrived at a pragmatic short-term solution that addresses our international customers' requests for greater security within Notes. However, we continue to argue vigorously that, due to clear and present threats to our global information systems, all interests would be well-served by widespread use of strong, high-grade cryptography. Without substantial rethinking of U.S. cryptography policy, particularly as it pertains to export controls, our global and national economic security is at risk.

Of course, a temporary compromise often ends up being what we live with forever. We just need to wait and see what happens.

Never Talk about Religion or Politics

To avoid discussions of religion or politics is always a good policy in polite society. Unfortunately, the politics of e-mail security may well affect what kind of encryption products you can get and how private your e-mail may be in the future. Law enforcement agencies around the world are appalled at wide-spread public use of encryption and are trying their best to control it. The following controls, for example, are among those employed in the United States and elsewhere:

- ✔ Export of strong cryptographic software is illegal in the United States.

- ✔ The United States is pressuring software manufacturers to adopt encryption standards that include mandatory key escrow so that the government can get at your secret keys.

- The European Union is considering restrictions on cryptography that include mandatory key escrow.
- France and Russia have banned cryptography outright.
- Many other countries are considering such a ban.

What is key escrow?

Key escrow is a new class of encryption technologies in which a master key that can read all your messages is split into two pieces and the pieces are stored for safekeeping with two different *escrow agents* — special organizations that promise not to give out your key information without proper authorization. This type of technology appeals primarily to the following types of individuals:

- Those who run large organizations and who fear an employee may abscond with the keys needed to decode vital data.
- Representatives of law-enforcement and intelligence agencies who need to read the messages of people considered a threat to society.

The U.S. government's first attempt to push key escrow, the *Clipper chip,* never caught on. Clipper was an attempt to get everyone to use special encryption hardware, developed by the National Security Agency, that had built-in key escrow. The U.S. government is now proposing a new standard called *software key escrow.* Under the new standard, e-mail software vendors can get approval for encryption software under the following circumstances:

- The software automatically sends copies of your keys to approved key escrow agents.
- The encryptor is designed so that you cannot defeat the escrow feature by some clever trick.
- The encryption uses keys no longer than 64 bits so that the government can still crack it, though with some difficulty.

The European Union is working on a software key escrow standard of its own.

Some people consider software key escrow to be a reasonable compromise that may finally allow encryption technology to see widespread use. Civil-liberties groups and many people on the Internet, however, are horrified by the idea of key escrow, likening it to the police demanding a key to your home to keep in case they ever need to search it.

The key escrow battle is far from over. Stay tuned.

But what about the Fourth Amendment to the Constitution of the United States?

The Fourth Amendment reads in its entirety:

"The right of the people to be secure in their persons, houses, papers, and effects, against unreasonable searches and seizures, shall not be violated, and no warrants shall issue, but upon probable cause, supported by oath or affirmation, and particularly describing the place to be searched, and the persons or things to be seized."

Can you find where it says that you must send your mail in a form that the government can read? We can't either.

What can happen if I don't use encryption?

A stolen customer list could cost you sales. A leaked positive HIV test could ruin a person's life. An investigative reporter's field notes on the Cali drug cartel could get her killed. The more severe the consequences of data compromise, the more carefully the data needs to be protected.

In some cases, the law requires you to protect information. A publicly traded company, for example, had better not allow any outsider to see its quarterly financial results before these results are made public. A psychiatrist may be liable if she fails to protect her clients' treatment records. Europe has especially strict data-privacy laws. In the United Kingdom, for example, the Data Protection Act of 1984 provides penalties for anyone who stores personal information on any computer and fails to take reasonable measures to prevent disclosure of that information.

If you have government-classified information to communicate, the National Security Agency or your local equivalent tells you what to do about it. You had better listen to them — not to us.

Top Ten E-Mail Security Tips

Here are ten tips on how to how to better protect your e-mail. For more ideas, see the section "Common Sense and Cryptography" in *Internet Secrets* (IDG Books Worldwide, Inc.).

- ✔ Always use randomly selected keys, passwords, and pass phrases. Never use single dictionary words or your favorite literary quotes.
- ✔ Never perform encryption, decryption, or key generation on a multiuser computer or on a computer connected to a network.

✔ Don't connect your sensitive internal network to the Internet without a firewall.

✔ The best way to perform encryption, decryption, or key generation is on a battery-powered laptop with no cables plugged in.

✔ Floppy disks, tapes, and hard disks that contain sensitive information are very difficult to erase completely. Follow the disposal guidelines listed in the sidebar in the preceding section.

✔ Spend ten times more money, time, and effort on physical security than you do on encryption.

✔ Take security seriously, day in and day out. Don't be careless and don't be cute.

✔ Don't print sensitive e-mail messages on remote laser printers.

✔ Remember that copies of your e-mail probably exist on backup tapes at both the sender's and the receiver's computers.

✔ Be careful not to violate U.S. export laws if you live in the United States (or you are a U.S. citizen who plans on coming home).

What about anonymous remailers?

Several sites on the Internet offer anonymous remailing services. If you are unwilling to reveal your true identity when sending mail or posting news, you can send your message to one of these sites. The sites strip off all identifying information in your message's header and then repost the message with a randomly assigned pseudonym. Some sites enable recipients to use that same pseudonym in replying to you.

How safe are these services? Here's what the one in Finland, anon.penet.fi, writes about its service:

> Short of having everyone run a public-key crypto system such as PGP, there is no way to protect users from malicious administrators. You have to trust my personal integrity. Worse, you have to trust the administrators on every mail-routing machine on the way, as the message only becomes anonymous once it reaches my machine. Malicious

sysadmins and crackers could spy on SMTP mail channels, sendmail queues, and mail logs. But as there are more than 3,000 messages being anonymized every day, you have to be pretty perverted to scan everything.

Let's get real. Electronic intelligence services are omnivorous. They specialize in collecting information that can be used years later. They keep warehouses full of tapes of intercepted traffic, in the hope that some snippet will come in handy someday. With so many messages from people letting their electronic hair down, remailers are a juicy target. You can bet that more than one foreign security agency must be collecting all the e-mail going to and coming from every remailer that it can tap, including the mail before it becomes anonymous. One good lead to someone who can be blackmailed 10 years from now would be worth the effort. Sorry, but that's the world we live in.

Chapter 23

Pretty Good Privacy (PGP)

● ●

In This Chapter

▶ Getting a copy of PGP

▶ Creating a good secret pass phrase

▶ Making your public and secret keys

▶ Encrypting and decrypting messages

▶ Signing messages

● ●

*P*GP, which stands for *Pretty Good Privacy*, is a freeware encryption program with a very loyal following. The program was first written by Phil Zimmermann and released in 1991. It is now being improved by a team of programmers working worldwide and coordinating their work over the Internet. Here are some thing you should know about PGP:

- ✔ PGP is free only for noncommercial use.

- ✔ A commercial version of PGP is available in North America from Viacrypt Corp.

- ✔ Most experts consider PGP very secure if used correctly.

- ✔ PGP enables you to make your own public and secret key pairs.

- ✔ PGP public keys are distributed and certified via an informal network called "the web of trust," which is kind of like the letters of introduction popular in the pre-electronic era.

- ✔ For three years, Philip Zimmermann, the developer of PGP, was threatened with federal prosecution in the United States for his actions. Charges were finally dropped in January 1996.

See Chapter 22 in this book and the sections "Commonsense and Cryptography" and "Privacy on the Net" in *Internet Secrets* (IDG Books Worldwide, Inc.), for more on the Philip Zimmermann story.

Software that protects your messages by using encryption is more difficult to use than regular e-mail software, and the current version of PGP, PGP 2.6.2, is not as easy to use as it could be. Unfortunately, however, for many e-mail users who want real security, PGP is the only game in town.

PGP's most obvious defect is that it is not well integrated with your e-mail program. A variety of freeware and shareware PGP add-on programs out there attempt to fix this problem. None that we know about work all that well. The developers of PGP are aware of the problem and are due to release a new version, PGP 3.0, that fixes many usability problems.

In this chapter, we describe how to use the basic command line version of PGP that runs on a PC under MS-DOS and, of course, in a DOS window under Microsoft Windows 3.1 and Windows 95. We also describe how to use MacPGP2.6.2, which runs on almost any Apple Macintosh computer.

Getting Ready to Use PGP

Setting up PGP is more complicated than setting up most application programs. Before you can start using PGP, you must take the following steps:

1. **Get a current version of PGP that works on your computer.**
2. **Unpack and install PGP on your computer.**
3. **Make up a good secret pass phrase.**
4. **Create your own public and private keys.**
5. **Validate your public key.**
6. **Give copies of public key to your friends.**
7. **Get copies of your friends' public keys.**

Each of these steps takes some effort to get right. Make yourself comfortable and we'll go through them one at a time.

Encryption technology is beset by legal issues, both in the United States and in many — if not most — foreign countries. We believe that you have a legal right to use PGP in the United States, but we are not lawyers and cannot give legal advice. We suggest that you consult a lawyer if you have legal questions. But be aware that lawyers who are knowledgeable in this field are few and far between.

Getting a current version of PGP that works on your computer

How you can legally obtain a copy of PGP and which version to get depends on who and where you are. Before you blame the complexity of what you are about to read on the Byzantine minds of the developers of PGP, realize that this system is probably the best they could come up with, given U.S. export laws and the maze of patents and copyrights that apply to PGP.

You are a U.S. citizen currently living in the United States

If you are a U.S. citizen or permanent resident and live in the United States right now, you have the following three choices for obtaining PGP:

- ✔ Buy the commercial version of PGP from Viacrypt, 9033 N. 24th Avenue, Suite 7, Phoenix, AZ 85021. Send them e-mail at `viacrypt@acm.org` for more information.

- ✔ Get a copy from a friend who has PGP. As far as we can determine, this is perfectly legal if your friend knows you are a U.S. citizen. You may want to get a copy of the Immigration and Naturalization Service's Form I-9 to find out what the INS considers valid proof of citizenship.

- ✔ Download a copy of the PGP program over the Internet. This option is the one most people use. In the rest of this section, we tell you how.

Sites that distribute PGP take special precautions to verify that you live in the United States and agree to obey U.S. export restrictions. These sites also ask you to acknowledge a license from RSA Data Security, Inc., which holds many of the patents on Public Key Cryptography used in PGP.

The primary North American distribution site for PGP is the Massachusetts Institute of Technology (MIT) in Cambridge, MA. If you have Netscape Navigator or another World Wide Web browser, perhaps the easiest way to get PGP is to go to the MIT PGP Web page at the following location:

```
http://web.mit.edu/network/pgp.html
```

You are asked to answer the following four questions:

1. Are you a citizen or national of the United States or a person who has been lawfully admitted for permanent residence in the United States?

2. Do you agree not to export PGP 2.6.2, or RSAREF to the extent incorporated therein, in violation of the export control laws of the United States of America as implemented by the United States Department of State Office of Defense Trade Controls?

3. Do you agree to the terms and conditions of the RSAREF license (in /pub/ PGP/rsalicen.txt)?

4. Will you use PGP 2.6.2 solely for noncommercial purposes?

If you said "yes" to all the above, if MIT can figure out from your Internet address that you are in the United States, and if you started at the right time, you can down load PGP or MacPGP without much fuss.

Yes, that's right, we said "started at the right time." To make sure that you can get PGP only by going through the listed procedure, MIT changes the name of the directory where the PGP software is kept every 30 minutes. The name changes at the hour and on the half-hour. If you don't get everything you need before the name change, you must start over. So a good idea is to begin this little treasure hunt just after the hour (say, between 3 and 3:10 p.m.) or just after the half-hour (say, between 3:30 and 3:40 p.m.) to give yourself as much time as possible to download the program. The PGP files should download in under 12 minutes on a good day.

If you don't have Web access but do have both telnet and FTP access, you can telnet to `net-dist.mit.edu` and login as `getpgp`. You are asked the same questions. If you pass the test, you are then given the magic name for the PGP distribution directory that is valid at that moment.

You then have until the end-of-the-half-hour pumpkin time to FTP on over to `net-dist.mit.edu`, login as `anonymous`, enter your e-mail address as the password, `cd` to the magic directory name you were given, and `get` the right files. Pheew.

If you only have e-mail, you can try using the FTP-via-e-mail methods described in Chapter 24, but you may have difficulty negotiating the anti-export features at most PGP repositories.

If you live in Canada

The method for PGP distribution to Canada is a little bit different. If you're using a Web browser, go to MIT's Canada page at the following address:

```
http://web.mit.edu/network/pgp-form-canada.html
```

You are asked a set of questions oriented to Canadian residents. From there on, the procedure is the same as for the U.S. residents, as described in the preceding section.

If you live outside North America

People living outside of the U.S. and Canada in countries that permit PGP use can obtain PGP over the Internet pretty much without restriction. The primary international distribution site is at the following address:

```
http://www.ifi.uio.no/~staalesc/PGP/home.html
```

If you plan on using the international version for commercial purposes, you need to get an end user license for the IDEA encryption technology that PGP uses. Prices start at $15 per user for up to 50 users. For information, send e-mail to `IDEA@ascom.ch` or check their Web page at `http://www.ascom.ch/systec`. The Viacrypt version for commercial use in North America includes the required IDEA license.

Why shouldn't North American users download PGP2.6.2i from an international site? Well, a big fuss arose over PGP's use of patented RSA technology. The deal that settled everyone down required that things be set up the way they are. If you use the international version in North America, you risk the ire of RSADSI for violating their patents.

Which version of PGP should I get?

If you live in North America and own a Macintosh with a 68020, 68030 or 68040 processor or a PowerMac, get MacPGP2.6.2. If you own an older, 68000-based Macintosh, get MacPGP2.6.

If you have a IBM PC or compatible, get PGP2.6.2 for DOS.

If you live outside North America, get the international versions. They have similar names but end in an *i* — for example, PGP2.6.2i.

For a more complete and up-to-date list of download locations and available versions, see "Where To Get The Pretty Good Privacy Program (PGP) FAQ" at the following address:

```
ftp://ftp.netcom.com/pub/mp/mpj/getpgp.asc
```

If you use Microsoft Windows, you can get one of a number of Windows front ends to PGP. You still need PGP 2.6.2 for DOS, but you can access the program by using the Windows front end to provide a graphical interface.

The most popular Windows front ends are available for free over the Internet. They include the following programs:

- **PGP Windows Shell.** The latest version is V. 2.1. The developer, Aegis Research, says that the shell works with Windows 3.1, Windows 95, and Windows NT.

- **PGP Winfront.** Developed by Ugali International. Corp., the latest version of this front end is V. 3.1.

- **Private Idaho.** This utility for PGP and anonymous remailing for Windows e-mail software was written by Joel McNamara. The latest beta version is v. 2.6b. Private Idaho enables you to send and receive encrypted e-mail in standard Internet format.

You can find links to all these front ends and more at the following Web page:

```
http://www.primenet.com/~shauert/pgpwins.htm
```

Making up a good secret pass phrase

Before you make your public and secret keys, you need a *pass phrase*. Because just walking up to a computer and copying someone's secret key file is so easy, the designers of PGP added a feature that stores the secret key in a coded form. To unlock this coded secret key, you must type in the right pass phrase.

Pass phrases, as used in PGP, were invented by Sigmund Porter in 1982. They can be longer than the typical 8- to 10-character password and are used to give added security.

A lot of mumbo-jumbo has been written on how to make up your pass phrase. We have a simple prescription: Just pick five words at random from a dictionary. A password chosen this way provides very good protection for your secret key — better than most PGP users enjoy — and five words is not too much to remember or too long to type in each time you need it.

A pass phrase word list

A dictionary of very short words, designed to simplify picking out random words by using ordinary dice, is available from the Internet at the following Web address:

```
http://dummies.com/diceware.wordlist.asc
```

The word list is indexed so that words can be randomly selected by tossing five dice. The list is made up of short English words, abbreviations, and easy-to-remember character strings. The average length of each word is about 4.2 characters. The longest words are 6 characters. The list is based on a longer word list posted to the Internet by Peter Kwangjun Suk.

Using the list

Each word in the list is preceded by five numbers ranging between 1 and 6, corresponding to the marks on an ordinary die (which is the singular term for *dice*, if you didn't already know). To pick a random word, just shake a die in a glass, throw it five times, write down the five numbers, and then look up the numbers in the word list. If, for example, you rolled five dice and they came up 2, 1, 1, 2, 4, your next pass phrase word is *clip*. Repeat this process until you have five words. Those five words are your pass phrase.

Nineteenth-century security precautions are in order here: Make sure that you are alone. Close the curtains. Write your words on a hard surface, not on a pad. Burn your notes and pulverize the ashes after you memorize your pass phrase.

The following are some sample pass phrases generated by using this list:

```
le puddly flame hang
cohn jewett ewe epic jones
creek 36th broom foggy evade cogent
```

Pass phrases are case sensitive, which means that the following two phrases are *not* the same:

```
early think vy haul book
Early Think Vy Haul Book
```

Some people encourage you to use weird capitalization in your pass phrase to make it more secure. We think that doing this just makes remembering and accurately typing your pass phrase too hard and is not worth the trouble. Add a sixth word if you are paranoid.

Creating your own public and private (secret) keys

Before you make your keys, you must tell PGP where to put them. (If you have gotten this far, you may have some scatological ideas for this, but just take a deep breath and go on.) PGP stores keys in special files called *key rings*. Normally, you keep your key rings on your hard disk with the rest of PGP. If you like, you can keep PGP on your hard disk, but keep your key rings on a floppy disk stored in a safe place.

Should I write down my pass phrase?

Most authorities say that you should never write down your pass phrase. We don't agree. Most of us just are not that confident of our ability to memorize passwords and phrases, especially those for infrequently used accounts. The risk of someone trying to steal your secret key is theoretical for most of us. The risk of forgetting is all too real.

At best, losing a pass phrase means the hassle of creating a new key pair, revoking the old key, and distributing the new public key. At worst, the loss could result in your inability to read important mail in time to act on it — or even losing valuable data files forever. As a result, even people who know better may choose a short pass phrase that is easy to remember — and equally easy to guess.

If writing down your pass phrase spurs you to pick a stronger pass phrase, we say to go ahead and write it down — but keep it in a safe place. What's a safe place? Your wallet; a secret hiding place at home; or, if you have a great many paper files, a random file folder (but *not* one labeled "Pass Phrase"). For high-security situations, a bank safe-deposit box is a good choice. *Never store your pass phrase on or near your computer.*

If you use the DOS version of PGP, copy CONFIG.TXT to the floppy disk along with the key rings. PGP creates the other files it needs. You also need to set your PGPPATH environment variable so that PGP can find the files it needs. To do so, add the following lines to your AUTOEXEC.BAT file:

```
SET PGPPATH=C:\PGP
SET PATH=C:\PGP;%PATH%
SET TZ=EST5EDT
```

(These lines specify that PGP and the key rings are on your hard disk.)

Alternatively, add the following lines:

```
SET PGPPATH=A:\
SET PATH=C:\PGP;%PATH%
SET TZ=EST5EDT
```

These lines specify that your key rings are on your floppy disk A: drive.

The first line in each set of code tells PGP where to find the key rings and CONFIG.TXT. The second line tells your system where to find PGP. The third line specifies your local time zone; see the file DOC\SETUP.DOC that comes with PGP for a more complete list.

Now reboot your system.

For MacPGP users, insert the diskette you want to use (if any), choose Options⇨Set Key ring, click the button next to the key ring you want to set, and click Do It. Then select the disk and folder where you want your key rings located and click Open.

For quick Help at any time, enter **pgp -h** at the DOS prompt. In MacPGP, choose Apple⇨Help from the menu bar.

Making your keys

This is the big moment. You are now ready to create your very own public and private PGP key pair.

On DOS PGP, enter the command **pgp -kg** at the DOS prompt. On MacPGP choose Key⇨Generate Key. PGP prompts you for the rest of the information it needs. You are asked to enter the following three items of information:

- Your pass phrase.
- Your user ID, which is then associated with the key. The preferred form is *First-name Last-name <email@address>* — for example, `Allen Dulles <oss@dummies.com>`

✔ The size of your public key. (See the section "How big should my public key be?" in Chapter 22.) Most PGP users choose 1,024 bits, which is more than enough for anyone whose computer is not under armed guard 24 hours a day.

Back up your secret key

Your private or secret key is stored in your secret key ring file. You need to make a backup copy of this file on a floppy disk of its own and keep the disk in a safe place. Better yet, make two backup copies and store them in different locations. If you lose your secret key, *no one* can recreate it for you.

Validating your public key

The first thing you need to do is to sign your public key. Remember way back when we told you that can use PGP to sign documents? Well, you also sign public keys. Signing a public key is a way of saying, "I know the person to whom this key belongs." Signing a public key does not mean that you vouch for the person's integrity — or even like the person. This action means only that you know that the person is who he or she claims to be.

A big problem with all this public key stuff is knowing that a public key really came from the person whose name is on it. Other advocates of public key technology are proposing complex hierarchies in which your key is registered with some big organization that signs your key. The big organization's key is signed by some bigger agency and so on up to some super-duper master certifying agency, maybe at the UN or something.

Spin a Web of Trust

Well the developers of PGP don't like that concept. They believe that having such agencies for signing keys centralizes control of your electronic identity into the hands of big business and big government. (The U.S. Post Office, for example, is thinking of getting into the key certificate business.) So the PGP gang came up with a different, more organic approach called the *Web of Trust*.

The Web of Trust — which has nothing to do with the Internet's World Wide Web, by the way — works by having people sign the keys of people they know. If you have enough signers, and I have enough signers, and all the signers have enough signers, the chances are good that we may have a signer in common. If so, we can be pretty confident that we each are who we say we are. For example, Bill knows Bob who knows Sally. Bill also know Marko who knows Irena who knows Ofer. So Sally can know who Ofer is. The Web of Trust is a nice concept, and no one can revoke your keys because you didn't pay your parking tickets. We hope that it catches on.

In any case, the first step in the Web of Trust is to sign your *own* key. Signing your own key just proves to the world that your public key comes from someone who has the matching secret key and prevents some of the arcane (no, not arcade — *arcane*) games that cryptographers spend much of their time worrying about. (Remember the guy who was paranoid until the day *they* got him?) To sign your key just enter the following at the DOS prompt, substituting your actual name for *yourname*:

```
pgp -ks yourname
```

In MacPGP, choose Key∫Certify key and follow the instructions.

The second thing you need to do is to copy your public key off your key ring and put it into a little text file of its own that you can give on a floppy disk to someone or paste into an e-mail message. An example of a public key is displayed in Chapter 22. To extract your public key as a text file, enter the following at the DOS prompt, substituting your name for *yourname* and your key's file name for *keyfilename*:

```
pgp -kxa yourname keyfilename
```

In MacPGP, choose Key⇨Extract keys and follow the instructions.

If a friend who already has PGP is helping you set up, ask that friend to sign your public key, and then you can sign his or her key. See the section "Get your key certified" later in this chapter.

Dust for fingerprints

While you're fussing with your keys, you should need to extract your *key fingerprint* as well. Suppose that someone who knows you calls you up and says, "Hey ol' buddy, I got this here public key that has your name on it. Is it really yours?" You could sit there on the phone while he reads your public key back to you:

"Small 'M,' capital 'Q,' capital 'C," small 'Y,' number '9,' <yawn>. . . ."

A public key can have hundreds of letters in it. Sitting there listening to them is a *big* drag.

To solve this problem, PGP enables you to run one of those mush-up hash functions over your public key and display the answer. The result is called a *key fingerprint*. As with human fingerprints, the chance that two PGP users would ever have the same key fingerprints is so small as to be practically nonexistent. Key fingerprints contain only 32 letters and numbers, and the letters are all the same case. Arnold's PGP fingerprint, for example, looks like this:

```
FA C3 82 FB 05 5E 03 1A  34 04 79 EA 9E 76 7B 67
```

If you were checking up on this key, you'd need to read only these 32 letters and numbers over the phone, which is only a minor drag.

PGP fanatics put their key fingerprints on their business cards, their stationary, their e-mail signatures, their front doors, and so on.

To see your PGP fingerprint, type the following at the DOS prompt:

```
pgp -kvc yourname
```

In MacPGP, choose Key⇨Fingerprint Key and then select your key from the list in the dialog box that appears.

A good idea is to write down your fingerprint in a handy place, such as in your address book so that you can verify your public key at any time.

Exchanging public keys with your friends

Your friends need your public key to send you coded messages. (When we say *friends*, we really mean anyone with whom you want to communicate in private). You can safely give your public key to anyone — friend, stranger or enemy. On the other hand, if someone knocks on your door and says that she is from the phone company, your bank, Dummies Central, or whatever and asks to see your *secret* key, you slam the door. Now. Got that?

You can get your public key to someone in the following ways:

- ✔ **In person.** Just copy the little public key file we described earlier onto a floppy disk and hand it to the person. You can even send the disk by postal mail or express delivery service. As you're probably a bit confused by now, here's what you enter at the DOS prompt to copy the file:

- ✔ **By e-mail.** Include the file *keyfilename* in a message and e-mail it. See the chapter in this book that describes the e-mail program you use to learn how to include a file in your message. If you can't figure out how to send a file with your message, try opening *keyfilename* in a word processor program, copy all the text to the Clipboard, and paste the text into a new e-mail message.

- ✔ **Use a PGP key server.** We discuss this option in the section "Key servers at your service" later in this chapter.

In theory, you could mail or fax someone a hard copy printout of your key and have her type it in, but keys can be a few hundred characters long, so typing one exactly right is very difficult and *very* tedious.

Adding a key

If a friend gives you her public key, you need to add it to your public key ring file. Adding a new key to your public key ring is actually easier than adding a metal key to one of those circle rings, where you have to pry up one end, slip the hole in the key under that half of the circle, and slide the key all the way along until it snaps off the other end.

If you are given a file *newfilename* with a key in it that you want to add to your public key ring, enter the following at the DOS prompt:

```
pgp -ka newfilename
```

In MacPGP, choose Key⇨Add keys and select *newfilename* from the dialog box.

You are asked if you want to certify this key. Do *not* do so unless you know the person, and she personally handed you the key file on disk, or you have verified the key fingerprint over the phone with the person and you recognized her voice.

The PGP distribution should come with a file called KEYS.ASC. This file contains the public keys of several PGP honchos. Adding the keys in this file to your public key ring is good practice and you can use the keys to verify that the copy of PGP you have is valid.

To add these big-shots' keys to your key ring, type the following at the DOS prompt:

```
pgp -ka keys.asc
```

In MacPGP, choose Key⇨Add keys and then select keys.asc.

How do you know that the KEYS.ASC file itself hasn't been tampered with? Type the following at the DOS prompt:

```
pgp -kvc "Philip R. Zimmermann <prz@acm.org>"
```

In MacPGP, choose Key⇨Fingerprint key, select your public key ring in the dialog box, and then select Philip R. Zimmermann from the list.

PGP should reply with the following information:

```
looking for user ID "Philip R. Zimmermann <prz@acm.org>".
Type bits/keyID    Date       User ID
pub 1024/C7A966DD 1993/05/21 Philip R. Zimmerman <prz@acm,org>
```

```
        Key fingerprint =   9E 94 45 13 39 83 5F 70 7B E7
        D8 ED C4 BE 5A A6
1 matching key found.
```

Because the other keys in KEYS.ASC are signed by Phil, if the key fingerprint you get matches that in the preceding example, you (and your copy of PGP) are safe.

Well, you're sort of safe. Anyone clever enough to make a doctored version of PGP could have it recognize that you are checking its signature and print out the "all clear" message. You really ought to get PGP from two independent sources and use each to check the other. If you are a gentle, laid-back, trusting sort of soul, this crypto stuff should cure you of that really fast.

Get your key certified

To get your key certified, first extract a copy of your key by entering the following at the DOS prompt:

```
pgp -kxa yourname yourname.asc
```

In MacPGP, choose Key⇨Extract keys and follow the instructions given.

Give *yourname.asc* to a friend who has PGP. That person adds your key to her key ring by typing the following at the DOS prompt:

```
pgp -ka yourname.asc
```

In MacPGP, she must choose Key⇨Add keys and follow the instructions given.

PGP asks her if she wants to certify this key. She answers "yes" and enters her personal pass phrase. She now extracts a fresh copy of your key from her key ring by typing the following at the DOS prompt:

```
pgp -kxa yourname yourname.asc
```

In MacPGP, she must choose Key⇨Extract keys.

She then gives the key back to you on a floppy disk. You add it back into your key ring by typing the following at the DOS prompt:

```
pgp -ka yourname.asc
```

In MacPGP, choose Key⇨Add keys.

You now have a signature on your key. From now on, anybody who knows your friend, trusts her, and has a copy of her public key knows that your public key is legitimate.

Naturally, you want to return the favor and sign her key.

Get your key certified remotely

Suppose that your friend is a long distance away, but you still want to exchange signatures. Simply send your key to your friend by e-mail. She adds your key to her key ring as before, but she *doesn't* certify it because she has no way to know that the key wasn't tampered with on the way.

Both of you get the key's fingerprint. Remember that a PGP key fingerprint is a string of 32 letters and numbers. (See the section "Dust for fingerprints," earlier in this chapter.) Now call your friend on the phone, make sure that you recognize her voice, and read her the 32 letters and numbers in the fingerprint. If the fingerprint matches what she has, she knows that she has a legitimate copy of your key. She can now sign your key, extract it, and e-mail it back to you. You then add it to your public key ring as before.

What a pretty key ring!

To view all the keys in your public key ring, enter the following at the DOS prompt:

```
pgp -kv
```

In MacPGP, choose Key⇨View Key ring and select your public key ring in the file dialog box.

To view all the keys in your public key ring, along with who has certified each key, enter the following at the DOS prompt:

```
pgp -kvv
```

In MacPGP, choose Key⇨View Key ring, select your public key ring in the file dialog box, and, in the next dialog box that appears, select the Show Signatures Also check box.

Key servers at your service

A number of universities and other organizations around the world operate public PGP *key servers* on a volunteer basis. These key servers enable you to submit your key and look for keys submitted by others. You can submit and search for keys by Internet FTP or by e-mail.

Most of the organizations that run these key servers make no attempt whatsoever to verify the keys. (One exception, however, is Four11, which does ask for some ID and then signs your public key. But Four11 also charges a $20 fee to list your public key. Four11 is on the Web at http:/www.Four11.com, or send e-mail to info@Four11.com.)

Most key servers process requests from you that are sent as e-mail messages. You give the server one command per message. Commands are entered on the subject line of your message, as in the following example:

```
To: pgp-public-keys@pgp.mit.edu
From: Arnold Reinhold@world.std.com
Subject: help
```

You only need to send your key to one volunteer server. That server forwards your Add request to the other servers automatically.

To add your key to a key server, for example, or to update your key if it is already there, send a message similar to the following to any server:

```
To: pgp-public-keys@keys.us.pgp.net
        From: Arnold Reinhold@world.std.com
        Subject: add
—BEGIN PGP PUBLIC KEY BLOCK—
Version: 2.6.2

mQCPAy9MyROAAAEEANejhFb64tLhD1xa/kOmLHRPuXNW2vVvjaOluCX1Ntcu7EWA
K8PnmWqruEOWflkBA42g6iwta9B/Bm8JOYfkk6T7CrnAeBN/IuepQa4uJXXk7AqO
whO3vF8TzPk6STIJAPTQ9CWQ+6MHnwmDk9RzDwxtnS8dMKGXiWtruC2sMYShABEB
AAGOKOFybm9sZCBHLiBSZWluaG9sZCA8cmVpbmhvbGRAd29ybGQuc3RkLmNvbT6J
AJUDBRAwwLyzkGCWpQlZ7KkBARKaBADCggEzWe2tLvHn9/QkSfPnTMJhXiSDzz6V
K2Xwzyo/TElV632ZNQ6yQ9IMRObQAs95LNwwd4iGPoeZ3OCqNvqaGkU4fJjz6gW9
v/szgwOfINa9lsRtfOJWvKyBiq9J9JC/q9mA6T7mmhDsoWXJZ6/h49AeNF2KCszE
LyybOtAgAokAlQMFEC925FzVMiHPX2OluQEBxCMD/33cCtdo6yGPWdCddZlx+aBh
tTrat81WwYc2QfIdSphryVeP5nK95YOmsR+94ESgKEzpJQGIYJsK8ZLsu7AaQrYE
CNHkQhe6EkW/Oy4t4X36Yx3qufwKmP4jc5WCliT6o4T+RpCidbrGm3mw91oWJexV
UBp4apxK/rRPaZX7AgoriQCVAwUQLOzKK2truC2sMYShAQELTAQAyOAbV87SYPAJ
tzm3iJwBkcxDoBE/VOdY29H9ZgKSGnebVSySqKpeo5rJq+XFr1sDZ7cZyYacOpaR
FcCFE7sAZoy7bLTMBu6KbhX5YndWqRL+uT8xkNscugPi6O9RTo7lroMeA847TuQ7
fl9tYFB25HpDWeKh+CR2Gh3mf4LnvCc=
=M7fR
—END PGP PUBLIC KEY BLOCK—
```

Most key servers accept the commands shown in Table 23-1.

Table 23-1	Server Commands
Command	*Meaning*
ADD	Your PGP public key. (Key to add is the body of the message.)
INDEX *userid*	List of all the PGP keys that match the user ID.
VERBOSE INDEX *userid*	List of matching PGP keys, along with any signatures they may have.
GET *userid*	Get just that one key.
MGET *pattern*	Get all keys that match *pattern*.

You should normally send e-mail key server requests to the following address:

```
pgp-public-keys@keys.pgp.net
```

Use `ftp.pgp.net:pub/pgp/` for FTP access to key servers.

Using PGP

This section tells you how you actually use PGP.

Sending George a secret message

Assume that you have George's public key on your key ring. (See the section "Adding a key," earlier in this chapter, if you don't). First, type your message in a file and save it as a text file. (We use *textfile* in the following examples as a substitute for whatever name you choose for the file). Now enter the following at the DOS prompt:

```
pgp -esat textfile "George"
```

In MacPGP, choose File⇨Encrypt/Sign and choose the name of the file you want to encrypt.

What if someone steals your secret key?

If you have reason to believe that your secret key was compromised, the only thing you can do is revoke your public key, create a new pair of PGP keys, and circulate the revocation file containing your new public key as widely as possible. To revoke your public key, enter the following at the DOS prompt:

pgp -kd *yourkeyid*

In MacPGP, choose Key⇨Disable/Reenable key.

PGP asks if you really want to do this and then prompts for your pass phrase. You then extract an ASCII copy of your now-revoked key and distribute it widely, just as you did after you first made it. You also need to make a new key pair for yourself, extract the public key, and distribute the new public key at the same time. After you revoke your own key, you cannot re-enable it, despite what the Mac command name implies.

Notice that you need both your secret key and pass phrase to revoke your key. If you lose either of them, you're stuck. This situation is why we recommend that you make at least two backup copies of your secret key and why we think that writing your pass phrase down and keeping it somewhere safe is okay.

PGP prompts you for your pass phrase and then creates the file *textfile.asc*, encrypted and signed by you, suitable for mailing.

The letters in the magic incantation for DOS, in the preceding example, have the following meanings:

> e = encrypt
> s = sign
> a = ASCII output
> t = files are text

Leave out the *s* if you don't want to sign the document you are encrypting. Leave out the *t* if the original file is not an ASCII text file.

If you tell PGP that a file is a text file, PGP handles the file's end-of-line characters, which vary from computer to computer, in a way that should work on any computer.

Signing a document

You can sign a document as part of the encryption process, or you can sign a document while leaving the body of the document unencrypted. You can even produce a signature file that is independent of the document.

To sign a text file without encrypting it, enter the following at the DOS prompt:

```
pgp -sat textfile
```

In MacPGP, choose File➪Sign Only and select the text file you want to sign.

PGP asks for your pass phrase and then adds a PGP signature, similar to the one in the following example, to the end of the text file, as follows:

```
—BEGIN PGP SIGNATURE—
Version: 2.6

iQCVAwUBMArBSGtruC2sMYShAQEwEwQAzNIpRm29UXQwpT9AGctbnn4GrRibWCt
rgSUJaCYn+fP3NMalYUbEbljd+AbWXACuLSUCagKPEoC2vu6fzpO7h2q6TAFewrn
JAHFLJHIfvhUXKsQF84BbWdvK6u+qaDjJeTlvTrD4L2dUlEAOOtOVa9ntwPmzt+l
dHzeD3JBHFY=
=akuU
—END PGP SIGNATURE—
```

Signing a file separately

Sometimes, you want the signature file to be separate from the signed document. You may, for example, want to protect a binary file from viruses and tampering in the way PGP distributions are protected.

To sign a file separately, just enter the following at the DOS prompt:

```
pgp -sba binfile
```

In MacPGP, choose File⇨Sign Only and then select the file you want to sign — for example, **binfile**. Then mark the Create Separate Signature File check box in the dialog box.

This action produces a new file, named *binfile.asc,* which is the signature to binfile. Any modifications to binfile makes the signature invalid.

The letters in the magic incantation for DOS, in the preceding example, have the following meanings:

> s = sign
> b = break signature from file
> a = ASCII output

Reading encrypted files and verifying signatures

PGP is pretty clever in reading files. If you open a file in PGP, the program decrypts that file (if encrypted) or verifies the signature (if the file has one). If the file is signed and encrypted, PGP performs both functions. You just enter the following at the DOS prompt:

```
pgp thefilename
```

In MacPGP, choose File⇨Open/Decrypt and then select the file you want to open from the file dialog box.

You are asked for your pass phrase if the file is encrypted. You are also asked where to put the output file. The output file is the actual signed document, decrypted if necessary. You can open the output file in any word processor. Most e-mail programs also enable you to open the file.

MacPGP has a handy option that decrypts to MacPGP's display window. This option enables you to view a message without writing an unencrypted version to disk.

A bug was found in older versions of PGP that affects plain text signatures. The following line is meant to be followed by a *blank* line:

```
—BEGIN PGP SIGNED MESSAGE—
```

A signed document can be tampered with by adding text in front of that blank line.

Always examine the output of PGP when verifying a document signed with versions before 2.6.2. The input may be tampered with, but the output cannot be.

Verifying a separate signature

You verify the signature on a separate file by giving PGP both file names.

As an exercise, check the signature on the copy of PGP you downloaded. Enter the following at the DOS prompt:

```
pgp pgp262i.asc pgp262i.zip
```

In MacPGP, first choose File⇨MacBinarize and then select the file MacPGP2.6.2-130v1-inner. Next, choose File⇨Open/Decrypt and select the signature file in the file dialog box — in this case, MacPGP2.6.2-130v1-inner.asc. PGP then asks you what the the signature applies to. Select MacPGP2.6.2-130v1-inner.bin.

PGP should tell you about a good signature from one Jeffrey I. Schiller. PGP also warns you that Jeffrey I. Schiller's signature hasn't been certified by anybody you know. This warning is normal.

Mac users can now drag the MacPGP2.6.2-130v1-inner.bin file into the Trash. We needed the file only to check the signature.

Can the NSA Crack PGP?

This question, regarding the NSA's ability to undo PGP encryption, is a perennial one on Internet newsgroups such as sci.crypt and alt.security.pgp. The *NSA,* of course, is the United States National Security Agency. NSA is the largest code-breaking outfit in the world, getting a big piece of the United States' $29 billion annual budget for intelligence. The days when the NSA's mere existence was a secret, however, are long gone. The agency has a nice World Wide Web home page at the following address:

```
http://www.nsa.gov:8080
```

The NSA certainly can crack PGP if you use a key length of 512 bits or less. But what if you use the 1,024-bit key size we recommend? The truth is that no one outside the NSA can say for sure. No techniques that have been published are even remotely close to breaking keys that big. And the 128-bit session keys seem equally impregnable. Our gut feeling is that the NSA cannot crack the codes used in PGP. Is our gut feeling worth much? Probably not.

If the NSA really wants to obtain data encrypted with PGP, can they do so? More often than not, we think, they can. Isn't that a contradiction? The NSA knows all those tricks and probably some we haven't thought of. To achieve the level of security PGP is capable of takes discipline. Remember, however, that PGP promises only pretty good privacy. Without more attention to security than an average person is likely to stand for, that is all PGP can provide. It's a tough world.

Chapter 24

The Internet by E-Mail

* *

In This Chapter

▶ FTP by mail

▶ Archie by mail

▶ Gopher by mail

▶ Other services by mail

* *

*T*he Internet contains many *mail servers* that provide access to various services. You send an e-mail message to the server telling it what you want, and it sends back a response, which — with any luck — will actually be what you asked for. Retrieving information this way isn't as quick as the *native* connection to these services (Netscape for the World Wide Web, for example), but it's a lot better than nothing. A few services that we list are *only* available by e-mail.

TIP

Mail server tips

✔ Most servers respond quickly (within a few minutes) after you send a request. But some, particularly the FTP-by-mail servers described later in the chapter, are very heavily loaded and can take days to respond. Patience is a virtue.

✔ If your mail program automatically adds a signature to your message, tell it not to do so to your request messages because servers won't understand the signature.

✔ You can usually send multiple requests in a single message. Put each on a separate line.

✔ Most servers ignore the Subject: line of your message, so requests must be in the body of the message. But to keep life interesting, a few servers *require* that the request be in the Subject: line. Read the descriptions for each server carefully.

Mailing Many Makes of Files

Some servers return files of nontext information, such as programs and digitized images or sounds. The servers use the same file mailing techniques, MIME and uuencoding, that we discuss in Chapters 3 and 5. If you receive a nontext file from a server, handle the file the same way that you handle an attached file received from anyone else. (See "A picture is worth a million bytes" in Chapter 3 and "I'm So Attached to You" in Chapter 5 for the details.)

FTP by Mail

FTP, File Transfer Protocol, is the Internet's way of letting you retrieve files from public archives all over the Net. For example, thousands of archives exist with hundreds of thousands, maybe millions, of files ranging from software to pictures to the text of *Alice in Wonderland*.

Several systems offer FTP by mail. These servers are all very slow, frequently taking several days to respond, but they're a lot better than nothing. The two most widely available services are FTPMAIL and BITFTP.

The most confusing thing about FTP-by-mail is that two separate computers other than your computer are involved: the one providing the FTP-by-mail service and the one where the files actually reside. Any FTP-by-mail server can retrieve files available on any FTP server.

FTPMAIL

FTPMAIL is a system originally written at Digital Equipment's lab in California and is now available at the sites listed in Table 24-1. Use the site closest to you to minimize the load on expensive international network links.

Table 24-1	Sites Where FTPMAIL Is Available
Site	*Country*
ftpmail@cs.uow.edu.au	Australia
ftpmail@ccc.uba.ar	Argentina
ftpmail@ieunet.ie	Ireland
ftpmail@ftp.luth.se	Sweden
ftpmail@ftp.sunet.se	Sweden

Site	Country
ftpmail@nctuccca.edu.tw	Taiwan
ftpmail@doc.ic.ac.uk	United Kingdom
ftpmail@info.census.gov	United States
ftpmail@oak.oakland.edu	United States
ftpmail@ftp.dartmouth.edu	United States
ftpmail@ftpmail.ramona.vix.com	United States

You send FTPMAIL a list of commands that tell who you are, what system you want to retrieve your files from, and what files you want. The commands should include a *reply-to command* (if you're not sure, the return address on your mail gives your correct address) followed by *open* and other commands to specify what to retrieve.

Before trying to retrieve any files from an FTPMAIL server, first send it a one-line message containing

```
help
```

This verifies that the server is still available and gets you a list of the exact commands that the server supports. All of the FTPMAIL servers are more or less the same, but they all have minor differences that can trip up the unwary. The standard FTPMAIL commands are listed in Table 24-2.

Table 24-2	An FTPMAIL Cheat Sheet
Command	**Description**
reply-to *address*	Where to send the response.
open *host user password*	Where to FTP to. The default user is anonymous, and the default password is your e-mail address, usually the correct values to use for public FTP archives. At some sites this is connect rather than open.
cd *directory*	Change directory.
ls *directory*	List directory, short form. Default directory is the current directory.
dir *directory*	List directory, long form. Default directory is the current directory.
get *file*	Retrieve that file and mail it to you.

(continued)

Table 24-2 (continued)

Command	Description
compress	Compress returned files or directory listings with UNIX compress.
gzip	Compress returned files or directory listings with GNU gzip.
uuencode	Encode binary files using uuencode, the default. (See Chapter 5.)
btoa	Encode non-text files using btoa (an older uuencode-like system).
mime	Encode non-text files using MIME.
force uuencode	Encode all files using uuencode.
force btoa	Encode all files using btoa.
force mime	Encode all files using MIME.
size *nnn*[K|M]	Set the size pieces in which a large file will be returned. For many mail systems, 64K is a good value. On some servers, this command is `chunksize`.
mode binary	Get subsequent files in binary (non-text) mode. (Default.)
mode ascii	Get subsequent files in ASCII (text) mode.
quit	Ignore any following lines (useful if you can't suppress your signature).

Let's say that you want to retrieve a file called `rfc821.txt` that is in the directory `rfc` on the server `ds.internic.net`. (This is one of the RFC documents we discussed at the end of Chapter 5.) You send a message to one of the FTPMAIL servers containing the following lines:

```
open ds.internic.net
cd pub
get rfc821.txt
quit
```

This says to go to the host `ds.internic.net`, go to the directory `pub` and return the file `rfc821.txt`. Because this is a text file, it'll be returned as a regular text e-mail message.

You can get a list of files in a directory on a particular server in much the same way. To get a list of all the RFC documents, send this message:

```
open ds.internic.net
ls pub
quit
```

If your computer can handle files compressed by the `gzip` compression utility (most UNIX systems have gzip itself, and the popular Windows shareware WinZip can decode gzip files), you can request to receive the document in a more compact form by sending this message:

```
open ds.internic.net
gzip
mime
cd pub
get rfc821.txt
quit
```

This tells the server to compress the file using gzip and then send it as a MIME attached file. When you receive the response, you un-gzip the received file to recover the original. The gzip-ed version of the file is considerably smaller than the original, so if you receive mail via a dial-up connection, a gzip-ed version of a file will download considerably faster than the plain text. Non-text files in most archives are already stored compressed, so gzip-ing won't help them any.

BITFTP

BITFTP is another FTP-by-mail system originally written for BITNET, an older network mostly containing IBM mainframe computers. BITFTP is now available to any user with Internet mail access. From the list of servers below, use the server closest to you.

- ✔ bitftp@pucc.princeton.edu (United States)
- ✔ bitftp@vm.gmd.de (Germany, available to European users only)
- ✔ bitftp@plearn.edu.pl (Poland)

As with FTPMAIL, send a message containing `help` to a server before you retrieve files so that you can verify the availability of the server and find out about its particular commands. The standard BITFTP commands are listed in Table 24-3.

Also, as with FTPMAIL, the message you send should contain commands to specify the host, a USER command to log in, and then other commands to retrieve files, but of course the syntax is slightly different.

Here's the general sketch of what you send to BITFTP:

```
FTP hostname UUENCODE
USER username [password]
... commands ...
QUIT
```

The UUENCODE tells the server to uuencode binary files. (Other options are not pertinent to Internet users.) The most commonly used user name is anonymous, a general name that you can use on systems for which you don't need a personal account or a password.

Table 24-3	A BITFTP Cheat Sheet
Command	*Description*
ACCT *acctinfo*	Sends an ACCT command to the host to specify an account. Useful only in special cases.
ASCII	Retrieves files as text.
BINARY	Retrieves files as non-text.
CD *dir*	Changes to given directory.
DIR	Lists entries in current directory.
EBCDIC	Retrieves files in EBCDIC (used on IBM mainframes).
GET *filename*	Retrieves the specified file.
LS *dir*	Lists files in a directory.
MODE S|B	Retrieves files in Stream or Block mode. (Stream, the default, is almost always what you want.)
PWD	Prints current directory name.
QUIT	Ends session, disregards anything else in the message (useful if you can't suppress your signature).
SYSTEM	Prints the name of the FTP host's operating system.
TYPE A|I|B|E|F	Retrieved files are in ASCII ("A"), image ("I"), Kanji Shift JIS ("B"), EBCDIC ("E"), or EBCDIC IBM Kanji ("F"). By far the most common are A for text files and I for non-text files.

For the RFC example in the preceding section, you'd send this:

```
FTP rs.internic.net UUENCODE
CD pub
GET rfc821.txt
QUIT
```

Unlike FTPMAIL, BITFTP doesn't offer compression or any file attachment scheme other than uuencoding.

What FTP servers are there?

Now that you know how to get files from FTP servers by mail, you have to find out what the FTP servers are. Fortunately, a large list is available from a mail server. To get this list, send a message to mail-server@rtfm.mit.edu and in the message put:

```
send usenet/news.answers/ftp-list/sitelist/part1
send usenet/news.answers/ftp-list/sitelist/part2
send usenet/news.answers/ftp-list/sitelist/part3
... and so on up to ...
send usenet/news.answers/ftp-list/sitelist/part21
```

Each part of the list is 60,000 characters long, so unless you're sure you want a lot of mail in your mailbox, you should start by getting one or two parts of the sitelist and then get more after the first parts arrive.

The same server has lots and lots of FAQ (Frequently Asked Questions) documents available. To get the one that talks about FTP, send a message containing this line:

```
send usenet/news.answers/ftp-list/faq
```

Archie by Mail

Archie is a service that helps you find servers that contain files available for FTP. You send Archie a request consisting primarily of a filename or a text pattern that specifies an approximate filename, and the server sends back a list of matching names and the FTP hosts where the files are available. Once you know which server has your file, you can use FTP-by-mail to retrieve the actual file.

Many Archie servers exist around the world. Pick a nearby one from Table 24-4.

Table 24-4	Archie Servers
Address	*Country*
archie@archie.doc.ic.ac.uk	United Kingdom
archie@archie.hensa.ac.uk	United Kingdom
archie@archie.univie.ac.at	Austria
archie@archie.funet.fi	Finland
archie@archie.th-darmstadt.de	Germany
archie@archie.rediris.es	Spain
archie@archie.luth.se	Sweden
archie@archie.unipi.it	Italy
archie@archie.au	Australia
archie@archie.uqam.ca	Canada
archie@archie.sogang.ac.kr	Korea
archie@archie.ncu.edu.tw	Taiwan
archie@archie.unl.edu	USA
archie@archie.internic.net	USA
archie@archie.rutgers.edu	USA
archie@archie.ans.net	USA
archie@archie.sura.net	USA

Archie servers support all sorts of complicated options, as you can see in Table 24-5, but for most purposes the only command you need is find, which is the way you ask the Archie server to search for a filename. Here's an example:

```
find winzip
```

You may want to use a few other commands before you use the find command:

✔ set maxhits 50: Normally, Archie returns a maximum of 100 files that match your request. You can set the number higher or lower. Usually a few dozen hits is more than plenty — how many different places do you need to find copies of the same thing? (You want Archie to find enough places so that at least one of them will be in your country — to avoid slow international file retrievals.)

✔ `compress`: Compress and uuencode the results. If you can handle uuencoded mail (as Eudora can) and can decode UNIX *compress* format archives (using either compress itself or a program like WinZip, which knows about compress), this command can make the returned message smaller and hence faster to download to your PC.

Table 24-5	An Archie Cheat Sheet
Command	*Description*
find *name*	Returns files that match that name.
whatis *name*	Returns entries from the "whatis" descriptive database that match that name.
compress	Compresses and uuencodes the response.
set *options*	Set optional parameters. Plain "set" returns all current settings.
servers	Returns a list of Archie servers.
path *addr*	Returns the response to that address rather than to the return address on the request.
help	Sends a help message.
quit	Disregards anything else in the message.

Gopher by Mail

Gopher is a networked menu system that was a predecessor to the better known World Wide Web. The Gopher system organizes all of its information into pages that contain menu items. Some items refer to other menus, while some are documents and other kinds of files.

Gophermail returns gopher pages by e-mail. It is a nicely designed service so that you can go from one page to the next easily by responding to the pages sent by the server.

Servers currently include the following:

✔ `gophermail@ncc.go.jp` (Japan)
✔ `gopherpp.shsu.edu` (Texas, USA)
✔ `gophermail@cr-df.rnp.br` (Brazil)
✔ `gophermail@eunet.cz` (Czech Republic)
✔ `gopher@nig.ac.jp` (Japan)

Start by sending an empty message to one of the servers. The server should send you back a copy of its home page, as shown in Figure 24-1. To retrieve any entry from that page, merely mail back the page it sent you with an X in front of each menu item that you want. When the server returns subsequent pages, you can, in turn, send those pages back with Xs in front of the items you want.

Figure 24-1:
The Gopher
home page
from Sam
Houston
State
University.

```
Mail this file back to gopher with an X before the menu items that you want.
If you don't mark any items, gopher will send all of them.
For best results, remove this message and all e-mail headers above it prior
to returning it to the GopherMail server.
1. Sam Houston State University Information/
2. Current Time and Weather in Huntsville, Texas, USA.
3. Daily Almanac (from UChicago).
4. Iconomics (SHSU Network Access Initiative Project)/
5. Information by Subject Area/
6. DIU Library Prototype Demonstration Area/
7. Network-based Information and References/
8. Other Gopher and Information Servers in the World/
9. TeX-related Materials/
10. Literate Programming Library/
11. VMS Gopher-related file library/
12. Veronica (search menu items in most of GopherSpace)/
13. Professional Sports Schedules from culine.Colorado.edu/
14. anonymous ftp archives on Niord.SHSU.edu/
15. anonymous ftp archives on ftp.shsu.edu/
16. Texas Legislative Gopher/
17. GopherMail @md Gopher via Electronic Mail!!
```

Some Gopher items are *search* items. To use a search item, you provide some words in the Subject: line of your message, and the Gopher server looks for items in an index that match your search words.

The most well-known Gopher searcher is Veronica, which searches through a large database of Gopher items. But there are many other indexes as well. If you select a search item, remember to put the words to search for in the Subject: line of your reply. (In the absence of search items, the Subject: line is ignored.)

For more details, send a message containing the word `help` to one of the Gophermail servers.

Other Servers on the Net

Many mail servers exist to return information from a particular source or of a particular type.

The Usenet FAQ archive

The Usenet-distributed bulletin board system contains thousands of discussion groups, many of which have Frequently Asked Question (FAQ) documents that answer to most common questions asked in those groups.

Nearly all the FAQs can be retrieved from `mail-server@rtfm.mit.edu`. FAQs are a treasure trove of useful information and often represent the distilled wisdom and opinions of many, many people interested in a particular topic.

- ✔ To get a list of newsgroups (topic areas) available, send `index usenet`.
- ✔ For a list of the FAQs for a particular newsgroup, send `index usenet/groupname`.
- ✔ To get a particular document, send `usenet/groupname/filename`.
- ✔ For general help, send `help` — as always.

Many FAQs are long enough that they are distributed in several parts. For example, the list of FTP servers discussed in "FTP by Mail" earlier in this chapter is in 21 files named `usenet/news.answers/ftp-list/sitelist/part1` through `part21`.

The daily discussions on usenet are too voluminous to be distributed by e-mail. (Do you really want 300 messages each day about the theory and practice of *Star Trek* in your mailbox?)

The InfoBot

The InfoBot is a mail server that provides a variety of services ranging from the extremely useful to the totally silly. Send `help` to `infobot@infomania.com` to get started. Services include:

- ✔ Looking up words in a large dictionary
- ✔ Looking up ham radio call signs
- ✔ City-by-city weather reports
- ✔ Translations of your documents into the distinctive dialect used by the Muppets' Swedish Chef (bork, bork, bork)
- ✔ Telephone area codes
- ✔ The "finger" service to ask about users on particular Internet hosts
- ✔ Several hundred digits of the value of π

New services are frequently added, and the help message will tell you about them.

Part VI
The Part of Tens

The 5th Wave   By Rich Tennant

"He should be all right now. I made him spend two and a half hours on a 'prisoners' chat line."

In this part . . .

No *Dummies* book would be complete without our handy lists of helpful hints. By the strangest coincidence, we have exactly *ten* hints in each list. (Note to the literal-minded: You may have to cut off and/or glue on some fingers to make your version of ten match up with ours. Perhaps it would be easier just to take our word for it.)

Chapter 25
The Ten Commandments of E-Mail

Thou shalt include a clear and specific subject line.

Thou shalt edit any quoted text down to the minimum needed.

Thou shalt read thine own message thrice before thou sendest it.

Thou shalt ponder how thy recipient shall react to thy message.

Thou shalt check thy spelling and thy grammar.

Thou shalt not curse, flame, spam, or USE ALL CAPS.

Thou shalt not forward any chain letter.

Thou shalt not use e-mail for any illegal or unethical purpose.

Thou shalt not rely on the privacy of e-mail, especially at work.

When in doubt, save thy message overnight.

The Golden Rule of E-Mail

That which thou findest hateful to receive, sendest thou not unto others.

Chapter 26
Ten E-Mail Messages *Not* to Send

$\bullet \bullet$

*Y*ears ago, we read a story about a motel on a canal that had a sign in the elevator that read "No Fishing From the Balcony." Guests just ignored the sign, so the hotel manager kept putting up bigger signs with sterner warnings, all to no avail. Finally, he sold the motel. The new owner took down the sign and no one ever thought to fish from a balcony again.

With this story in mind, we hesitantly present ten e-mail messages that we hope you will not emulate.

The Flame

```
To: pc-experts-list@server.com

Subject: Re: How do I back up my hard disk

Norbert Newbie wrote:

>I just got a new Zorch 686 for my birthday. The manual says
to back up my hard drive every day. How do I do that?
I'm sick of idiots like you wasting everybody's time by aksing
stupid, elementary queestions lik this. There's probably
nothing on your hard drive worth backing up anyway.
```

Maybe Norbert shouldn't have posted his question to this exalted group, but the e-mail writer just made things worse by sending the message out to everyone on the list. A polite e-mail reply just to Norbert might be appropriate. And if this person is such a *$%#@ expert, she could just give poor Norbert an answer or point him to a more appropriate list. Spell checking wouldn't hurt either.

The Good News Virus Hoax

```
> To: departments
> Subject: WARNING on Internet Email Virus
>
> There is a computer virus that is being sent across the
> Internet.  If you receive an e-mail message with the
> subject line "Good Times", DO  NOT read the message, DELETE
> it immediately.  Please read the messages below.
>
> Some miscreant is sending e-mail under the title "good
times" nation-wide.
> If you get anything like this, DON'T DOWNLOAD THE FILE! It
has a virus that rewrites your hard drive, obliterating
anything on it.  Please be careful and forward this mail to
anyone you care about—I have.
>
>        Subject: INTERNET VIRUS
>        Thought you might like to know...
>
> The FCC released a warning last Wednesday concerning a
> matter of major importance to any regular user of the
> InterNet.  Apparently, a new  computer virus has been
> engineered by a user of America Online that is  unparal-
> leled in its destructive capability.  Other, more well-
> known viruses such as Stoned, Airwolf, and Michaelangelo
pale in comparison to the prospects of this newest creation
by a warped mentality.
>
> What makes this virus so terrifying, said the FCC, is the
> fact that no program needs to be exchanged for a new com-
> puter to be infected.  It can be spread through the exist-
> ing e-mail systems of the InterNet.  Once a computer is
> infected, one of several things can happen.  If the
> computer contains a hard drive, that will most likely be
> destroyed.  If the program is not stopped, the computer's
> processor will be placed in an nth-complexity infinite
> binary loop - which can severely damage the processor if
> left running that way too long.  Unfortunately, most novice
> computer users will not realize what is happening until it
> is far too late...
```

This is a hoax. It's a self-perpetuating chain letter. Computer viruses are execut-
able programs and cannot be spread via text messages in e-mail. We include
most of the actual text here so that you might be able to spot it if it lands in
your inbox. Throw this message in the trash. Do not forward it. Send a kind
letter to the friend who so thoughtfully informed you and suggest that she buy a
copy of *Internet E-Mail For Dummies* so that she too can stay ahead of the pack.

The Chain Gang

```
To: ...

Subject: EARN BIG MONEY FAST

Could you use more cash? Just add your name to the bottom of
this message, send it to just 10 friends, and soon your bank
account will be in the six figures as the postman delivers
thousands of checks to your door each week...
```

The only thing dumber than sending a letter like this is giving them your money and passing the message on to your friends. Chain letters like this are illegal in most countries. (Hint: messages that say "this is not an illegal chain letter" always *are* illegal chain letters.) You are not likely to make any money from them, either, legally or not.

For a Free Good Time, Call . . .

```
To: ...

Subject: Have Fun by Phone for Free

Just call 011-234-1-23 45 67 89 No credit card needed.
```

There are all kinds of scams like this that are being run out of third world countries. The gimmick is that you are charged $3 or more for each minute of the international phone call (that 011 is the international access code in North America) that you make. The foreign phone company gives the scam artists a cut. And unlike 900 number charges, you can't get them taken off your phone bill.

Exporting PGP

```
To: monami@le-net.fr

Subject: Latest version of PGP

So we can chat in private in the future, I've attached the
binary file for the latest version of PGP to this message.
```

First of all, exporting PGP from the U.S. without a license is seriously illegal, and we know you don't have a license because the State Department won't give you one. In fact, what you did is a felony. Second, PGP is illegal in France, so you might just have gotten your friend in hot water. See Chapter 23 for information on how you and most of your friends can get PGP legally.

The Dying Boy Hoax

```
To: ...

Subject: Dying Boy Wants Business cards

A boy in England who is dying of leukemia wants to get into
the Book of Records for receiving as many business cards as
possible. Send your card to...
```

The actual boy who first made this request was cured, thank goodness, and he really, REALLY doesn't want any more cards.

The Modem Tax Hoax

```
To: ...

Subject: Fight the modem tax

Congress is planning to tax your modem to pay for the
Internet. Call, write, or fax...
```

There once was a proposal for a modem tax back in 1987, but it never got far. If we could only tax messages like this!

Subscribe Message to the Wrong Address

```
To: foo-l@server.com

Subject:

subscribe FOO-L
```

The problem here is that you are sending your subscription request to the mailing list's *list* address, not to its *administrative* address. The administrative address, which in this case is probably `listserv@server.com`, is where `subscribe` and `unsubscribe` messages should go. This is not a great way to introduce yourself to everyone on the list — although everybody *will* get a copy.

The Cause

```
To: fellow-coworkers@myjob.com

Subject: Save the Polyesters

Did you know that some manufacturers require their employees
to wear polyester socks? I am sure all of you find this abuse
horrifying and will be glad to sign this electronic petition
asking...
```

This cause may be very dear to your heart, but you should not assume that it will be as great a concern to people you work with or to the people on a mailing list that has nothing to do with this issue.

The Grabber

```
To: foo-l@server.com

Subject: SEX!!!

This isn't really about sex, I just wanted to get everyone's
attention so that I can tell you about...
```

Well, you probably did, and we're sure they think highly of you and will give what you say the serious consideration it deserves.

The Subject Is Everything

```
To: email@dummies.com

Subject: Please tell me what my e-mail address is. Just got
your book as a gift last week and it looks great so far. I
recommended it to several of my friends and plan to send a
copy to my parents. Have a great day.
```

We enjoy getting fan mail, but it is generally considered a good idea to put the text of your message in the message body, *not* in the subject line. Put a concise, informative desciption of your message in the subject line, please.

It's Hard to Ignore 15,000 Messages

```
To: foo-l@server.com

Subject: Ignore this message

I just want to see if my e-mail program works.
```

It may only take the subscribers to this list a few seconds to drag your message to the trash, but you are still being very inconsiderate for wasting their time. If you really want to test out a new mail system, just send a message to email@dummies.com. Our robot will confirm receipt and tell you your e-mail address. Add your thoughts about this book since we do read those messages.

Chapter 27
Ten Great Messages to Send

Having told you in Chapter 26 what not to send, here are ten e-mail messages that we hope you will emulate.

Long Time No See

```
To: janed@server.com
From: Marco@provider.com
Subject: Hi!

Saw your name on feline-1 and I wondered if you are the same
Jane Dodi who sat next to me in French at Newtown High?
```

Thank You

```
To: nimbus-team@myjob.com
From: marco
Subject: Thanks

I was really surprised by the birthday cake yesterday at
lunch. Thanks for all the good wishes. Turning 50 didn't hurt
a bit!
```

I'm Mad and I Won't Take It Any More

```
To: jim_congressman@house.gov
From: janed@server.com
Subject: Proposed Federal Budget

I am writing to let you know my views on the draft federal
budget for 1999. In my opinion, it is very important that our
nation take seriously the clear imperative to redress the
long standing requirements we face as we enter the coming
century, nay, millennium, for a forceful and sharply focused
policy on...
```

Good Work

```
To: lorena@myjob.com
From: boss
Subject: Simson contract

Nice job. Thanks for all the extra hours you put in. Sue was
really pleased.
```

I Was Once New at This Too

```
To: nnewbie@server.com
From: joe-expert
Subject: Re: How do I back up my hard disk

Norbert Newbie wrote:

>I just got a new Zorch 686 for my birthday. The manual  says
>to back up my hard drive every day. How do I do that?

Your Zorch 686 comes with a built-in backup program. Just
double-click on the Backup icon in the Zorch Tools window.

BTW, pc-experts-list is not the best place for this sort of
question. Next time try zorch-l.

Also you might also want to pick up a copy of Zorch For
Dummies from IDG Books. Don't take this the wrong way :-)
Dummies books are well written and really try to take the
user's point of view.
```

Please Fix This

```
To: customer-feedback@zorch.com
From: nnewbie@server.com
Subject: Zorch 686 User Manual

On page 36, your Zorch 686 User Manual says to back up the
hard disk every day, but nowhere does it tell you how, and
the word "backup" is not in the index.
```

I'm Sorry

```
To: nnewbie@server.com
From: steve-expert
Subject: My apologies

I am really sorry I posted that nasty reply to your message
asking how to back up your Zorch 686 hard drive. pc-experts-
list may not have been the right place for you to post your
message, but that's no excuse for what I wrote. I guess I was
just having a bad day.

We have a Zorch at work and the backup utility is mentioned
on p. 52 of the manual, though I noticed it wasn't in the
index.
```

Lost Mail

```
To: arnold@server.com
From: johnl@server.com
Subject: Re: Errata for Chapter 3

Wrong johnl!
You probably meant to send this to johnl at some other sys-
tem, not here. Maybe you left off the domain part of the "To"
address.
```

Umm, Hi, We Haven't Met But . . .

```
To: janed@server.com
From: richard@eastdunk-tel.ma.us
Subject: RE: SF in Podunk seeks friend

I saw your message on the podunk-l mailing list and I know
how hard it can be to meet people in this area. I live about
30 miles away in Eastdunk. Let me tell you a little about
myself...
```

Let Us Know How We're Doing

```
To: email@dummies.com
From: you
Subject: E-mail For Dummies

Really liked your book, but I wish you had explained how
to...
```

Chapter 28

Ten Cats and Dogs: Mailing Lists You Can Chew On

· ·

*W*e present here, for your e-mail edification and enjoyment, several sets of polar opposite e-mail mailing lists.

Cats and Dogs: Some People Claim to Like Both

FELINE-L: The amazing cat fancier's mailing list offers support, love, and feline skullduggery for the serious cat lover. This list averages about 150 messages per day.

To subscribe, send the message: `sub FELINE-L` *yourfirstname yourlastname*
to: `listserv@psuvm.psu.edu`

CANINE-L: The dog lover's list. Lots of people like dogs, it seems.

To subscribe, send the message: `sub CANINE-L` *yourfirstname yourlastname*
to: `listserv@psuvm.psu.edu`

Macintosh and PC

Mac-L: The Macintosh questions and discussion list. Not sponsored by Apple.

To subscribe, send the message: `sub MAC-L` *yourfirstname yourlastname*
to: `listserv@yalevm.cis.yale.edu`

TIDBITS: An excellent newsletter for Macintosh users.

To subscribe, send the message: `sub TIDBITS` *yourfirstname yourlastname*
to: `listserv@ricevm1.rice.edu`

WinNews: All Windows 95 stuff. Tips and hints. New products. General propaganda.

To subscribe, send the message: `subscribe winnews` to: `enews99@microsoft.nwnet.com` (The subject should be blank.)

WIN95-L: Windows 95 Give-And-Take List

To subscribe, send the message: `sub WIN95-L` *yourfirstname yourlastname* to: `listserv@peach.ease.lsoft.com`

New and Old

New-List: This handy list lets you know about new mailing lists as they appear. (Note: the first part of the domain name is spelled "vee em one.")

To subscribe, send the message: `sub NEW-LIST` *yourfirstname yourlastname* to: `listserv@vm1.nodak.edu`

ARCH-L: General archaeology list, covering all aspects of archaeology worldwide.

To subscribe, send the message: `SUBSCRIBE ARCH-L` *yourfirstname yourlastname* to: `listserv@tamvm1.tamu.edu`

Single and Married

SINGLES: A forum to discuss issues related to the single life, including flirting.

To subscribe, send the following message: `subscribe SINGLES` to: `majordomo@indiana.edu`

WME-L: Worldwide Marriage Encounter Discussion.

To subscribe, send the message: `sub WME-L` *yourfirstname yourlastname* to: `listserv@american.edu`

Republican and Democrat

REPUB-L: To subscribe, send the message: `sub REPUB-L` *yourfirstname yourlastname* to: `listserv@vm.marist.edu`

CDLIST: College Democrats Discussion and Information Group

To subscribe, send the message: `sub CDLIST` *yourfirstname yourlastname*
to: `listserv@gwuvm.gwu.edu`

CLINTON: Discussion of Bill Clinton's Presidency

To subscribe, send the message: `sub CLINTON` *your firstname yourlastname*
to: `listserv@vm.marist.edu`

Jocks and Couch Potatoes

D-SPORT: Sports for Persons with Disabilities

To subscribe, send the message: `sub D-SPORT` *yourfirstname yourlastname*
to: `listserv@sjuvm.stjohns.edu`

SPORTSOC: Sociological aspects of sports discussion

To subscribe, send the message: `sub SPORTSOC` *yourfirstname yourlastname*
to: `listserv@vm.temple.edu`

SCREEN-L: Film and TV Studies Discussion List

To subscribe, send the message: `sub SCREEN-L` *yourfirstname yourlastname*
to: `listserv@ua1vm.ua.edu`. (That's a numeral one between "ua" and "vm.")

FRIENDS: List about the NBC Comedy *Friends.*

To subscribe, send the message: `sub FRIENDS` *yourfirstname yourlastname*
to: `listserv@listserv.dartmouth.edu`

Near and Far

Roadside mailing list: The discussions on this list concern great cheesy tourist attractions across the U.S. They focus on those that are still in operation but would also enjoy tales of gone-but-not-forgotten ones.

To subscribe, send the message: `SUBSCRIBE ROADSIDE` *yourfirstname yourlastname* to: `listproc@echonyc.com`

Earth and Sky mailing list: "Earth and Sky" is a radio broadcast on public radio stations. It covers questions on geology, earth science, and astronomy, and many of the questions are sent in by listeners. The transcripts of the radio broadcasts are sent out once a week along with references and sometimes additional information on a topic.

To subscribe, send the message: subscribe EARTHANDSKYH *youremailaddress* to: majordomo@lists.utexas.edu

Serious and Funny

E-POETRY: Electronic Poetry Distribution List

To subscribe, send the message: sub E-POETRY *yourfirstname yourlastname* to: listserv@ubvm.cc.buffalo.edu.

TOPTEN: David Letterman's Top-Ten lists from his TV program. It's the single most popular known mailing list with over 90,000 subscribers.

To subscribe, send the message: sub TOPTEN *yourfirstname yourlastname* to: listserv@listserv.clark.net

HUMOR: University of Georgia, Athens, Humor List

To subscribe, send the message: sub HUMOR *yourfirstname yourlastname* to: listserv@uga.cc.uga.edu

Quick and Dead

ECENET-L: Early childhood education/young children (0–8)

To subscribe, send the message: sub ECENET-L *yourfirstname yourlastname* to: listserv@vmd.cso.uiuc.edu

ROOTS-L: General Genealogy List

To subscribe, send the message: sub ROOTS-L *yourfirstname yourlastname* to: listserv@mail.eworld.com

JEWISHGEN: Jewish Genealogy Discussion Group

To subscribe, send the message: sub JEWISHGEN *yourfirstname yourlastname* to: listserv@mail.eworld.com

Part VII

Glossary and
Appendixes

The 5th Wave   By Rich Tennant

The embarrassment of
Laptop Static Cling

In this part . . .

You can learn a lot about where the e-mail you get is coming from if you can recognize the country codes and understand zones for domain names. We give you two references to help you figure out where your mail is coming from. We also describe what's on the CD-ROM that's included with this book. But before any of the appendixes, we provide you with a glossary defining all of the techie terms mentioned in this book.

Glossary

account: Computers used by more than one person use accounts to keep track of (and bill) who's doing what on the system. When you sign up with an Internet service provider, you're given an account name that allows you access.

address: The letters and numbers that tell an e-mail message where to go. It usually looks like `username` or `username@ hostname`, where `username` is your username, login name, or account number, and `hostname` is the Internet's name for the computer or Internet provider you use. The former is called a *local address;* the latter is called an *Internet address*. The *Internet E-Mail For Dummies* address, for example, is `email@dummies.com` because its username is `email` (for this book) and it's on a system named `dummies.com`.

See Chapter 3 for more information about addresses, including yours, and Chapter 20 to learn how to find out other people's addresses.

AFAIK: As Far As I Know.

All-in-One: An office automation system, including e-mail, that runs on Digital Equipment Corp. (DEC) computers.

America Online (AOL): A public Internet provider. If you have an account on AOL, your Internet address is `username@ aol.com`, where `username` is your account name. See Chapter 11 to learn how to use America Online to send e-mail.

anonymous FTP: A method of using the FTP program to log on to another computer to copy files, even though you don't have an account on the other computer. When you log on, you enter `anonymous` as the username and your address as the password, and you get access to publicly available files. See Chapter 24 for information about FTP-ing via e-mail.

AppleLink: An e-mail and bulletin board service developed by Apple Computer to communicate with its suppliers and large customers.

archive: A file that contains a group of files which have been compressed and glommed together for efficient storage. You have to use a program like PKZip, tar, or Stuffit to get the original files back out. See Chapter 5.

ARPANET: Started in 1969, ARPANET is the original ancestor of the Internet, funded by the U.S. Department of Defense's Advanced Research Projects Agency. ARPANET was dismantled several years ago.

article: A posting to a mailing list. That is, a message someone sends to the mailing list to be readable by everyone who reads the mailing list. See Chapter 21 for information about mailing lists.

ASCII: *A*merican *S*tandard *C*ode for *I*nformation *I*nterchange. Basically, the code computers use to represent letters, numbers, and special characters. Uses 7 or 8 bits per letter. Almost the same as *ISO Latin*.

ASCII armor: A way of coding binary files for data transmission so that they only use 64 common ASCII characters and so are less likely to be smashed by uncooperative mail systems.

AT&T Mail: A commercial e-mail system that connects to the Internet. If you have an AT&T Mail account, your Internet address is `username@attmail.com`, where `username` is your account name.

AUP: *A*cceptable *U*se *P*olicy; a set of rules describing which sorts of activities are permitted on a network. The most restrictive AUP was the one on the NSFNET that prohibited most commercial and non-academic use. The NSFNET AUP is no longer in force, although many people erroneously believe that it is.

automatic mailing list: A mailing list maintained by a computer program, usually one named LISTSERV or Majordomo. *See also* mailing list. Chapter 21 provides information about how to use mailing lists.

bang path address: An old-fashioned method of writing network addresses. UUCP, an old, cruddy mail system, used to use addresses that contained exclamation points (!) — also called *bangs* by computer types — to string together the parts of the address. Forget about them.

baud: Technically the number of *symbols* per second that a modem sends down a phone line. Many people incorrectly use baud as a synonym for bps (bits per second). John hates this, but he is the only one who seems to care.

Baudot: An older, five-bit code used for sending digital messages. Used in TTY and TDD equipment. Named after the inventor of the teletype machine.

BBS: Bulletin-board system; a system that lets people read each other's messages and post new ones.

BFN : Bye For Now. A TLA.

binary file: A file containing information that consists of more than just text. Examples include an archive, a picture, sounds, a video clip, a spreadsheet, or a word-processing document (which includes formatting codes in addition to characters).

bit: The smallest unit of measure for any kind of information. Bits can be on or off and are used in various combinations in computers to represent different kinds of data. Many bits (usually eight) form a byte. Bytes are often used to represent single letters, numbers, and punctuation.

BITFTP: The most widely available FTP-by-mail server. *See also* FTP-by-mail.

bitmap: Lots of teeny, tiny, little dots put together to make a picture. Screens (and paper) are divided into thousands of little, tiny bits, each of which can be turned on or off. These little bits are combined to create graphical representations. *GIF* and *JPG* files are the most popular kind of bitmap files on the Net.

BITNET: A network of mostly IBM mainframes that connects to the Internet. If you have an account on machine `xyzvm3` on the BITNET and your username on the machine is `abc`, your Internet mail address is `abc@xyzvm3.bitnet`; or if your system isn't well-informed about BITNET, `abc%xyzvm3.bitnet@cunyvm.cuny.edu`.

BIX: A commercial system formerly run by *Byte* magazine and now run by Delphi. If you have a BIX account, your Internet address is `username@bix.com`, where `username` is your account name.

bps: *B*its *p*er *s*econd. A measure of how fast data is transmitted. Usually used to describe modem speed. Not quite the same as *baud*.

browser: A super-duper, all-singing, all-dancing program that lets you read information on the World Wide Web. Netscape's browser Navigator 2.0 and Netcom's browser Netcruiser can also do e-mail.

BTW: *By The Way.* Another silly acronym, BTW.

bulletin-board system: An electronic message system that enables you to read and post messages. *See also* BBS.

byte: A series of bits, usually eight. Computer storage is often measured in bytes. *Kilo*byte means 1024 bytes; *Mega*byte means 1024 kilobytes (about a million bytes); *Giga*byte means 1024 megabytes (about a billion bytes).

CCITT: The old name for the international committee that set worldwide communication specifications. It's now called ITU-T — unless they've changed it again.

Cipher: A set of rules for scrambling up a message so that no one can read it without a key. See Chapter 22.

CIX: The Commercial Internet Exchange, an association of Internet providers who agree to exchange traffic without *AUP*-type restrictions.

classified: Information that has be designated Confidential, Secret, or Top Secret under U.S. or some other countries' secrecy laws.

client: A computer that uses the services of another computer (such as e-mail, Usenet, Gopher, FTP, Archie, or the World Wide Web.) If your computer is a PC or Macintosh and you dial in to another system, your computer becomes a client of the system you dial in to.

client/server model: A division of labor between computers. Computers that provide a service other computers can use are known as servers. Servers provide such services as e-mail, FTP, or the World Wide Web. If you don't have these services on your very own machine, you can connect to these machines and use these services and thereby become a client.

clipper chip: A standard for data encryption that uses a secret algorithm developed by the NSA, featuring key escrow.

code: Assignment of meaning to symbols used in communication — for example, "One if by land, two if by sea." If the meanings are kept secret, the code becomes a form of encryption.

com: When these letters appear in the last part of an address (`email@dummies.com`, for example), it indicates that the host computer is run by a company rather than by a university or governmental agency. It also means that the host computer is probably in the United States.

communications program: A program you run on your personal computer that enables you to call up and communicate with other computers. It's a rather broad term, but most people use it to mean a program that makes your computer pretend to be a terminal (that's why they are also known as *terminal programs* or *terminal emulators*). The most commonly used communications programs on PCs are Windows Terminal (because it's free with Windows), CrossTalk, and ProComm, though there are lots of others. Macintosh owners often use Zterm or Microphone.

compression program: Software used to squeeze files together so that they take up less room and are easier to transfer from one location to another. Favorite compression programs include PKZip and Stuffit. The opposite of compression is expansion or decompression.

CompuServe: An online e-mail and information provider that also gives you Internet access. If your CompuServe account number is 7123,456, your Internet address is 7123.456@compuserve.com (notice the period in the account number). See Chapter 12 for info on how to use CompuServe's e-mail services.

country code: The last part of a geographic address, which indicates which country the host computer is in. An address that ends in ca is Canadian, for example, and one that ends in us is in the United States. For a complete list, see Appendix A.

daemon: A mysterious little program that runs while you're not looking and takes care of things you would rather not know about. When your e-mail does not go through, you may get a long message from a mail daemon. If you are really clever, you might be able to figure out what it means.

DB-25: The style of data plug on most modems and PC serial ports. They are shaped like a 2-inch high, skinny letter *D* with 25 pins. (Macs use a smaller, round plug.)

Delphi: An e-mail and information provider that includes access to lots of Internet services. If you have an account on Delphi, your Internet address is user name@ delphi.com, where username is your account name. See Chapter 5 of our *MORE Internet For Dummies* to learn how to use Delphi to access the Internet.

DES: A cipher first proposed in 1975 by the U.S. Government for protection of non-classified data. Controversial because of its short, 56-bit key length, it is still widely used even though it can be broken. A newer version, called triple DES or 3DES, is considered strong.

digest: A compilation of the messages that have been posted to a mailing list over the past few days. Many people find it more convenient to receive one big message than a bunch of individual ones (see Chapter 21).

digital: Refers to information that has been converted to a pattern of ones and zeros or bits.

digital signature: A string of bits that is added to a message, which can only be created by someone with that message and a particular secret key.

directory: A structure, sort of like a file folder (and called a folder in the Macintosh world). A special kind of file used to organize other files. Directories are lists of other files and can contain other directories (known as subdirectories) that contain still more files. UNIX, DOS, and Windows systems all use directory structures. The more stuff you have, the more you need directories in which to organize it. Directories enable you to organize files hierarchically.

discrete logarithm: A method for public key cryptography that relies on the difficulty of undoing (hold your nose) exponentiation in cyclic groups.

domain: The official Internet-ese name of a computer or group of computers on the Net. It's the part of an Internet address that comes after the @. *Internet E-Mail For Dummies* Central is email@dummies.com, for example, and its domain name is dummies.com.

domain name server: (Or just *name server* or abbreviated as *DNS.*) A computer on the Internet that translates between Internet domain names, such as xuxa.iecc.com, and Internet numerical addresses, such as 140.186.81.2.

download: To bring software from a remote computer "down" to your computer.

dumb terminal: A screen and a keyboard and not much else. It sort of resembles a PC without the computer. Dumb terminals connect to other computers and use their data and their computing power. When you use your computer to dial into another computer (ignoring SLIP and PPP connections for the moment), your computer generally acts like a dumb terminal and relies on the computer you've dialed into for processing the requests you make.

dynamic routing: A method of addressing information on the Internet (not just mail messages, but all information) so that if one route is blocked or broken, the information can take an alternative route. Pretty darned clever. The U.S. Department of Defense built this method into the design of the Internet for the benefit of the military to resist enemy attack. It's also useful when nonmilitary networks are attacked by errant backhoes.

e-mail: Electronic mail (also called *e-mail* or just *mail*) messages sent by way of computers that talk to each other. For the basics of sending and receiving e-mail, see Chapter 3.

Easylink: An e-mail service formerly run by Western Union and now run by AT&T. If you have an Easylink account, your Internet address is `1234567@eln.attmail.com`, where `1234567` is your account number.

edu: When these letters appear in the last part of an address (in `info@mit.edu`, for example), it indicates that the host computer is run by an educational institution, probably a college or university. It also means that the host computer is probably in the United States.

elliptic curves: A method for public key cryptography that relies on the difficulty of undoing certain polynomial transformations. Not to be confused with morphing.

elm: An easy-to-use UNIX mail reader. Another good one is Pine. See Chapter 16 for information on Pine.

emoticons: *See* smileys.

encryption: Converting a message into a form that can only be understood by the desired recipient, usually by means of a code or cipher.

etiquette: Proper behavior or courtesy. See Chapter 4 for tips on e-mail etiquette.

Eudora: A mail-handling program that runs on the Macintosh and under Windows. Originally a shareware program, it is now sold by QualComm. Eudora Light is still available free; Eudora Pro sells for about $65. See Chapters 8 and 9 in this book to learn how to get and use it.

eWorld: An Internet and e-mail service developed by Apple Computer.

expansion program: Software used to expand a file that has been compressed. Favorite expansion programs include UNZIP and Unstuffit.

FAQ: *F*requently *A*sked *Q*uestions. A collection of answers to questions that come up regularly in an Internet newsgroup or mailing list. The collection of FAQ's at `rtfm.mit.edu` forms a vast, up-to-date, online encyclopedia.

To read an entire book of frequently asked questions about the Internet, get *Internet FAQs* (IDG Books Worldwide, Inc.).

Fax modem: Modems that enable you to send and receive faxes in addition to ordinary computer-type data. Fax is short for facsimile, a technology that uses ordinary phone lines to send copies of printed material from place to place. If you stick fax technology on your computer, what you send may never touch paper. It can go from your computer to theirs or to their fax machine if they don't have a computer.

feature creep: *See* version creep. Avoid creeps of all kinds.

FIDONET: A worldwide network of bulletin-board systems (BBSs). Each individual BBS is called a *node* on FIDONET and has a three- or four-part numeric address in the form *1:2/3* or *1:2/3.4* (who the heck thought of this?). To send Internet mail to someone on FIDONET, address it to `firstname.last name@p4.f3.n2.z1.fidonet.org` (for nodes with four-part names) or `firstname.lastname@f3.n2.z1` (for nodes with three-part names), substituting the addressee's username for `firstname.lastname`.

file: A collection of information (data or a software program, for example) treated as a unit by computers. Files have names and are organized into directories or folders.

file-transfer protocol: A method of transferring one or more files from one computer to another on a network or phone line. The idea of using a protocol is that the sending and receiving programs can check that the information has been received correctly. The most commonly used dial-up protocols are Xmodem, Ymodem, Zmodem, and Kermit. The Internet has its own file-transfer protocol, called FTP (clever name, huh?), to transfer files among computers on the Net. See Chapter 24 for information on how to use FTP via e-mail.

finger: A program that displays information about someone on the Internet. On most UNIX systems, the command tells you who is logged on right now. On most Internet hosts, it tells you the actual name and perhaps some other information, based on the person's Internet address and the last time she logged on.

firewall: A system has a firewall around it if it lets only certain kinds of messages in and out from the rest of the Internet. If an organization wants to exchange mail with the Internet, for example, but it doesn't want nosy college students using the telnet system to log in and read everyone's files, its connection to the Internet can be set up to prevent incoming telnets.

folder: A structure, sort of like a file folder, used to group items of a like nature. E-mail programs enable you to store your mail in folders for easy retrieval.

freenet: A free online system. Wow! The first one, created at the University of Cleveland, is called the Cleveland Freenet, offering local community information and limited access to the Internet. Lots of other freenets have sprung up, and because you can telnet from one to another, if you can access one, you can access them all. For a list of freenets, see Chapter 2.

FTP: *File-Transfer Protocol*; also the name of a program that uses the protocol to transfer files all over the Internet. See Chapter 24 for information on how to use FTP via e-mail.

FTP-by-mail: A method by which you can send a mail message to a server computer to request that a file be mailed to you by way of e-mail. This is a way to get files over the Net, slowly, if you have access only to e-mail (see Chapter 24 for more information).

FTP server: An Internet host computer that stores files which can be retrieved by FTP. Some FTP servers also accept uploads of files.

gateway: A computer that connects one network with another when the two networks use different protocols. The UUNET computer connects the uucp network with the Internet, for example, providing a way for mail messages to move between the two networks. For more information about how gateways work, see Chapter 3 of *MORE Internet For Dummies.* Also an older name for what's now called a *router.*

GEnie: An online service run by General Electric. If you have an account on GEnie and your mail name (not your username!) is `ABC`, your Internet address is `ABC@genie.geis.com`.

GIF: A type of graphics file originally defined by CompuServe and now found all over the Net. GIF stands for *Graphics Interchange Format.* See Chapter 5 for suggestions about how to handle GIF files. Pronounced *JIF* unless you feel like saying *GIF.*

GKA: Government key access. A proposed standard that would insure that your government can get your encryption keys. Proponents claim it is needed for law enforcement; civil liberties groups find it abhorrent. *See* key escrow and Chapter 22.

GMT: Greenwich Mean Time. Often used in international communications. Also called UTC, Z, or Zulu time. GMT does *not* change during the summer. GMT is 5 hours later than Eastern Standard Time.

gov: When these letters appear in the last part of an address (`cu.nih.gov`, for example), it indicates that the host computer is run by some part of a government body, probably the U.S. federal government, rather than by a company or university. (Your tax dollars at play!) Most `gov` sites are in the United States.

Group 3: The standard for sending fax messages everyone uses these days. There is a *Group 4* fax standard waiting in the wings that could provide much higher quality over the Internet.

host name: The name of a computer on the Internet. *See also* Domain.

HTTP: *HyperText Transfer Protocol,* which is the way World Wide Web pages are transferred over the Net (see Chapters 4 and 5). Also see Chapter 15 of *MORE Internet For Dummies* for more details about how to read the World Wide Web from a PC with Windows. Web addresses start with "`http://`"

hypertext: A system of writing and displaying text that enables the text to be linked in multiple ways, to be available at several levels of detail, and to contain links to related documents. Hypermedia can also contain pictures, sounds, video — you name it. The World Wide Web uses hypertext.

icon: A little picture on your computer screen intended to represent something bigger, such as a program, a choice of action, or object.

IDEA: A cipher used to encrypt messages in PGP. Patented by Ascom Tech AG in Switzerland. Considered very strong.

IETF: *Internet Engineering Task Force.* The hard working volunteers who set the standards that make the Internet work. Much more effective than the ISO. For example, IETF insists that you make a working model before you propose a standard.

IMO, IMHO, IMNSHO: *I*n *My O*pinion; *I*n *My H*umble Opinion; *I*n *My N*ot *So H*umble Opinion.

Internet: An interconnected bunch of computer networks, including networks in all parts of the world. See *The Internet For Dummies,* 3rd Edition for more information.

Internet Explorer: Microsoft's Web browser. If you have a Microsoft Network account, you can download it or you can buy it as part of Microsoft PLUS!

Internet Protocol: *See* IP.

Internet service provider (ISP): A shell access or SLIP/PPP service that enables you to use the Internet on a paying (by the month or hour) basis. If you need to find one, check *The Internet For Dummies,* 3rd Edition for a partial listing and helpful hints.

Internet Society: An organization dedicated to supporting the growth and evolution of the Internet. You can contact it at isoc@isoc.org.

InterNIC: The Internet *N*etwork *I*nformation *C*enter, a repository of information about the Internet. It is divided into two parts: Directory Services, run by AT&T in New Jersey, and Registration Services, run by Network Solutions in Virginia. It's funded partially by the National Science Foundation and partially by fees charged to register Internet domains.

To find out more about it, point your Web browser at http://rs.internet.net. To FTP information from InterNIC, try ftp.internic.net.

interrupt character: A key or combination of keys you can press to stop whatever is happening on your computer. You might find that you have started something and don't want to wait for it to finish. Common interrupt characters are Ctrl-C and Ctrl-D. Telnet's usual interrupt character is Ctrl-].

IP: *I*nternet *P*rotocol, a scheme that enables information to be routed from one network to another as necessary. Don't worry: You don't have to know any more about it. For a long and tedious discussion, see Chapter 2 of *MORE Internet For Dummies.*

ISDN: *I*ntegrated *S*ervices *D*igital *N*etwork. A faster, digital phone service that operates at speeds of up to 128 kilobits per second. See *ISDN For Dummies* to learn how the phone companies have fouled this up.

ISO: *I*nternational *S*tandards *O*rganization. A multinational, independent body formed to define international standards for, among other things, network communications. Often a little late in coming to terms with the reality of what's already in place.

ISO Latin: A character code very much like ASCII. You're allowed to write English and other languages (as well as Latin) using it.

ITAR: *I*nternational *T*raffic in *A*rms Regulations. Old name for the U.S. State Department rules that limit export of machine guns, poison gas, and encryption software.

ITU-T: The International Telecommunications Union (an agency of the United Nations) committee that sets worldwide communication specifications. It used to be called CCITT.

Kermit: A file-transfer protocol developed at Columbia University and available for a variety of computers, from PCs to mainframes. See Chapter 4 of *MORE Internet For Dummies* for more information about file-transfer protocols.

key: A string of bits that tell an encryption program exactly how to do its thing. You need one key to encrypt a message, another to decrypt it. Sometimes both keys are the same (*symmetric* keys).

key escrow: Handing over your secret encryption keys to some organization (a key escrow *agent*) who will hold them so that your government can get them with a court order (or even without, some suspect). *See* GKA.

link: A connection. Two computers can be linked together. Also can refer to a pointer to a file that exists in another place. Rather than have a copy of a particular file reside in many places, for example, some file systems (the ones in UNIX, for example) enable a filename to point to another file. Finally, a link can refer to a hypertext link in a Web page that connects one page to another.

LISTSERV: A family of programs that automatically manage mailing lists, distributing messages posted to the list, adding and deleting members, and so on without the tedium of someone doing it manually. The names of mailing lists maintained by LISTSERV usually end with -L. See Chapter 21 for information about how to get on and off LISTSERV mailing lists.

list server: A program that automatically manages mailing lists. *See also* LISTSERV. See Chapter 21.

LOL: *Laughing Out Loud.* A TLA.

Lotus Notes: A distributed database and groupware package from IBM that includes encrypted e-mail. See Chapter 18.

MacTCP: TCP/IP for the Macintosh. Not very interesting except that you can't put your Mac on the Internet without it.

mail: In this book, electronic mail or *e-mail*. Other types of mail include *voice mail,* which you probably already know and hate, and postal mail, known in the cyber world as *snail* mail or *dead-tree* mail, which consists of pieces of paper stuffed in envelopes with postage stamps on the outside. For a detailed description, buy this book.

mail server: The computer that provides mail services. A mail server usually sends mail out for you (using a system called SMTP) and may also enable you to download your mail to a PC or Mac by using a protocol called POP. See Chapters 8, 9, and 10 in this book to learn how to use Eudora and Netscape Navigator 2.0 to grab your mail from a mail server.

mailing list: A special kind of e-mail address for a computer that remails any incoming mail to a list of *subscribers*. Each mailing list has a specific topic, so you subscribe to the ones of interest (see Chapter 21).

mainframe: A large computer usually sold complete with all its peripherals and often a closed architecture (meaning not friendly to other vendors' products). Usually housed in a special room with glass walls, false floors, and air conditioning. Often refers to large, old IBM computers.

Majordomo: Like LISTSERV, a program that handles mailing lists. See Chapter 21 in this book and Chapter 20 of *MORE Internet For Dummies.*

MCI Mail: A commercial e-mail system linked to the Internet. If you have an MCI Mail account, you have both a username and a seven-digit user number. Your Internet address is `1234567@mcimail.com` or `username@mcimail.com`, substituting your own username or number, of course.

Watch out when you're addressing mail by name on MCI Mail — more than one person may have the same name! Numbers are safer. If a name is ambiguous, MCI Mail returns a message that gives some hints about how to find the user you want.

message: Some information that one person wishes to send to another. The content of e-mail.

Microsoft Network (MSN): A commercial online service run by Microsoft and usable only if you have Windows 95. If your MSN username is `BillGates`, your Internet e-mail address is `billgates@msn.com`. See Chapter 14 for info on how to use MSN's e-mail services.

mil: When these letters appear in the last part of an address (`wsmrsimtel20@ army.mil`, for example), it indicates that the host computer is run by some part of the U.S. military. Note that the computer may or may not be located in the U.S.

MIME: *M*ultipurpose *I*nternet *M*ail *E*xtension used to send pictures, word processor files, and anything else other than straight text through e-mail. Netscape Navigator 2.0, Eudora, Pine, and other hip e-mail programs support MIME.

mirror: An FTP server that provides copies of the same files as another server. Some FTP servers are so popular that other servers have been set up to mirror them and spread the FTP load on to more than one site.

modem: A gizmo that lets your computer talk on the phone. Short for modulator/ demodulator. A modem can be internal (a board that lives inside your computer), external (a box that connects to your computer's serial port), or a PC Card. Unless it's a radio modem, you need a phone wire to connect the modem to your phone jack.

For tons of information about modems and how to use them, get *Modems For Dummies,* by Tina Rathbone.

moderated mailing list: A mailing list run by a moderator. See Chapter 21.

moderator: Someone who looks first at the messages posted to a mailing list or newsgroup before releasing them to the public. The moderator can nix messages that are stupid (in her opinion, of course), redundant, or inappropriate for that list or newsgroup (wildly off the topic or offensive, for example). Depending on whom you ask, this is editing or censorship, but the Internet is getting so big and crowded that non-moderated discussions can generate an amazing number of uninteresting messages.

Mosaic: A super-duper all-singing, all-dancing program that lets you read information on the World Wide Web. Comes in Windows, Mac, and UNIX flavors. See Chapter 15 in *MORE Internet For Dummies* to learn how to get, install, and use it. Similar to Netscape.

MS-DOS: The original Microsoft operating system for IBM-compatible personal computers. Made a young Harvard dropout named Bill Gates the richest person in the world.

MSN: *See* Microsoft Network.

name server: *See* domain name server.

NSA: *N*ational *S*ecurity *A*gency. Top Secret U.S. Government agency in charge of protecting U.S. communications and producing foreign intelligence from intercepted and decoded messages. *Bete noir* of the PGP crowd.

Netcom: A national Internet service provider whose browser, Netcruiser, provides e-mail services. See Chapter 15.

NetCruiser: A Web browser from Netcom that also provides e-mail services. See Chapter 15.

Netscape: The first company to scare Microsoft. Netscape's world-class World Wide Web browser has taken the planet by storm. Learn how to use it for e-mail in Chapter 10.

network: For our purposes, we are talking about a bunch of computers that are connected together. Those in the same or nearby buildings are called *local area networks;* those that are farther away are called *wide area networks.* When you interconnect a large number of networks all over the world, you get the Internet!

For more than you want to know about how networks are connected together into the Internet, see Chapters 2 and 3 in *MORE Internet For Dummies.*

networking conventions: Standards that everybody, or almost everybody, agrees to so that networks can talk to each other. Also large gatherings where people go to learn how to connect up their computers.

NIC: *N*etwork *I*nformation *C*enter. An NIC is responsible for coordinating a set of networks so that the names, network numbers, and other technical details are consistent from one network to another. The address of the one for the U.S. part of the Internet is internic.net.

node: A computer on the Internet, also called a *host.* Computers that provide a service, such as FTP sites or places that run Gopher, are also called *servers.*

NSFNET: The *N*ational *S*cience *F*oundation's former network, a part of the Internet devoted to research and education and funded by government money. It has gone away, replaced by pieces of commercial networks. ANS, the company that formerly ran the NSFNET, now belongs to America Online.

operating system: The basic software that runs on a computer and is responsible for all the ordinary things that a computer has to keep track of, such as files, disks, and printers. MS-DOS, Windows 95, UNIX, VMS, OS/2, and Mac OS System 7.5 are all operating systems. (Operating systems arouse great passions among computer types, much like football teams and diet programs do among other humans.)

parity: Once upon a time, someone had the idea that when you sent 7-bit data in 8-bit bytes, you could use the extra bit to detect errors. Nowadays, people use much more sophisticated ways to find and correct errors in digital communications, but the parity idea remains enshrined in many communications programs. Just say "none."

password or passphrase: A secret code used to keep things private. Your account on the system that connects you to e-mail is no doubt protected by a password. Be sure to pick a code that is not obvious, preferably combining numbers and letters so as to thwart any untoward activity. Passphrases are longer than passwords and can contain multiple words for added security.

password file: The file in which all the passwords for a system are stored. Most systems are smart enough to keep passwords encoded so that even if someone gains access to this file, it isn't of much value.

PC Card or PCMCIA Card: A small electronics module, about the size of a fat credit card, that plugs into a special slot on your computer. Often used for laptop modems. PCMCIA either refers to the joint committee of the *P*ersonal *C*omputer *M*anufacturers and *C*omputer *I*ndustry *A*ssociation trade groups that came up with the card's specifications, or it means Purchasers Can't Memorize Computer Industry Abbreviations.

PEM: *P*rivacy *E*nhanced *M*ail. A standard for encrypted e-mail, similar to but not compatible with PGP.

PGP: A popular e-mail and file encryption program developed by Phil Zimmermann and the subject of Chapter 23. PGP stands for *P*retty *G*ood *P*rivacy.

Pine: A UNIX-based e-mail program inspired by another UNIX e-mail program called elm. (It stands for *pine is not e*lm.) Pine is easy to use, at least for a UNIX program; it's described in Chapter 16.

Pipeline: An Internet provider in New York City (`pipeline.com` is its address) that works with a special Windows communications program, also called Pipeline. It uses its own protocol to talk to this program, which enables it to display everything in a nice Windows-y way. Several other providers around the country use the Pipeline program, giving it different names to avoid consistency.

PKZip: A file-compression program that runs on PCs. PKZip creates a *ZIP file* that contains compressed versions of one or more files. To restore them to their former size and shape, you use PKUnzip. *PK,* by the way, stands for Phil Katz, who wrote the program. PKZip and PKUnzip are shareware programs available from many FTP sites. If you use the programs, you are honor-bound to send Mr. Katz a donation (the program will tell you the address).

If you use a Windows computer, you will probably prefer WinZip, which has nice Windows-y menus and buttons. You can get it via FTP from `ftp.winzip.com` in the

`/winzip` directory, or from nearly every BBS in the world. See Chapter 24.

POP: *P*ost *O*ffice *P*rotocol, a system by which a mail server on the Internet lets you pick up your mail and download it to your PC or Mac. There have been several versions, but POP-3 is the one nearly everyone uses.

port number: On a networked computer, an identifying number assigned to each program that is chatting on the Internet. The program that handles incoming telnet sessions uses port 23, for example, and the program that handles some other service has another number. You hardly ever have to know these numbers — the Internet programs work this stuff out among themselves.

PPP: *P*oint-to-*P*oint *P*rotocol, a scheme for connecting two computers over a phone line (or a network link that acts like a phone line). Like *SLIP,* only better. See Chapter 2 of *MORE Internet For Dummies.*

Prodigy: A large online system run by IBM and Sears. If you have a Prodigy account, your Internet address is `username@` `prodigy.com` (substitute your username for `username`). See Chapter 13.

Profs: An office automation system, including e-mail, that runs on IBM mainframes.

protocol: Rules for communicating that two computers agree on. When you use a file-transfer protocol, for example, the two computers involved (the sender and the receiver) agree on a set of signals that mean "go ahead," "got it," "didn't get it, please re-send," and "all done."

The Internet involves lots of different protocols that help computers with different jobs interact with each other.

public key cryptography: A really neat encryption system that uses two keys: your *public key,* which you can tell to anyone and is used to encrypt messages sent to you; and your *secret key* that you tell to no one and lets you read those messages. See Chapter 22. Techniques for public key cryptography include RSA, discrete logarithms, and elliptic curves.

RC4: A cipher developed by Ron Rivest for RSADSI that is used in Netscape Navigator 2.0. The version of this cipher with 40 bit keys is considered weak enough that you can export it from the U.S. (You still have to say "May I?")

RIPEM: An e-mail encryption program based on PEM. Not as popular as PGP.

rot13: A very simple cipher invented by Julius Caesar that is used on the Internet to encrypt potentially offensive material such as off-color jokes.

ROTFL, ROTFLOL: *R*olling *O*n *T*he *F*loor, *L*aughing. *R*olling *O*n *T*he *F*loor, *L*aughing *O*ut *L*oud.

RSA: A technique for public key cryptography that relies on the apparent difficulty of breaking up a big number into prime factors.

RSADSI: *R*SA *D*ata *S*ecurity, *I*nc. A company that promotes RSA public key encryption technology and controls key patents in the field.

RTFM: *R*ead *T*he *M*anual. A suggestion made by people who feel that you have wasted their time asking a question that you could have found the answer to by looking it up.

A well-known and much-used FTP site named rtfm.mit.edu contains up-to-date FAQs for all Usenet newsgroups, by the way.

secret key: The key you never tell to anyone. (Everyone knows about the one under your doormat.) *See* public key cryptography.

security: In the computer world, a means to allow access to only those who should have it. Security includes the use of passwords to protect your account.

serial port: The place on your computer where you can plug in a modem or other serial device. Often confused with the place where giant corn flakes ships dock.

server: A computer that provides a service to other computers on a network. An e-mail server, for example, lets people use e-mail.

service provider: An organization that provides access to e-mail and possibly the Internet. Your service provider might be a commercial online service such as America Online or CompuServe, a shell provider, or your school or workplace.

shareware: Computer programs that are easily available for you to try with the understanding that if you decide to keep the program, you will pay for it and send the requested amount to the shareware provider specified in the program. In this honor system, a great deal of good stuff is available, and voluntary compliance makes it viable.

signature: The line or lines at the end of a message that say who sent it. Some mailers let you make up a signature file that is then added to all outgoing e-mail. *See also* digital signature.

SLIP: Short for *S*erial *L*ine *I*nternet *P*rotocol, a software scheme for connecting a computer to the Internet over a serial line. For example, if you can run SLIP on your personal computer and you call up an

Internet provider that does SLIP, your computer is *on the Internet;* it's not just a terminal — it's right on it. You can telnet and FTP to other computers; when you get files, they arrive back on your PC, not on the Internet provider's computer.

For instructions about how to run SLIP on your computer, see Chapter 9 of *MORE Internet For Dummies.*

smileys: A short group of characters used to express emotions and irony in an e-mail message. Some people think they're fun :-) while others find them dumb :-(. Also called *emoticons.* See Chapter 4 for a list of common smileys.

SMTP: *S*imple *M*ail *T*ransfer *P*rotocol, the optimistically named method by which Internet mail is delivered from one computer to another.

socket: A logical "port" a program uses to connect to another program running on another computer on the Internet. You might have an FTP program using sockets for its FTP session, for example, while Eudora connects by way of another socket to get your mail.

software: Computer programs that make computers usable as something other than a paperweight. Compare to *hardware.*

spam: Originally a meat-related, sandwich-filling product. The word now refers to the act of posting inappropriate commercial messages to a large number of unrelated, uninterested Usenet newsgroups or mailing lists.

spoiler: Used in the subject line of a message to warn that the message contains information that you may not want to know, like the ending of a movie or the solution to a puzzle.

SprintMail: An e-mail system provided by Sprintnet and formerly named Telemail. Believe it or not, if you have a SprintMail account, your Internet address is `/G=firstname/S=lastname/O=company/C=countrycode/A=TELEMAIL/@sprint.com`. Substitute your first name, last name, company name, and country code (`us` for United States folks).

SSL: *S*ecure *S*ocket *L*ayer. A scheme proposed by Netscape to allow secure connections over the Internet, including e-mail.

string: A bunch of characters strung together, such as "Internet E-Mail For Dummies." Strings are composed of any characters available in the character set being used, typically all letters, digits, and punctuation.

Stuffit: A compression program for the Mac.

subdirectory: A directory within a directory.

substring: A piece of a string. *See also* string.

System 7.5: The latest, most feature-laden, Macintosh operating system, which includes built-in TCP/IP support.

TCP/IP: The system that networks use to communicate with each other on the Internet. It stands for *T*ransfer *C*ontrol *P*rotocol/*I*nternet *P*rotocol, if you care. See Chapters 2 and 3 of *MORE Internet For Dummies* for the gory details.

TDD: *T*elecommunications *D*evice for the *D*eaf. *See also* TTY.

telnet: A program that lets you log in to other computers on the Net.

terminal: In the olden days, a terminal was a thing that consisted of a screen, a keyboard, and a cable that connected it to a computer. These days, not many people (not many people *we* know) use terminals because personal computers are so cheap. Why have a brainless screen and keyboard when you can have your own computer on your desk?

Of course, there are still many times when you want to connect to a big computer somewhere. If you have a personal computer, you can run a program that makes it *pretend* to be a brainless screen and keyboard — the program is called a *terminal emulator, terminal program,* or *communications program.*

terminal emulator: *See* communications program and also terminal.

terminal program: *See* communications program and also terminal.

Tessera card: A PC Card that contains the clipper chip. Used by the U.S. government and others to protect e-mail and other data. Features *key escrow.* See Chapter 22.

text file: A file that contains only characters, with no special formatting characters, graphical information, sound clips, video, or what have you. Most computers store their text by using a system of codes named *ASCII,* so this type of file is also known as an *ASCII text file.* See Chapter 3.

third party: Sometimes you buy your computer from one place and your operating software from somewhere else, but you find that you still need other hardware or software pieces to make it all work. The people from whom you buy those other pieces are known as third-party vendors.

thread: An article posted to a mailing list or Usenet newsgroup, together with all the follow-up articles, the follow-ups to follow-ups, and so on.

Organizing articles into threads makes it easier to choose which articles in a newsgroup you want to read.

TLA: *T*hree *L*etter *A*cronym (or *A*bbreviation).

TIA: *T*he *I*nternet *A*dapter, nifty software that makes your regular dial-up account look like a SLIP or PPP account.

Also, *T*hanks *I*n *A*dvance, for the acronymophiles.

TTY: Teletypewriter. A method for visual communication over the telephone that is used by the Deaf and hard of hearing and their friends. TTY uses the ancient Baudot code which turns out to be ideal in some ways even though it is slow. Also know as TDD. See Chapter 6.

Unicode : A standard for encoding all the writing styles used in the world today, including Chinese, Japanese, and Korean, and all alphabets. Takes two bytes per character, if you were wondering. Designed to facilitate international communications, including e-mail.

UNIX: An operating system developed by the phone company back when it was a monopoly. Enjoying something of a come back because it gives good Internet. Caution: UNIX was designed for use by trained professionals. Do not attempt to use it at home.

For the complete truth about UNIX, get a copy of *UNIX For Dummies,* 2nd Edition.

upload: To put your stuff on somebody else's computer.

URL: *U*niform *R*esource *L*ocator, a way of naming network resources and originally for linking pages together in the World Wide Web. Luckily, you don't have to know much about them — only the people who *write*

Web pages really have to fool with them. They have some features in common with e-mail addresses but serve different purposes. URLs are often case sensitive.

Usenet: A system of thousands of distributed bulletin boards called *newsgroups*. A competitor for mailing lists. You read the messages by using a program called a *newsreader*. See *The Internet For Dummies,* 3rd Edition for an introduction to newsgroups and a list of some interesting ones.

UUCP: An elderly and creaky mail system still used by some UNIX systems. UUCP stands for *UNIX-to-UNIX-copy*. UUCP mail address contain exclamation points rather than periods between the parts (and they are in reverse order), a method known as *bang path addressing.* Whenever possible, use regular Internet addresses instead.

uuencode/uudecode: Programs that encode files to make them suitable for sending as e-mail. Because e-mail messages must be text, not binary information, *uuencode* can disguise non-text files as text so that you can include them in a mail message. When the message is received, the recipient can run *uudecode* to turn it back into the original file. A pain in the mouse to use compared to MIME. For more information, see Chapter 5.

UUNET: A formerly nonprofit organization which, among other things, runs a large Internet site that links the UUCP mail network with the Internet and has a large and useful FTP file archive. You may encounter it in addresses that contain `uunet.uu.net` at the end.

UTC: *U*niversal *C*oordinated *T*ime. Another name for GMT.

V.32bis: The code word for a fast modem — one that talks at a speed of 14,400 bits per second. "bis" is French for "and-another." See Chapter 2.

V.34: The code word for really fast modems that talk at 28,800 bps. See Chapter 2.

VAX/VMS: Digital Equipment Coprorations's major computer line over the last 15 years was the VAX; its proprietary operating system is known as VMS. Its e-mail system was part of a package called All-in-One. (Vaxen are now passé, replaced by DEC's new Alpha line.)

version creep: A problem that occurs when lots of people add features to programs that people are already using. Unless care is taken to keep programs compatible, sooner or later the program you're using doesn't talk to its "new and improved cousin" until you get the latest and greatest version that should make everybody happy 'til they add more features again. Also called *feature creep.*

viewer: A program used by MIME, Gopher, WAIS, or World Wide Web client programs to show you files that contain stuff other than text. For example, you might want viewers to display graphics files, play sound files, or display video files.

virus: Software that infects other software and causes damage to the system on which the infected software is run. You should download software only from reputable servers and use a virus checker regularly. Safe software is everyone's business. Viral infection can be deadly. Don't let it happen to you.

VT100: The model number of a terminal made some 15 years ago by Digital Equipment Corporation. Why do you care? Because many computers on the Internet expect to talk to VT-100-type terminals, and many communications programs can pretend to be (emulate) VT-100 terminals.

Web: The World Wide Web. "The Web" is a term of endearment used by those intimate with the World Wide Web.

Web page: The basic building block of the World Wide Web. Information displayed on a Web page can include highly sophisticated graphics, audio, and video. Web pages are linked together to form the World Wide Web.

Web server: An Internet host computer that stores Web pages and responds to requests to see them. Web servers talk to Web browsers by using a language named HTTP.

Web site: A location on the World Wide Web. It means the same as a Web page or Web server, depending on whom you ask.

WELL: The WELL (the Whole Earth 'Lectronic Link) is a public Internet provider in Sausalito, California. You can contact it at info@well.sf.ca.us.

whois: A command on some systems that tells you the actual name of someone, based on the person's username. *See also* finger. See Chapter 20

WinSock: WinSock (short for *Windows Sock*ets) is a standard way for Windows programs to work with TCP/IP. You use it if you connect your Windows PC directly to the Internet, either with a permanent connection or with a modem by using SLIP or PPP. *The Internet For Windows For Dummies Starter Kit* comes with a free trial version of a whole set of WinSock software, including programs for e-mail, the Web, Gopher, FTP, and telnet.

WinZip: A Windows-based program for zipping and unzipping ZIP files in addition to other standard types of archive files. WinZip is shareware, and you can get it from the Net from http://www.winzip.com.

World Wide Web (WWW): A hypermedia system that lets you browse through lots of interesting information. See *The Internet For Dummies,* 3rd Edition. The best-known WWW browser is Netscape, with Microsoft Explorer and Mosaic distant seconds.

WYSIWYG: *What You See Is What You Get.* Refers to document-generation software, like word processors, where the screen image you are working on looks just the way your document will look when it is finally printed.

X.25: A protocol that defines packet switching. You shouldn't care. The thing that TCP/IP is much better than.

X.400: An ISO standard of e-mail. Like SMTP but designed by international bureaucrats.

X.500: An ISO standard for e-mail "white pages" directory services

Xmodem: A file-transfer protocol developed ages ago by Ward Christiansen to check for errors as files are transferred. It has since been superseded by Ymodem and Zmodem, but many programs (especially Windows Terminal) still use it. See *The Internet For Dummies,* 3rd Edition for information about transferring files.

XON/XOFF: One way for your computer to say *wait a sec* when data is coming in too fast from your modem.

Ymodem: A file-transfer protocol that is faster than Xmodem but not as powerful (nor as complicated) as Zmodem.

Z: A code letter for Greenwich Mean Time (GMT). You might see 1730Z in an e-mail header. It just means 5:30 p.m. GMT or 9:30 a.m. P.S.T. *See also* Zulu.

ZIP file: A file that has been created by using WinZip, PKZip, or a compatible program. It contains one or more files that have been compressed and glommed together to save space. To get at the files in a ZIP file, you usually need WinZip, PKUnzip, or a compatible program. Sometimes you may get a self-extracting file, which is a ZIP file that contains the unzipping program right in it. Just run the file (type the name of the file at the command line), and it unzips itself.

For information about how to get and set up WinZip on a Windows computer, see *The Internet For Dummies,* 3rd Edition.

Zmodem: A fast file-transfer protocol defined by Chuck Forsberg, used by many programs. With Zmodem, you can transfer several files with one command, and the names of the files are sent along with them. Some communications programs (such as ProComm) can detect when a Zmodem transfer has begun and automatically begin receiving the files. We think it deserves Best of Breed in the file transfer arena.

Zulu: Another name for Greenwich Mean Time (GMT). The word Zulu represents the letter Z in the standard phonetic alphabet used in radio communications: "Let's have lunch at seventeen fifteen Zulu." "Roger that."

Appendix A

Countries on the Internet, by Country Code

• •

*T*his table lists all the countries and country-like areas in the world, alphabetically by the two-letter code used in geographically-based domain names.

The access codes are as follows: I: Full Internet access; M: E-mail only; X: No connection.

Code	Access	Country
AD	X	Andorra (Principality of)
AE	I	United Arab Emirates
AF	X	Afghanistan (Islamic Republic of)
AG	I	Antigua and Barbuda
AI	M	Anguilla
AL	X	Albania (Republic of)
AM	I	Armenia
AN	M	Netherlands Antilles
AO	M	Angola (People's Republic of)
AQ	I	Antarctica
AR	I	Argentina (Argentine Republic)
AS	X	American Samoa
AT	I	Austria (Republic of)
AU	I	Australia
AW	M	Aruba
AZ	M	Azerbaijan
BA	M	Bosnia-Herzegovina
BB	I	Barbados

Code	Access	Country
BD	M	Bangladesh (People's Republic of)
BE	I	Belgium (Kingdom of)
BF	M	Burkina Faso (formerly Upper Volta)
BG	I	Bulgaria (Republic of)
BH	M	Bahrain (State of)
BI	X	Burundi (Republic of)
BJ	X	Benin (People's Republic of)
BM	I	Bermuda
BN	X	Brunei Darussalam
BO	M	Bolivia (Republic of)
BR	I	Brazil (Federative Republic of)
BS	M	Bahamas (Commonwealth of the)
BT	X	Bhutan (Kingdom of)
BV	X	Bouvet Island
BW	M	Botswana (Republic of)
BY	I	Belarus
BZ	M	Belize
CA	I	Canada
CC	X	Cocos (Keeling) Islands
CF	X	Central African Republic
CG	M	Congo (Republic of the)
CH	I	Switzerland (Swiss Confederation)
CI	M	Cote d'Ivoire (Republic of)
CK	M	Cook Islands
CL	I	Chile (Republic of)
CM	M	Cameroon (Republic of)
CN	I	China (People's Republic of)
CO	I	Colombia (Republic of)
CR	I	Costa Rica (Republic of)
CU	M	Cuba (Republic of)
CV	X	Cape Verde (Republic of)
CX	X	Christmas Island (Indian Ocean)

Code	Access	Country
CY	I	Cyprus (Republic of)
CZ	I	Czech Republic
DE	I	Germany (Federal Republic of)
DJ	X	Djibouti (Republic of)
DK	I	Denmark (Kingdom of)
DM	X	Dominica (Commonwealth of)
DO	I	Dominican Republic
DZ	I	Algeria (People's Democratic Republic of)
EC	I	Ecuador (Republic of)
EE	I	Estonia (Republic of)
EG	I	Egypt (Arab Republic of)
EH	X	Western Sahara
ER	M	Eritrea
ES	I	Spain (Kingdom of)
ET	M	Ethiopia (People's Democratic Republic of)
FI	I	Finland (Republic of)
FJ	I	Fiji (Republic of)
FK	X	Falkland Islands (Malvinas)
FM	X	Micronesia (Federated States of)
FO	I	Faroe Islands
FR	I	France (French Republic)
GA	X	Gabon (Gabonese Republic)
GD	M	Grenada
GE	M	Georgia (Republic of)
GF	M	French Guiana
GH	M	Ghana (Republic of)
GI	X	Gibraltar
GL	I	Greenland
GM	M	Gambia (Republic of the)
GN	M	Guinea (Republic of)
GP	M	Guadeloupe (French Department of)
GQ	X	Equatorial Guinea (Republic of)

Code	Access	Country
GR	I	Greece (Hellenic Republic)
GT	M	Guatemala (Republic of)
GU	I	Guam
GW	X	Guinea-Bissau (Republic of)
GY	M	Guyana (Republic of)
HK	I	Hong Kong
HM	X	Heard and McDonald islands
HN	I	Honduras (Republic of)
HR	I	Croatia
HT	M	Haiti (Republic of)
HU	I	Hungary (Republic of)
ID	I	Indonesia (Republic of)
IE	I	Ireland
IL	I	Israel (State of)
IN	I	India (Republic of)
IO	X	British Indian Ocean Territory
IQ	X	Iraq (Republic of)
IR	I	Iran (Islamic Republic of)
IS	I	Iceland (Republic of)
IT	I	Italy (Italian Republic)
JM	I	Jamaica
JO	M	Jordan (Hashemite Kingdom of)
JP	I	Japan
KE	M	Kenya (Republic of)
KG	M	Kyrgyz Republic
KH	X	Cambodia
KI	M	Kiribati (Republic of)
KM	X	Comoros (Islamic Federal Republic of the)
KN	X	Saint Kitts and Nevis
KP	X	Korea (Democratic People's Republic of)
KR	I	Korea (Republic of)
KW	I	Kuwait (State of)

Code	Access	Country
KY	X	Cayman Islands
KZ	I	Kazakhstan
LA	X	Lao People's Democratic Republic
LB	M	Lebanon (Lebanese Republic)
LC	M	Saint Lucia
LI	I	Liechtenstein (Principality of)
LK	I	Sri Lanka (Democratic Socialist Republic of)
LR	X	Liberia (Republic of)
LS	M	Lesotho (Kingdom of)
LT	I	Lithuania
LU	I	Luxembourg (Grand Duchy of)
LV	I	Latvia (Republic of)
LY	X	Libyan Arab Jamahiriya
MA	M	Morocco (Kingdom of)
MC	I	Monaco (Principality of)
MD	I	Moldova (Republic of)
MG	M	Madagascar (Democratic Republic of)
MH	M	Marshall Islands (Republic of the)
MK	I	Macedonia (Former Yugoslav Republic of)
ML	M	Mali (Republic of)
MM	X	Myanmar (Union of)
MN	M	Mongolia
MO	I	Macau (Ao-me'n)
MP	X	Northern Mariana Islands (Commonwealth of the)
MQ	X	Martinique (French Department of)
MR	X	Mauritania (Islamic Republic of)
MS	X	Montserrat
MT	M	Malta (Republic of)
MU	M	Mauritius
MV	X	Maldives (Republic of)
MW	M	Malawi (Republic of)
MX	I	Mexico (United Mexican States)

Code	Access	Country
MY	I	Malaysia
MZ	I	Mozambique (People's Republic of)
NA	M	Namibia (Republic of)
NC	M	New Caledonia
NE	M	Niger (Republic of the)
NF	X	Norfolk Island
NG	M	Nigeria (Federal Republic of)
NI	I	Nicaragua (Republic of)
NL	I	Netherlands (Kingdom of the)
NO	I	Norway (Kingdom of)
NP	M	Nepal (Kingdom of)
NR	M	Nauru (Republic of)
NT	X	Neutral Zone (between Saudi Arabia and Iraq)
NU	M	Niue
NZ	I	New Zealand
OM	X	Oman (Sultanate of)
PA	I	Panama (Republic of)
PE	I	Peru (Republic of)
PF	M	French Polynesia
PG	M	Papua New Guinea
PH	I	Philippines (Republic of the)
PK	M	Pakistan (Islamic Republic of)
PL	I	Poland (Republic of)
PM	X	Saint Pierre and Miquelon (French Department of)
PN	X	Pitcairn Island
PR	I	Puerto Rico
PT	I	Portugal (Portuguese Republic)
PW	X	Palau (Republic of)
PY	M	Paraguay (Republic of)
QA	X	Qatar (State of)
RE	I	Réunion (French Department of)
RO	I	Romania

Code	Access	Country
RU	I	Russian Federation
RW	X	Rwanda (Rwandese Republic)
SA	M	Saudi Arabia (Kingdom of)
SB	M	Solomon Islands
SC	M	Seychelles (Republic of)
SD	X	Sudan (Democratic Republic of the)
SE	I	Sweden (Kingdom of)
SG	I	Singapore (Republic of)
SH	X	Saint Helena
SI	I	Slovenia
SJ	I	Svalbard and Jan Mayen islands
SK	I	Slovakia
SL	M	Sierra Leone (Republic of)
SM	X	San Marino (Republic of)
SN	M	Senegal (Republic of)
SO	X	Somalia (Somali Democratic Republic)
SR	M	Suriname (Republic of)
ST	X	São Tomé and Principe (Democratic Republic of)
SV	M	El Salvador (Republic of)
SY	X	Syria (Syrian Arab Republic)
SZ	M	Swaziland (Kingdom of)
TC	X	Turks and Caicos Islands
TD	X	Chad (Republic of)
TF	X	French Southern Territories
TG	M	Togo (Togolese Republic)
TH	I	Thailand (Kingdom of)
TJ	M	Tajikistan
TK	X	Tokelau Islands
TM	M	Turkmenistan
TN	I	Tunisia
TO	M	Tonga (Kingdom of)
TP	X	East Timor

Code	Access	Country
TR	I	Turkey (Republic of)
TT	M	Trinidad and Tobago (Republic of)
TV	M	Tuvalu
TW	I	Taiwan, Province of China
TZ	M	Tanzania (United Republic of)
UA	I	Ukraine
UG	M	Uganda (Republic of)
UK	I	United Kingdom (Official country code is GB, but domain is UK)
UM	X	United States Minor Outlying Islands
US	I	United States (United States of America)
UY	I	Uruguay (Eastern Republic of)
UZ	I	Uzbekistan
VA	X	Vatican City State (Holy See)
VC	M	Saint Vincent and the Grenadines
VE	I	Venezuela (Republic of)
VG	X	Virgin Islands (British)
VI	I	Virgin Islands (U.S.)
VN	M	Vietnam (Socialist Republic of)
VU	M	Vanuatu (Republic of, formerly New Hebrides)
WF	X	Wallis and Futuna Islands
WS	M	Samoa (Independent State of)
YE	X	Yemen (Republic of)
YT	X	Mayotte
YU	M	Yugoslavia (Socialist Federal Republic of)
ZA	I	South Africa (Republic of)
ZM	I	Zambia (Republic of)
ZR	X	Zaire (Republic of)
ZW	I	Zimbabwe (Republic of)

Appendix B
Zones for Domain Names

• •

*T*he last part of an Internet domain name is the *zone*. For example, in the name www.dummies.com, the zone is com. There are two kinds of zones: three-letter generic zones and two-letter geographic zones.

Generic Zones

There is a small, fixed set of generic zones. Computers in these zones may be anywhere in the world, although in practice, most of them are in the United States.

Zone	Description
arpa	Obsolete, now used only for a few internal network names
com	Commercial organizations
edu	Four-year universities and similar educational organizations (Two-year colleges, high schools, and elementary schools use geographic zones, covered later in this appendix.)
gov	U.S. Federal government organizations
int	International organizations (notably NATO)
mil	U.S. military organizations
net	Networking organizations
org	Catch-all for organizations that don't fit anywhere else, such as non-profits and professional societies

Geographic Zones

Every country in the world and quite a few country-like geographic places have a two-letter geographic zone code. For example, aq is the code for Antarctica, so scott.aq is a computer in Antarctica. (It really is. Brr.) Each country has its own rules for what the structure of names within its zone is. Some countries are quite formal, while others (particularly smaller countries) assign names more haphazardly. Appendix A lists the two-letter country codes alphabetically by code. See Chapter 21 of *MORE Internet For Dummies,* 2nd Edition for more information on geographic domains.

The U.S. Domain

Any host within the United States can register within the U.S. domain at no charge. The U.S. domain is organized geographically by state, as in this example:

```
iecc.cambridge.ma.us
```

The component before us is the two-letter state code for the state where the host is, and the component before that is the name of the city or town.

As special cases, federal government agencies may be registered within fed.us, and "distributed national institutes" may be registered within dni.us.

Within each state, conventions exist for computers in government and educational organizations:

- ✔ A city or other local government registers in *name*.CI.*locality*.*state*.US.
- ✔ A county or parish government registers in *name*.CO.*locality*.*state*.US.
- ✔ A state government registers in *name*.STATE.*state*.US.
- ✔ A public elementary or high school registers in *name*.K12.*state*.US.
- ✔ A private elementary or high school registers in *name*.PVT.K12.*state*.US.
- ✔ A community college registers in *name*.CC.*state*.US.
- ✔ A technical college registers in *name*.TEC.*state*.US.
- ✔ A library registers in *name*.LIB.*state*.US.
- ✔ An organization with no single location within the state registers as *name*.GEN.*state*.US.

In all of the preceding cases, *name* can have multiple parts. For example, a computer at the P.S.123 elementary school in the New York City school district might be called alpha.ps123.nyc.k12.ny.us.

Appendix C

What's on the CD-ROM?

● ●

*T*his book includes a CD-ROM with e-mail programs of use to both Windows and Macintosh users. In this appendix, you'll find out what programs we included, what they are for, and how to install them.

For You Windows Users

If you stick the *Internet E-Mail For Dummies* CD-ROM into the CD-ROM drive of a computer running Windows (Windows 3.1 or Windows 95 — your choice), you see three directories:

- ✔ EUDORALT: Contains Eudora Light, the excellent e-mail program described in Chapters 8 and 9.

- ✔ NETCOM: Contains NetCruiser, the program that lets you sign up for and use a Netcom account, including e-mail, the World Wide Web, Usenet newsgroups, and online chatting. Doing e-mail with Netcom and NetCruiser is described in Chapter 15.

- ✔ WINCIM: Contains WinCIM, the program that lets you sign up for and use a CompuServe account, including e-mail, the World Wide Web, Usenet newsgroups, and lots of CompuServe-specific services. CompuServe Mail is described in Chapter 12.

The next three sections tell you how to install and use each of these programs.

Eudora Light for Windows

Eudora Light is a terrific e-mail program that you can use with your SLIP or PPP account. The program requires Windows 3.1, 3.11, or 95, a SLIP or PPP account, WinSock-compatible connection software (like Trumpet WinSock), and 4.5MB of free disk space (3.7 of which is the documentation). Your Internet provider must have a POP3-compatible mail server for your incoming mail and a SMTP mail gateway for your outgoing mail (most do). Ask your provider for the host name of the SMTP mail gateway.

Installing Eudora Light — Windows 3.1

Follow these steps if you are installing Eudora Light on a PC with Windows 3.1:

1. **Open the File Manager.**

2. **Insert the *Internet E-Mail For Dummies* CD-ROM into your CD-ROM drive.**

3. **Click on the Maximize button on any window you see inside the File Manager's own window.**

4. **Click on the drive button on the toolbar near the top of the screen that represents your CD-ROM drive.**

   Most of you will use drive D as your CD-ROM drive.

5. **Click once on the EUDORALT folder.**

6. **Choose File⇨Copy from the File Manager menu bar.**

   The From box shows D:\EUDORALT (if your CD-ROM drive isn't drive D, you see another drive letter).

7. **In the To: box, type in C:\ (substitute your drive letter if different than C) and click on the OK button.**

   The folder EUDORALT will be copied to your hard drive.

8. **Close the File Manager.**

9. **Open the Program Manager, and from its menu bar, choose File⇨New.**

10. **Choose the Program Group button and then click on OK.**

11. **In the Description box, type** Eudora Light **and then click on OK.**

12. **With the new Eudora Light program group window open, choose File⇨New.**

13. **Choose the Program Item button and then click on OK.**

14. **In the description box, type** Eudora Light.

15. **In the command line box, type** C:\EUDORALT\EUDORA.EXE. **(Substitute your hard drive letter if different.)**

16. **In the working directory box, type** C:\.

17. **Click on the OK button.**

18. **Add the following environment variable to your AUTOEXEC.BAT file by inserting a line like this:**

```
SET TMP=C:\TMP (or some temp directory)
```

To add a line to your AUTOEXEC.BAT file, edit it using Notepad, WordPad, or another text editor. If your AUTOEXEC.BAT file already contains a line beginning *SET TMP=*, then leave the file alone. If no line begins with *SET TMP=*, then add the line. Make sure that the C:\TMP directory exists.

Installing Eudora Light — Windows 95

Follow these steps if you are installing Eudora Light on a PC with Windows 95:

1. **Insert the *Internet E-Mail For Dummies* CD-ROM in your computer's CD-ROM drive.**

2. **Double-click on the My Computer icon.**

3. **Double-click on the icon representing your CD-ROM drive. A window appears that shows the Eudoralt folder.**

4. **Click and hold the left mouse button down on the Eudoralt folder.**

5. **With the mouse button still held down, move the mouse pointer on top of the icon in the My Computer window that represents your hard disk so that the icon is highlighted; then let go of the mouse button.**

   Windows 95 copies the folder and its contents to your drive.

6. **Double-click on your hard disk icon in My Computer.**

7. **Double-click on the Eudoralt folder.**

8. **Click and hold the left mouse button down on the icon named Eudora.**

9. **With the mouse button still held down, move the mouse pointer on top of the Start button on the Windows 95 toolbar and then let go of the mouse button.**

   Windows 95 will create a shortcut for Eudora in the Start menu.

10. **Add the following environment variable to your AUTOEXEC.BAT file by inserting a line like this:**

```
SET TMP=C:\TMP (or some temp directory)
```

To add a line to your AUTOEXEC.BAT file, edit it using Notepad, WordPad, or another text editor. If your AUTOEXEC.BAT file already contains a line beginning *SET TMP=*, then leave the file alone. If no line begins with *SET TMP=*, then add the line. Make sure that the C:\TMP directory exists.

Setting up Eudora Light (Windows 3.1 and Windows 95)

After you've installed Eudora Light, take the following steps to configure the program:

1. **Run Eudora by double-clicking its icon.**

   Before you can use Eudora, you have to tell it how to collect your incoming mail and send outgoing mail.

   If you are running Eudora for the first time, the Settings window will automatically appear (as shown in Figure C-1). If it doesn't, choose Special⇨Settings from the menu bar.

   The Getting Started category is selected from the list of categories along the left side of the window, so the window displays getting-started-type settings.

2. **In the POP Account box, type your e-mail address.**

3. **In the Real Name box, type your real name.**

   Eudora will insert your name, in parentheses, after your return address in your outgoing messages.

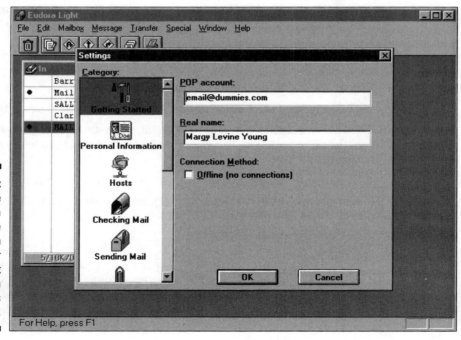

Figure C-1:
To configure Eudora Light, type information about your Internet provider in the Settings window.

4. **Click the Sending Mail icon on the list of categories so that you see the settings that apply to the way you send e-mail.**

5. **In the SMTP Server box, type the host name of your Internet provider's mail gateway.**

   This computer is the one that Eudora sends your outgoing mail to for distribution to the Internet.

6. **Click OK to close the Settings window.**

For more information about how to use Eudora, see Chapters 8 and 9. If you want to read the Eudora Light manual, open the file EUDORA.DOC in your Eudora program directory. The file is in Microsoft Word 6 format, which most word processors can read.

NetCruiser

Netcom is a national Internet provider that gives you free NetCruiser software for signing up and using your account. To use the NetCruiser for Windows software on this CD-ROM, you need Windows 3.1, 3.11, or Windows 95, 4MB RAM, and 4MB of disk space. And, of course, you need a modem that runs at least at 9600 bps and a credit card to charge your Netcom account to.

This copy of NetCruiser contains a special code that waives the usual $25 sign-up fee.

Note that Macintosh NetCruiser was due to be released shortly after the time this book was printed. You can check on the availability of the Macintosh version by calling Netcom at 408-983-5950.

Here's how to install the NetCruiser software using the *Internet E-Mail For Dummies* CD-ROM. Make sure that your modem is on (if it's an external modem with a switch) and that you aren't running any other communications software (such as a fax program).

1. **Use File Manager, My Computer, or Windows Explorer to see a list of the files on your CD-ROM.**

2. **Double-click the NETCOM directory to see the files it contains; then double-click the file SETUP.EXE.**

   The NetCruiser Setup program runs, asking what directory to install the software in. The setup program suggests C:\NETCOM.

3. **Edit the installation directory if you don't like the program's suggestion; then click Continue.**

   The setup program installs all the NetCruiser program files in the directory you chose. If the program finds a copy of a file named WINSOCK.DLL, it may ask whether it can update your AUTOEXEC.BAT file to make sure that the NetCruiser software will work: Click Yes.

   When the program is installed, you are ready to register for your new Netcom account. Click the Start Registration button and follow the directions. You can also refer to the Netcom card that comes with the CD-ROM packet, as it also includes information about fees and billing.

Congratulations! You've got a Netcom account and you are ready to cruise. Double-click the NetCruiser icon in Program Manager (in Windows 3.1) or in the Netcom folder on your desktop (in Windows 95). If you need to reach Netcom, call 408-983-5950 or fax 408-983-1537.

If you live in a rural area, Netcom's nearest access number may be a long-distance phone call away. You can avoid the long-distance charges by accessing Netcom through its 800 number, which is 800-784-3638. Netcom does charge 8 cents per minute for using its 800 line, but in many cases, this fee is less than the cost of a long-distance call to the nearest city with a local Netcom access number. By the way, you can also use the 800 number to reach Netcom if you're on the road and don't know the local Netcom access number for the city (or foreign country) you happen to be in.

WinCIM: The CompuServe Information Manager

The WinCIM program allows you to sign up for and use an account with CompuServe Information Services, an online service provider. You can sign up for a free trial account to see if you like CompuServe — we do! To use WinCIM, you need Windows 3.1 or Windows 95, 4MB free on your hard disk, a modem, and a credit card with which to pay for your new CompuServe account.

To install WinCIM and sign up for an account, put the *Internet E-Mail For Dummies* CD-ROM in your drive and follow these steps:

1. **In File Manager, My Computer, or Windows Explorer, look at the list of files on the CD-ROM.**

2. **Double-click the WINCIM directory to see its files; then double-click the WCINST.EXE program you find.**

The WinCIM installation program takes a minute or two to set up. Then it displays a window telling you that it's ready to begin.

3. **Click the Next button.**

   The program asks whether you already have a WINSOCK.DLL program that connects to CompuServe. You probably don't. Unless you're sure that you do, leave the Install WinSock option selected.

4. **Click Next again.**

   You see the WinCIM Installation window. You can choose the directory in which to install the software, and you can choose which parts of WinCIM to install.

5. **If you don't already have a CompuServe account, make sure that the Install Signup option is selected. Then click Next.**

   The installation program installs the WinCIM program with the options you chose. It creates a program group (in Windows 3.1) or a folder (in Windows 95) with icons for CompuServe Information Manager (that's WinCIM).

   If you chose to install the sign-up program, WinCIM asks if you want to sign up now.

6. **Click Yes to sign up for an account.**

   If you want to sign up later, click No. You can run the sign-up program later by double-clicking the Membership Sign Up program icon.

7. **Follow the directions to sign up for an account.**

For more information, refer to the CompuServe card that comes with the CD-ROM packet or call CompuServe at 800-336-6823.

For You Mac Users

If you stick the *Internet E-Mail For Dummies* CD-ROM into the CD-ROM drive of a Macintosh-compatible computer running Mac OS System 7 or later, you see two folders:

- ✔ Eudora Light: Contains Eudora Light, the excellent e-mail program described in Chapters 8 and 9.

- ✔ MacCim 2.4.3: Contains MacCIM, the program that lets you sign up for and use a CompuServe account, including e-mail, the World Wide Web, Usenet newsgroups, and lots of CompuServe-specific services. CompuServe Mail is described in Chapter 12.

The next two sections tell you how to install and use Eudora Light and MacCIM.

Eudora Light for Macs

Eudora Light is a terrific e-mail program that you can use with your SLIP or PPP account. The program requires Mac OS System 7 or later, MacTCP (which comes with System 7.5 and is available from Apple if you have an earlier version of System 7), a SLIP or PPP account, and the appropriate Mac interface program like InterSLIP or MacPPP (your Internet provider should be able to help you with these). Your Internet provider must have a POP3-compatible mail server for your incoming mail and a SMTP mail gateway for your outgoing mail (most do). Ask your provider for the host name of the SMTP mail gateway.

To install Eudora, put the *Internet E-Mail For Dummies* CD-ROM in your drive and follow these steps:

1. **Drag the Eudora Light folder from the CD-ROM onto your hard disk and then double-click on the Eudora Light folder icon to see its contents.**

   The Eudora README file has information on potential incompatibilities between Eudora and other applications.

2. **Run Eudora by double-clicking its icon.**

   Before you can use Eudora, you have to tell it how to collect your incoming mail and send outgoing mail.

   If you are running Eudora for the first time, the Settings window will automatically appear. If it doesn't, choose Special⇨Settings from the menu bar.

   The Getting Started category is selected from the list of categories along the left side of the window, so the window displays getting-started-type settings.

3. **In the POP Account box, type your e-mail address.**

4. **In the Real Name box, type your real name.**

   Eudora will insert your name, in parentheses, after your return address in your outgoing messages.

5. **If you are using a SLIP or PPP connection, select the MacTCP button.**

6. **Click the Sending Mail icon on the list of categories so that you see the settings that apply to the way you send e-mail.**

7. **In the SMTP Server box, type the host name of your Internet provider's mail gateway.**

   This computer is the one that Eudora sends your outgoing mail to for distribution to the Internet.

8. **Your e-mail address should be entered in the Return Address field.**

   You will also see a bunch of options with check boxes next to each. You can leave them the way they are for now. Turn on Balloon Help to find out more about what each option does.

9. **Click OK to close the Settings window.**

For more information about how to use Eudora, see Chapters 8 and 9. If you want to read the Eudora Light manual, double-click on the Eudora 1.5.1 Manual.sea file in your Eudora Light folder. The file is a self-extracting archive that expands to a Microsoft Word 6 format document, which many word processors can read.

MacCIM: The CompuServe Information Manager

The MacCIM program allows you to sign up for and use an account with CompuServe Information Services, an online service provider. You can sign up for a free trial account to see if you like CompuServe — we do! To use MacCIM, you need System 6 or System 7 (or later), 2MB free on your hard disk, 1.3MB of free RAM, a modem, and a credit card with which to pay for your new CompuServe account.

To install MacCIM and sign up for an account, put the *Internet E-Mail For Dummies* CD-ROM in your drive and follow these steps:

1. **Double-click the MacCim 2.4.3 folder to see its files; then double-click the MacCIM Archive Installer program you find.**

   The CompuServe Self-Extracting Archive Installer displays a window telling you that it's ready to begin.

2. **Click the Install button.**

   The Installer creates a folder called CompuServe on your hard disk containing everything you need to use CompuServe.

3. **Double-click on the CompuServe folder to see its contents.**

   You see the CompuServe Information Manager Icon and an icon called SignUp.

4. **Double-click on the SignUp icon.**

5. **Follow the directions to sign up for an account.**

For more information, refer to the CompuServe card that comes with the CD-ROM packet or call CompuServe at 800-336-6823.

Index

IDG BOOKS WORLDWIDE LICENSE AGREEMENT

4. Limited Warranty. IDGB warrants that the Software and disc are free from defects in materials and workmanship for a period of sixty (60) days from the date of purchase of this Book. If IDGB receives notification within the warranty period of defects in material or workmanship, IDGB will replace the defective disc. IDGB's entire liability and your exclusive remedy shall be limited to replacement of the Software, which is returned to IDGB with a copy of your receipt. This Limited Warranty is void if failure of the Software has resulted from accident, abuse, or misapplication. Any replacement Software will be warranted for the remainder of the original warranty period or thirty (30) days, whichever is longer.

5. No Other Warranties. To the maximum extent permitted by applicable law, IDGB and the author disclaim all other warranties, express or implied, including but not limited to implied warranties of merchantability and fitness for a particular purpose, with respect to the Software, the programs, the source code contained therein and/or the techniques described in this Book. This limited warranty gives you specific legal rights. You may have others which vary from state/jurisdiction to state/jurisdiction.

6. No Liability For Consequential Damages. To the extent permitted by applicable law, in no event shall IDGB or the author be liable for any damages whatsoever (including without limitation, damages for loss of business profits, business interruption, loss of business information, or any other pecuniary loss) arising out of the use of or inability to use the Book or the Software, even if IDGB has been advised of the possibility of such damages. Because some states/jurisdictions do not allow the exclusion or limitation of liability for consequential or incidental damages, the above limitation may not apply to you.

7. U.S.Government Restricted Rights. Use, duplication, or disclosure of the Software by the U.S. Government is subject to restrictions stated in paragraph (c) (1) (ii) of the Rights in Technical Data and Computer Software clause of DFARS 252.227-7013, and in subparagraphs (a) through (d) of the Commercial Computer—Restricted Rights clause at FAR 52.227-19, and in similar clauses in the NASA FAR supplement, when applicable.

CD-ROM Installation Information

The *Internet E-Mail For Dummies* CD-ROM contains software for both Mac and Windows users. Mac users have access to CompuServe's MacCIM software and Eudora Light for Macs. Windows users have access to CompuServe's WinCIM software, Eudora Light for Windows, and Netcom's NetCruiser. You'll find thorough installation instructions for each program in Appendix C.

IDG BOOKS WORLDWIDE REGISTRATION CARD

RETURN THIS REGISTRATION CARD FOR FREE CATALOG

Title of this book: Internet E-Mail For Dummies ®

My overall rating of this book: ❑ Very good [1] ❑ Good [2] ❑ Satisfactory [3] ❑ Fair [4] ❑ Poor [5]

How I first heard about this book:

❑ Found in bookstore; name: [6] _____
❑ Advertisement: [8]
❑ Word of mouth; heard about book from friend, co-worker, etc.: [10]

❑ Book review: [7]
❑ Catalog: [9]
❑ Other: [11]

What I liked most about this book:
_____
_____

What I would change, add, delete, etc., in future editions of this book:
_____
_____

Other comments:
_____

Number of computer books I purchase in a year: ❑ 1 [12] ❑ 2-5 [13] ❑ 6-10 [14] ❑ More than 10 [15]

I would characterize my computer skills as: ❑ Beginner [16] ❑ Intermediate [17] ❑ Advanced [18] ❑ Professional [19]

I use ❑ DOS [20] ❑ Windows [21] ❑ OS/2 [22] ❑ Unix [23] ❑ Macintosh [24] ❑ Other: [25]_____
(please specify)

I would be interested in new books on the following subjects:
(please check all that apply, and use the spaces provided to identify specific software)

❑ Word processing: [26]
❑ Data bases: [28]
❑ File Utilities: [30]
❑ Networking: [32]
❑ Other: [34]

❑ Spreadsheets: [27]
❑ Desktop publishing: [29]
❑ Money management: [31]
❑ Programming languages: [33]

I use a PC at (please check all that apply): ❑ home [35] ❑ work [36] ❑ school [37] ❑ other: [38] _____

The disks I prefer to use are ❑ 5.25 [39] ❑ 3.5 [40] ❑ other: [41]_____

I have a CD ROM: ❑ yes [42] ❑ no [43]

I plan to buy or upgrade computer hardware this year: ❑ yes [44] ❑ no [45]

I plan to buy or upgrade computer software this year: ❑ yes [46] ❑ no [47]

Name: _____ Business title: [48] _____ Type of Business: [49] _____

Address (❑ home [50] ❑ work [51]/Company name: _____)

Street/Suite# _____

City [52]/State [53]/Zipcode [54]: _____ Country [55] _____

❑ **I liked this book!** You may quote me by name in future
IDG Books Worldwide promotional materials.

My daytime phone number is _____

IDG BOOKS

THE WORLD OF COMPUTER KNOWLEDGE

☐ YES!

Please keep me informed about IDG's World of Computer Knowledge.
Send me the latest IDG Books catalog.